R. F. Winch

Macaulay's Essays on William Pitt,

Earl of Chatham

R. F. Winch

Macaulay's Essays on William Pitt,
Earl of Chatham

ISBN/EAN: 9783337809812

Printed in Europe, USA, Canada, Australia, Japan

Cover: Foto ©ninafisch / pixelio.de

More available books at **www.hansebooks.com**

MACAULAY'S ESSAYS

ON

WILLIAM PITT

EARL OF CHATHAM

BY

R. F. WINCH, M.A.

AUTHOR OF "NOTES ON MACAULAY'S 'ESSAY ON BOSWELL'S LIFE
OF JOHNSON' AND 'ESSAY ON ADDISON'" ALSO OF
"GLOSSARY AND NOTES ON 'OLD MORTALITY'"

London
MACMILLAN AND CO., Limited
NEW YORK: THE MACMILLAN COMPANY
1898

All rights reserved

GLASGOW: PRINTED AT THE UNIVERSITY PRESS
BY ROBERT MACLEHOSE AND CO.

PREFACE.

IN the compilation of these Notes frequent use has been made of the following books:—Lecky's *History of England in the Eighteenth Century*, Mahon's *History of England* (1713-1783), Walpole's *Memoirs of George II.*, Walpole's *Memoirs of George III.*, Cates's *Dictionary of General Biography*, Lowe and Pulling's *Dictionary of English History*, *The Encyclopaedia Britannica*, Smith's *Antiquities of Westminster*.

When copying direct from these works I have generally acknowledged my authority: sometimes, however, when giving only a digest of their remarks I have omitted to do so: but it would be worse than foolish to pretend to any originality in a book of this kind.

I have to thank Sir G. O. Trevelyan, M.P., for kindly putting me in the way of acquiring the information contained in the Appendix. My thanks are also due to Mr. Jones, the Clerk of the Works at Westminster Hall, for showing me over all the buildings in his charge, and for allowing me to examine many valuable plans, which he has in his office, descriptive of Westminster, Palace Yard, and its various buildings at different periods of its history.

R. F. W.

TILSDEN, CRANBROOK,
October, 1898.

CONTENTS.

	PAGE
WILLIAM PITT, EARL OF CHATHAM—FIRST ESSAY,	1
EARL OF CHATHAM--SECOND ESSAY,	50
NOTES,	144
CHRONOLOGICAL TABLE,	220
APPENDIX,	224
INDEX TO NOTES,	226

WILLIAM PITT, EARL OF CHATHAM.

FIRST ESSAY, JANUARY 1834.

A History of the Right Honourable William Pitt, Earl of Chatham, containing his Speeches in Parliament, a considerable portion of his Correspondence when Secretary of State, upon French, Spanish, and American affairs, never before published; and an account of the principal events and persons of his time, connected with his life, sentiments, and administration. By the Rev. FRANCIS THACKERAY, A.M. 2 vols. 4to. London. 1827.

THOUGH several years have elapsed since the publication of this work, it is still, we believe, a new publication to most of our readers. Nor are we surprised at this. The book is large, and the style heavy. The information which Mr. Thackeray has obtained from the State Paper Office is new; but much of it is very uninteresting. The rest of his narrative is very little better than Gifford's or Tomline's Life of the second Pitt, and tells little or nothing that may not be found quite as well told in the Parliamentary History, the Annual Register, and other works equally common.

Almost every mechanical employment, it is said, has a tendency to injure some one or other of the bodily organs of the artisan. Grinders of cutlery die of consumption; weavers are stunted in their growth; smiths become blear-eyed. In the same manner almost every intellectual employment has a tendency to produce some intellectual malady. Biographers, translators, editors, all, in short, who employ themselves in illustrating the lives or the writings of others, are peculiarly exposed to the *Lues Boswelliana*, or disease of admiration. But we scarcely remember ever to have seen a patient so far gone in this distemper as Mr. Thackeray. He is not satisfied with forcing us to confess that Pitt was a great orator, a vigorous minister, an honourable and high-spirited gentleman. He will have it, that all virtues and all accomplishments met in his hero. In spite of Gods, men, and columns, Pitt must be a poet, a poet capable of producing a heroic poem of the first order; and we are assured that we ought to find many charms in such lines as these :—

"Midst all the tumults of the warring sphere,
  My light-charged bark may haply *glide*;
  Some gale may waft, some conscious thought shall cheer,
  And the small freight unanxious *glide.*"

Pitt was in the army for a few months in time of peace. Mr. Thackeray accordingly insists on our confessing that, if the young cornet had remained in the service, he would have been one of the ablest commanders that ever lived. But this is not all. Pitt, it seems, was not merely a great poet *in esse*, and a great general *in posse*, but a finished example of moral excellence, the just man made perfect. He was in the right when he attempted to establish an inquisition, and to give bounties for perjury, in order to get Walpole's head. He was in the right when he declared Walpole to have been an excellent minister. He was in the right when, being in opposition, he maintained that no peace ought to be made with Spain, till she should formally renounce the right of search. He was in the right when, being in office, he silently acquiesced in a treaty by which Spain did not renounce the right of search. When he left the Duke of Newcastle, when he coalesced with the Duke of Newcastle, when he thundered against subsidies, when he lavished subsidies with unexampled profusion, when he execrated the Hanoverian connection, when he declared that Hanover ought to be as dear to us as Hampshire, he was still invariably speaking the language of a virtuous and enlightened statesman.

The truth is that there scarcely ever lived a person who had so little claim to this sort of praise as Pitt. He was undoubtedly a great man. But his was not a complete and well-proportioned greatness. The public life of Hampden or of Somers resembles a regular drama, which can be criticized as a whole, and every scene of which is to be viewed in connection with the main action. The public life of Pitt, on the other hand, is a rude though striking piece, a piece abounding in incongruities, a piece without any unity of plan, but redeemed by some noble passages, the effect of which is increased by the tameness or extravagance of what precedes and of what follows. His opinions were unfixed. His conduct at some of the most important conjunctures of his life was evidently determined by pride and resentment. He had one fault, which of all human faults is most rarely found in company with true greatness. He was extremely affected. He was an almost solitary instance of a man of real genius, and of a brave, lofty, and commanding spirit, without simplicity of character. He was an actor in the Closet, an actor at Council, an actor in Parliament; and even in private society he could not lay aside his theatrical tones and attitudes. We know that one of the most distinguished of his partisans often complained that he could never obtain admittance to Lord Chatham's room till every thing was ready for the representation, till the dresses and properties were all correctly disposed, till the light was thrown with Rembrandt-like effect on the head of the illustrious performer, till the flannels had been arranged with the air of a Grecian drapery, and the crutch placed as gracefully as that of Belisarius or Lear.

Yet, with all his faults and affectations, Pitt had, in a very extraordinary degree, many of the elements of greatness. He had splendid talents, strong passions, quick sensibility, and vehement enthusiasm for the grand and the beautiful. There was something about him which ennobled tergiversation itself. He often went wrong, very wrong. But, to quote the language of Wordsworth,

"He still retained,
'Mid such abasement, what he had received
From nature, an intense and glowing mind."

In an age of low and dirty prostitution, in the age of Doddington and Sandys, it was something to have a man who might perhaps, under some strong excitement, have been tempted to ruin his country, but who never would have stooped to pilfer from her, a man whose errors arose, not from a sordid desire of gain, but from a fierce thirst for power, for glory, and for vengeance. History owes to him this attestation, that, at a time when any thing short of direct embezzlement of the public money was considered as quite fair in public men, he showed the most scrupulous disinterestedness, that, at a time when it seemed to be generally taken for granted that Government could be upheld only by the basest and most immoral arts, he appealed to the better and nobler parts of human nature, that he made a brave and splendid attempt to do, by means of public opinion, what no other statesman of his day thought it possible to do, except by means of corruption, that he looked for support, not, like the Pelhams, to a strong aristocratical connection, not, like Bute, to the personal favour of the sovereign, but to the middle class of Englishmen, that he inspired that class with a firm confidence in his integrity and ability, that, backed by them, he forced an unwilling court and an unwilling oligarchy to admit him to an ample share of power, and that he used his power in such a manner as clearly proved him to have sought it, not for the sake of profit or patronage, but from a wish to establish for himself a great and durable reputation by means of eminent services rendered to the state.

The family of Pitt was wealthy and respectable. His grandfather was Governor of Madras, and brought back from India that celebrated diamond which the Regent Orleans, by the advice of Saint Simon, purchased for upwards of two millions of livres, and which is still considered as the most precious of the crown jewels of France. Governor Pitt bought estates and rotten boroughs, and sat in the House of Commons for Old Sarum. His son Robert was at one time member for Old Sarum, and at another for Oakhampton. Robert had two sons. Thomas, the elder, inherited the estates and the parliamentary interest of his father. The second was the celebrated William Pitt.

He was born in November, 1708. About the early part of his life little more is known than that he was educated at Eton, and that at seventeen he was entered at Trinity College, Oxford. During the second year of his residence at the University, George the First died; and the event was, after the fashion of that generation, celebrated by the Oxonians in many very middling copies of verses. On this occasion Pitt published some Latin lines, which Mr. Thackeray has preserved. They prove that the young student had but a very limited knowledge even of the mechanical part of his art. All true Etonians will hear with concern that their illustrious school-fellow is guilty of making the first syllable in *labenti*[1] short. The matter of the poem is as worthless as that of any college exercise that was ever written before or since. There is, of course, much about Mars, Themis, Neptune, and Cocytus. The Muses are earnestly entreated to weep over the urn of Cæsar; for Cæsar, says the Poet, loved the Muses; Cæsar, who could not read a line of Pope, and who loved nothing but punch and fat women.

Pitt had been, from his school-days, cruelly tormented by the gout, and was at last advised to travel for his health. He accordingly left Oxford without taking a degree, and visited France and Italy. He returned, however, without having received much benefit from his excursion, and continued, till the close of his life, to suffer most severely from his constitutional malady.

His father was now dead, and had left very little to the younger children. It was necessary that William should choose a profession. He decided for the army, and a cornet's commission was procured for him in the Blues.

[1] So Mr. Thackeray has printed the poem. But it may be charitably hoped that Pitt wrote *labanti*.

But, small as his fortune was, his family had both the power and the inclination to serve him. At the general election of 1734, his elder brother Thomas was chosen both for Old Sarum and for Oakhampton. When Parliament met in 1735, Thomas made his election to serve for Oakhampton, and William was returned for Old Sarum.

Walpole had now been, during fourteen years, at the head of affairs. He had risen to power under the most favourable circumstances. The whole of the Whig party, of that
10 party which professed peculiar attachment to the principles of the Revolution, and which exclusively enjoyed the confidence of the reigning house, had been united in support of his administration. Happily for him, he had been out of office when the South-Sea Act was passed; and, though he does not appear to have foreseen all the consequences of that measure, he had strenuously opposed it, as he opposed all the measures, good and bad, of Sunderland's administration. When the South-Sea Company were voting dividends of fifty per cent., when a hundred pounds of their stock were
20 selling for eleven hundred pounds, when Threadneedle Street was daily crowded with the coaches of dukes and prelates, when divines and philosophers turned gamblers, when a thousand kindred bubbles were daily blown into existence, the periwig company, and the Spanish-jackass company, and the quicksilver-fixation-company, Walpole's calm good sense preserved him from the general infatuation. He condemned the prevailing madness in public, and turned a considerable sum by taking advantage of it in private. When the crash came, when ten thousand families were
30 reduced to beggary in a day, when the people in the frenzy of their rage and despair, clamoured, not only against the lower agents in the juggle, but against the Hanoverian favourites, against the English ministers, against the King himself, when Parliament met, eager for confiscation and blood, when members of the House of Commons proposed that the directors should be treated like parricides in ancient

Rome, tied up in sacks, and thrown into the Thames, Walpole was the man on whom all parties turned their eyes. Four years before he had been driven from power by the intrigues of Sunderland and Stanhope, and the lead in the House of Commons had been intrusted to Craggs and Aislabie. Stanhope was no more. Aislabie was expelled from Parliament on account of his disgraceful conduct regarding the South-Sea scheme. Craggs was saved by a timely death from a similar mark of infamy. A large minority in the House of Commons voted for a severe censure on Sunderland, who, finding it impossible to withstand the force of the prevailing sentiment, retired from office, and outlived his retirement but a very short time. The schism which had divided the Whig party was now completely healed. Walpole had no opposition to encounter except that of the Tories; and the Tories were naturally regarded by the King with the strongest suspicion and dislike.

For a time business went on with a smoothness and a despatch such as had not been known since the days of the Tudors. During the session of 1724, for example, there was hardly a single division except on private bills. It is not impossible that, by taking the course which Pelham afterwards took, by admitting into the Government all the rising talents and ambition of the Whig party, and by making room here and there for a Tory not unfriendly to the House of Brunswick, Walpole might have averted the tremendous conflict in which he passed the later years of his administration, and in which he was at length vanquished. The Opposition which overthrew him was an Opposition created by his own policy, by his own insatiable love of power.

In the very act of forming his Ministry he turned one of the ablest and most attached of his supporters into a deadly enemy. Pulteney had strong public and private claims to a high situation in the new arrangement. His fortune was immense. His private character was respectable. He was already a distinguished speaker. He had acquired official

experience in an important post. He had been, through all
changes of fortune, a consistent Whig. When the Whig
party was split into two sections, Pulteney had resigned a
valuable place, and had followed the fortunes of Walpole.
Yet, when Walpole returned to power, Pulteney was not
invited to take office. An angry discussion took place between the friends. The Ministry offered a peerage. It was
impossible for Pulteney not to discern the motive of such an
offer. He indignantly refused to accept it. For some time
10 he continued to brood over his wrongs, and to watch for an
opportunity of revenge. As soon as a favourable conjuncture arrived he joined the minority, and became the
greatest leader of Opposition that the House of Commons
had ever seen.

Of all the members of the Cabinet Carteret was the most
eloquent and accomplished. His talents for debate were of
the first order; his knowledge of foreign affairs was superior
to that of any living statesman; his attachment to the
Protestant succession was undoubted. But there was not
20 room in one Government for him and Walpole. Carteret
retired, and was, from that time forward, one of the most
persevering and formidable enemies of his old colleague.

If there was any man with whom Walpole could have
consented to make a partition of power, that man was Lord
Townshend. They were distant kinsmen by birth, near
kinsmen by marriage. They had been friends from childhood. They had been school-fellows at Eton. They were
country neighbours in Norfolk. They had been in office
together under Godolphin. They had gone into opposition
30 together when Harley rose to power. They had been persecuted by the same House of Commons. They had, after
the death of Anne, been recalled together to office. They
had again been driven out together by Sunderland, and had
again come back together when the influence of Sunderland
had declined. Their opinions on public affairs almost always
coincided. They were both men of frank, generous, and

compassionate natures. Their intercourse had been for many years affectionate and cordial. But the ties of blood, of marriage, and of friendship, the memory of mutual services, the memory of common triumphs and common disasters, were insufficient to restrain that ambition which domineered over all the virtues and vices of Walpole. He was resolved, to use his own metaphor, that the firm of the house should be, not Townshend and Walpole, but Walpole and Townshend. At length the rivals proceeded to personal abuse before a large company, seized each other by the collar, and grasped their swords. The women squalled. The men parted the combatants. By friendly intervention the scandal of a duel between cousins, brothers-in-law, old friends, and old colleagues, was prevented. But the disputants could not long continue to act together. Townshend retired, and, with rare moderation and public spirit, refused to take any part in politics. He could not, he said, trust his temper. He feared that the recollection of his private wrongs might impel him to follow the example of Pulteney, and to oppose measures which he thought generally beneficial to the country. He therefore never visited London after his resignation, but passed the closing years of his life in dignity and repose among his trees and pictures at Rainham.

Next went Chesterfield. He too was a Whig and a friend of the Protestant succession. He was an orator, a courtier, a wit, and a man of letters. He was at the head of *ton* in days when, in order to be at the head of *ton*, it was not sufficient to be dull and supercilious. It was evident that he submitted impatiently to the ascendency of Walpole. He murmured against the Excise Bill. His brothers voted against it in the House of Commons. The Minister acted with characteristic caution and characteristic energy; caution in the conduct of public affairs; energy where his own supremacy was concerned. He withdrew his Bill, and turned out all his hostile or wavering colleagues. Chesterfield was stopped on the great staircase of St. James's, and summoned to deliver up the staff which he bore as Lord Steward of the Household. A crowd of noble and powerful functionaries, the Dukes of Montrose and Bolton, Lord Burlington, Lord Stair, Lord Cobham, Lord Marchmont, Lord Clifton, were at the same time dismissed from the service of the Crown.

Not long after these events the Opposition was reinforced by the Duke of Argyle, a man vainglorious indeed and fickle, but brave, eloquent and popular. It was in a great measure owing to his exertions that the Act of Settlement had been peaceably carried into effect in England immediately after the death of Anne, and that the Jacobite rebellion which, during the following year, broke out in Scotland, had been suppressed. He too carried over to the minority the aid of his great name, his talents, and his paramount influence in his native country.

In each of these cases taken separately, a skilful defender of Walpole might perhaps make out a case for him. But when we see that during a long course of years all the footsteps are turned the same way, that all the most eminent of those public men who agreed with the Minister in their general views of policy left him, one after another, with sore and irritated minds, we find it impossible not to believe that the real explanation of the phænomenon is to be found in the words of his son, "Sir Robert Walpole loved power so much that he would not endure a rival." Hume has described this famous minister with great felicity in one short sentence,—"moderate in exercising power, not equitable in engrossing it." Kind-hearted, jovial, and placable as Walpole was, he was yet a man with whom no person of high pretensions and high spirit could long continue to act. He had, therefore, to stand against an Opposition containing all the most accomplished statesmen of the age, with no better support than that which he received from persons like his brother Horace or Henry Pelham, whose industrious mediocrity gave no cause for jealousy, or from clever adventurers, whose situation and character diminished the dread which their talents might have inspired. To this last class belonged Fox, who was too poor to live without office; Sir William Yonge, of whom Walpole himself said, that nothing but such parts could buoy up such a character, and that nothing but such a character could drag down such parts; and Winnington, whose private morals lay, justly or unjustly, under imputations of the worst kind.

The discontented Whigs were, not perhaps in number, but certainly in ability, experience, and weight, by far the most important part of the Opposition. The Tories furnished little more than rows of ponderous foxhunters, fat with Staffordshire or Devonshire ale, men who drank to the King over the water, and believed that all the fundholders were Jews, men whose religion consisted in hating the Dissenters, and whose political researches had led them to fear, like Squire Western, that their land might be sent over to Hanover to be put in the sinking-fund. The eloquence of these zealous squires, the remnant of the once formidable October Club, seldom went beyond a hearty Ay or No. Very few members of this party had distinguished themselves much in Parliament, or could, under any circumstances, have been called to fill any high office; and those few had generally, like Sir William Wyndham, learned in the company of their new associates the doctrines of toleration and political liberty, and might indeed with strict propriety be called Whigs.

It was to the Whigs in opposition, the patriots, as they were called, that the most distinguished of the English youth who at this season entered into public life attached themselves. These inexperienced politicians felt all the enthusiasm which the name of liberty naturally excites in young and ardent minds. They conceived that the theory of the Tory Opposition and the practice of Walpole's Government were alike inconsistent with the principles of liberty.

They accordingly repaired to the standard which Pulteney had set up. While opposing the Whig minister, they professed a firm adherence to the purest doctrines of Whiggism. He was the schismatic; they were the true Catholics, the peculiar people, the depositaries of the orthodox faith of Hampden and Russell, the one sect which, amidst the corruptions generated by time and by the long possession of power, had preserved inviolate the principles of the Revolution. Of the young men who attached themselves to this portion of the Opposition the most distinguished were Lyttelton and Pitt.

When Pitt entered Parliament, the whole political world was attentively watching the progress of an event which soon added great strength to the Opposition, and particularly to that section of the Opposition in which the young statesman enrolled himself. The Prince of Wales was gradually becoming more and more estranged from his father and his father's ministers, and more and more friendly to the patriots.

Nothing is more natural than that, in a monarchy where a constitutional Opposition exists, the heir-apparent of the throne should put himself at the head of the Opposition. He is impelled to such a course by every feeling of ambition and of vanity. He cannot be more than second in the estimation of the party which is in. He is sure to be the first member of the party which is out. The highest favour which the existing administration can expect from him is that he will not discard them. But, if he joins the Opposition, all his associates expect that he will promote them; and the feelings which men entertain towards one from whom they hope to obtain great advantages which they have not are far warmer than the feelings with which they regard one who, at the very utmost, can only leave them in possession of what they already have. An heir-apparent, therefore, who wishes to enjoy, in the highest perfection, all the pleasure that can be derived from eloquent flattery and profound respect will always join those who are struggling to force themselves into

power. This is, we believe, the true explanation of a fact
which Lord Granville attributed to some natural peculiarity
in the illustrious House of Brunswick. "This family," said
he at Council, we suppose after his daily half-gallon of
Burgundy, "always has quarrelled, and always will quarrel,
from generation to generation." He should have known
something of the matter; for he had been a favourite with
three successive generations of the royal house. We cannot
quite admit his explanation; but the fact is indisputable.
Since the accession of George the First, there have been four
Princes of Wales, and they have all been almost constantly in
Opposition.

Whatever might have been the motives which induced
Prince Frederick to join the party opposed to Sir Robert
Walpole, his support infused into many members of that
party a courage and an energy of which they stood greatly in
need. Hitherto it had been impossible for the discontented
Whigs not to feel some misgivings when they found themselves dividing, night after night, with uncompromising
Jacobites who were known to be in constant communication
with the exiled family, or with Tories who had impeached
Somers, who had murmured against Harley and St. John as
too remiss in the cause of the Church and the landed interest,
and who, if they were not inclined to attack the reigning
family, yet considered the introduction of that family as, at
best, only the less of two great evils, as a necessary but
painful and humiliating preservative against Popery. The
Minister might plausibly say that Pulteney and Carteret, in
the hope of gratifying their own appetite for office and for
revenge, did not scruple to serve the purposes of a faction
hostile to the Protestant succession. The appearance of
Frederick at the head of the patriots silenced this reproach.
The leaders of the Opposition might now boast that their
course was sanctioned by a person as deeply interested as
the King himself in maintaining the Act of Settlement, and
that, instead of serving the purposes of the Tory party, they

14   WILLIAM PITT, EARL OF CHATHAM.   [No. 1

had brought that party over to the side of Whiggism. It must indeed be admitted that, though both the King and the Prince behaved in a manner little to their honour, though the father acted harshly, the son disrespectfully, and both childishly, the royal family was rather strengthened than weakened by the disagreement of its two most distinguished members. A large class of politicians, who had considered themselves as placed under sentence of perpetual exclusion from office, and who, in their despair, had been almost ready
10 to join in a counter-revolution as the only mode of removing the proscription under which they lay, now saw with pleasure an easier and safer road to power opening before them, and thought it far better to wait till, in the natural course of things, the Crown should descend to the heir of the House of Brunswick, than to risk their lands and their necks in a rising for the House of Stuart. The situation of the royal family resembled the situation of those Scotch families in which father and son took opposite sides during the rebellion, in order that, come what might, the estate might not be
20 forfeited.

In April, 1736, Frederick was married to the Princess of Saxe Gotha, with whom he afterwards lived on terms very similar to those on which his father had lived with Queen Caroline. The Prince adored his wife, and thought her in mind and person the most attractive of her sex. But he thought that conjugal fidelity was an unprincely virtue; and, in order to be like Henry the Fourth and the Regent Orleans, he affected a libertinism for which he had no taste, and frequently quitted the only woman whom he loved for
30 ugly and disagreeable mistresses.

The address which the House of Commons presented to the King on the occasion of the Prince's marriage was moved, not by the Minister, but by Pulteney, the leader of the Whigs in Opposition. It was on this motion that Pitt, who had not broken silence during the session in which he took his seat, addressed the House for the first time. "A contemporary historian," says Mr. Thackeray, "describes Mr. Pitt's first speech as superior even to the models of ancient eloquence. According to Tindal, it was more ornamented than the speeches of Demosthenes and less diffuse than those of Cicero." This unmeaning phrase has been a hundred times quoted. That it should ever have been quoted, except to be laughed at, is strange. The vogue which it has obtained may serve to show in how slovenly a way most people are content to think. Did Tindal, who first used it, or Archdeacon Coxe and Mr. Thackeray, who have borrowed it, ever in their lives hear any speaking which did not deserve the same compliment? Did they ever hear speaking less ornamented than that of Demosthenes, or more diffuse than that of Cicero? We know no living orator, from Lord Brougham down to Mr. Hunt, who is not entitled to the same eulogy. It would be no very flattering compliment to a man's figure to say, that he was taller than the Polish Count, and shorter than Giant O'Brien, fatter than the *Anatomie Vivante*, and more slender than Daniel Lambert.

Pitt's speech, as it is reported in the Gentleman's Magazine, certainly deserves Tindal's compliment, and deserves no other.

It is just as empty and wordy as a maiden speech on such an occasion might be expected to be. But the fluency and the personal advantages of the young orator instantly caught the ear and eye of his audience. He was, from the day of his first appearance, always heard with attention; and exercise soon developed the great powers which he possessed.

In our time, the audience of a member of Parliament is the nation. The three or four hundred persons who may be present while a speech is delivered may be pleased or disgusted by the voice and action of the orator; but, in the reports which are read the next day by hundreds of thousands, the difference between the noblest and the meanest figure, between the richest and the shrillest tones, between the most graceful and the most uncouth gesture, altogether vanishes. A hundred years ago, scarcely any report of what passed within the walls of the House of Commons was suffered to get abroad. In those times, therefore, the impression which a speaker might make on the persons who actually heard him was every thing. His fame out of doors depended entirely on the report of those who were within the doors. In the Parliaments of that time, therefore, as in the ancient commonwealths, those qualifications which enhance the immediate effect of a speech, were far more important ingredients in the composition of an orator than at present. All those qualifications Pitt possessed in the highest degree. On the stage, he would have been the finest Brutus or Coriolanus ever seen. Those who saw him in his decay, when his health was broken, when his mind was untuned, when he had been removed from that stormy assembly of which he thoroughly knew the temper, and over which he possessed unbounded influence, to a small, a torpid, and an unfriendly audience, say that his speaking was then, for the most part, a low, monotonous muttering, audible only to those who sat close to him, that when violently excited, he sometimes raised his voice for a few minutes, but that it soon sank again into an unintelligible murmur. Such was the Earl of Chatham ; but such was not William Pitt. His figure, when he first appeared in Parliament, was strikingly graceful and commanding, his features high and noble, his eye full of fire. His voice, even when it sank to a whisper, was heard to the remotest benches ; and when he strained it to its full extent, the sound rose like the swell of the organ of a great cathedral, shook the house with its peal, and was heard through lobbies and down staircases, to the Court of Requests and the precincts of Westminster Hall. He cultivated all these eminent advantages with the most assiduous care. His action is described by a very malignant observer as equal to that of Garrick. His play of countenance was wonderful : he frequently disconcerted a hostile orator by a single glance of indignation or scorn. Every tone, from the impassioned cry to the thrilling aside was perfectly at his command. It is by no means improbable that the pains which he took to improve his great personal advantages had, in some respects, a prejudical operation, and tended to nourish in him that passion for theatrical effect which, as we have already remarked, was one of the most conspicuous blemishes in his character.

But it was not solely or principally to outward accomplishments that Pitt owed the vast influence which, during nearly thirty years, he exercised over the House of Commons. He was undoubtedly a great orator; and, from the descriptions of his contemporaries, and the fragments of his speeches which still remain, it is not difficult to discover the nature and extent of his oratorical powers.

He was no speaker of set speeches. His few prepared discourses were complete failures. The elaborate panegyric which he pronounced on General Wolfe was considered as the very worst of all his performances. "No man," says a critic who had often heard him, "ever knew so little what he was going to say." Indeed his facility amounted to a vice. He was not the master, but the slave of his own speech. So little self-command had he when once he felt the impulse, that he did not like to take part in a debate when his mind was full of an important secret of state. "I must sit still," he once said to Lord Shelburne on such an occasion; "for, when once I am up, every thing that is in my mind comes out."

Yet he was not a great debater. That he should not have been so when first he entered the House of Commons is not strange. Scarcely any person has ever become so without long practice, and many failures. It was by slow degrees, as Burke said, that the late Mr. Fox became the most brilliant and powerful debater that ever lived. Mr. Fox himself attributed his own success to the resolution which he formed when very young, of speaking, well or ill, at least once every night. "During five whole sessions," he used to say, "I

B

spoke every night but one ; and I regret only that I did not speak on that night too." Indeed, with the exception of Mr. Stanley, whose knowledge of the science of parliamentary defence resembles an instinct, it would be difficult to name any eminent debater who has not made himself a master of his art at the expense of his audience.

But as this art is one which even the ablest men have seldom acquired without long practice, so it is one which men of respectable abilities, with assiduous and intrepid
10 practice, seldom fail to acquire. It is singular that in such an art, Pitt, a man of splendid talents, of great fluency, of great boldness, a man whose whole life was passed in parliamentary conflict, a man who, during several years, was the leading minister of the Crown in the House of Commons, should never have attained to high excellence. He spoke without premeditation; but his speech followed the course of his own thoughts and not the course of the previous discussion. He could, indeed, treasure up in his memory some detached expression of a hostile orator, and make it the text
20 for lively ridicule or solemn reprehension. Some of the most celebrated bursts of his eloquence were called forth by an unguarded word, a laugh, or a cheer. But this was the only sort of reply in which he appears to have excelled. He was perhaps the only great English orator who did not think it any advantage to have the last word, and who generally spoke by choice before his most formidable opponents. His merit was almost entirely rhetorical. He did not succeed either in exposition or in refutation ; but his speeches abounded with lively illustrations, striking apophthegms,
30 well told anecdotes, happy allusions, passionate appeals. His invective and sarcasm were terrible. Perhaps no English orator was ever so much feared.

But that which gave most effect to his declamation was the air of sincerity, of vehement feeling, of moral elevation, which belonged to all that he said. His style was not always in the purest taste. Several contemporary judges pronounced it too florid. Walpole, in the midst of the rapturous eulogy which he pronounces on one of Pitt's greatest orations, owns that some of the metaphors were too forced. Some of Pitt's quotations and classical stories are too trite for a clever schoolboy. But these were niceties for which the audience cared little. The enthusiasm of the orator infected all who heard him; his ardour and his noble bearing put fire into the most frigid conceit, and gave dignity to the most puerile allusion.

His powers soon began to give annoyance to the Government; and Walpole determined to make an example of the patriotic cornet. Pitt was accordingly dismissed from the service. Mr. Thackeray says that the Minister took this step, because he plainly saw that it would have been vain to think of buying over so honourable and disinterested an opponent. We do not dispute Pitt's integrity; but we do not know what proof he had given of it when he was turned out of the army; and we are sure that Walpole was not likely to give credit for inflexible honesty to a young adventurer who had never had an opportunity of refusing anything. The truth is, that it was not Walpole's practice to buy off enemies. Mr. Burke truly says, in the Appeal to the Old Whigs, that Walpole gained very few over from the Opposition. Indeed that great minister knew his business far too well. He knew that for one mouth, which is stopped with a place, fifty other mouths will be instantly opened. He knew that it would have been very bad policy in him to give the world to understand that more was to be got by thwarting his measures than by supporting them. These maxims are as old as the origin of parliamentary corruption in England. Pepys learned them, as he tells us, from the counsellors of Charles the Second.

Pitt was no loser. He was made Groom of the Bedchamber to the Prince of Wales, and continued to declaim against the ministers with unabated violence and with increasing ability. The question of maritime right, then agitated between Spain, and England, called forth all his powers. He clamoured for war with a vehemence which it is not easy to reconcile with reason or humanity, but which appears to Mr. Thackeray worthy of the highest admiration. We will not stop to argue a point on which we had long thought that all well informed people were agreed. We could easily show, we think, that, if any respect be due to international law, if right, where societies of men are concerned, be anything but another name for might, if we do not adopt the doctrine of the Buccaneers, which seems to be also the doctrine of Mr. Thackeray, that treaties mean nothing within thirty degrees of the line, the war with Spain was altogether unjustifiable. But the truth is, that the promoters of that war have saved the historian the trouble of trying them. They have pleaded guilty. "I have seen," says Burke, "and with some care examined, the original documents concerning certain important transactions of those times. They perfectly satisfied me of the extreme injustice of that war, and of the falsehood of the colours which Walpole, to his ruin, and guided by a mistaken policy, suffered to be daubed over that measure. Some years after, it was my fortune to converse with many of the principal actors against that minister, and with those who principally excited that clamour. None of them, no not one, did in the least defend the measure, or attempt to justify their conduct. They condemned it as freely as they would have done in commenting upon any proceeding in history in which they were totally unconcerned." Pitt, on subsequent occasions, gave ample proof that he was one of those tardy penitents. But his conduct, even where it appeared most criminal to himself, appears admirable to his biographer.

The elections of 1741 were unfavourable to Walpole; and after a long and obstinate struggle he found it necessary to resign. The Duke of Newcastle and Lord Hardwicke opened a negotiation with the leading patriots, in the hope of forming an administration on a Whig basis. At this conjuncture, Pitt and those persons who were most nearly connected with him acted in a manner very little to their honour. They attempted to come to an understanding with Walpole, and offered, if he would use his influence with the King in their favour, to screen him from prosecution. They even went so far as to engage for the concurrence of the Prince of Wales. But Walpole knew that the assistance of the Boys, as he called the young patriots, would avail him nothing if Pulteney and Carteret should prove intractable, and would be superfluous if the great leaders of the Opposition could be gained. He, therefore, declined the proposal. It is remarkable that Mr. Thackeray, who has thought it worth while to preserve Pitt's bad college verses, has not even alluded to this story, a story which is supported by strong testimony, and which may be found in so common a book as Coxe's Life of Walpole.

The new arrangements disappointed almost every member of the Opposition, and none more than Pitt. He was not invited to become a placeman; and he therefore stuck firmly to his old trade of patriot. Fortunate it was for him that he did so. Had he taken office at this time, he would in all probability have shared largely in the unpopularity of Pulteney, Sandys, and Carteret. He was now the fiercest and most implacable of those who called for vengeance on Walpole. He spoke with great energy and ability in favour of the most unjust and violent propositions which the enemies of the fallen minister could invent. He urged the House of Commons to appoint a secret tribunal for the purpose of investigating the conduct of the late First Lord of the Treasury. This was done. The great majority of the inquisitors were notoriously hostile to the accused statesman. Yet they were compelled to own that they could find no fault in him. They therefore called for new powers, for a bill of indemnity to witnesses, or, in plain words, for a bill to reward all who might give evidence, true or false, against the Earl of Orford. This bill Pitt supported, Pitt, who had

himself offered to be a screen between Lord Orford and
public justice. These are melancholy facts. Mr. Thackeray
omits them, or hurries over them as fast as he can ; and, as
eulogy is his business, he is in the right to do so. But,
though there are many parts of the life of Pitt which it is
more agreeable to contemplate, we know none more
instructive. What must have been the general state of
political morality, when a young man, considered, and justly
considered, as the most public-spirited and spotless statesman
10 of his time, could attempt to force his way into office by
means so disgraceful !

The Bill of Indemnity was rejected by the Lords. Walpole withdrew himself quietly from the public eye ; and the
ample space which he had left vacant was soon occupied by
Carteret. Against Carteret Pitt began to thunder with as
much zeal as he had ever manifested against Sir Robert.
To Carteret he transferred most of the hard names which
were familiar to his eloquence, sole minister, wicked minister,
odious minister, execrable minister. The chief topic of Pitt's
20 invective was the favour shown to the German dominions of
the House of Brunswick. He attacked with great violence,
and with an ability which raised him to the very first rank
among the parliamentary speakers, the practice of paying
Hanoverian troops with English money. The House of
Commons had lately lost some of its most distinguished
ornaments. Walpole and Pulteney had accepted peerages ;
Sir William Wyndham was dead ; and among the rising men
none could be considered as, on the whole, a match for Pitt.

During the recess of 1744, the old Duchess of Marlborough
30 died. She carried to her grave the reputation of being
decidedly the best hater of her time. Yet her love had been
infinitely more destructive than her hatred. More than
thirty years before, her temper had ruined the party to
which she belonged and the husband whom she adored.
Time had made her neither wiser nor kinder. Whoever was
at any moment great and prosperous was the object of her

fiercest detestation. She had hated Walpole; she now hated Carteret. Pope, long before her death, predicted the fate of her vast property.

"To heirs unknown descends the unguarded store,
Or wanders, heaven-directed, to the poor."

Pitt was then one of the poor; and to him Heaven directed a portion of the wealth of the haughty Dowager. She left him a legacy of ten thousand pounds, in consideration of "the noble defence he had made for the support of the laws of England, and to prevent the ruin of his country."

The will was made in August. The Duchess died in October. In November Pitt was a courtier. The Pelhams had forced the King, much against his will, to part with Lord Carteret, who had now become Earl Granville. They proceeded, after this victory, to form the Government on that basis, called by the cant name of "the broad bottom." Lyttleton had a seat at the Treasury, and several other friends of Pitt were provided for. But Pitt himself was, for the present, forced to be content with promises. The King resented most highly some expressions which the ardent orator had used in the debate on the Hanoverian troops. But Newcastle and Pelham expressed the strongest confidence that time and their exertions would soften the royal displeasure.

Pitt, on his part, omitted nothing that might facilitate his admission to office. He resigned his place in the household of Prince Frederick, and, when Parliament met, exerted his eloquence in support of the Government. The Pelhams were really sincere in their endeavours to remove the strong prejudices which had taken root in the King's mind. They knew that Pitt was not a man to be deceived with ease or offended with impunity. They were afraid that they should not be long able to put him off with promises. Nor was it their interest so to put him off. There was a strong tie between him and them. He was the enemy of their enemy.

The brothers hated and dreaded the eloquent, aspiring, and imperious Granville. They had traced his intrigues in many quarters. They knew his influence over the royal mind. They knew that, as soon as a favourable opportunity should arrive, he would be recalled to the head of affairs. They resolved to bring things to a crisis; and the question on which they took issue with their master was, whether Pitt should or should not be admitted to office? They chose their time with more skill than generosity. It was when
10 rebellion was actually raging in Britain, when the Pretender was master of the northern extremity of the island, that they tendered their resignations. The King found himself deserted, in one day, by the whole strength of that party which had placed his family on the throne. Lord Granville tried to form a government; but it soon appeared that the parliamentary interest of the Pelhams was irresistible, and that the King's favourite statesman could count only on about thirty Lords and eighty members of the House of Commons. The scheme was given up. Granville went away
20 laughing. The ministers came back stronger than ever; and the King was now no longer able to refuse any thing that they might be pleased to demand. He could only mutter that it was very hard that Newcastle, who was not fit to be chamberlain to the most insignificent prince in Germany, should dictate to the King of England.

One concession the ministers graciously made. They agreed that Pitt should not be placed in a situation in which it would be necessary for him to have frequent interviews with the King. Instead, therefore, of making their
30 new ally Secretary-at-War as they had intended, they appointed him Vice-Treasurer of Ireland, and in a few months promoted him to the office of Paymaster of the Forces.

This was, at that time, one of the most lucrative offices in the Government. The salary was but a small part of the emolument which the Paymaster derived from his place.

He was allowed to keep a large sum, which, even in time of peace, was seldom less than one hundred thousand pounds, constantly in his hands; and the interest on this sum he might appropriate to his own use. This practice was not secret, nor was it considered as disreputable. It was the practice of men of undoubted honour, both before and after the time of Pitt. He, however, refused to accept one farthing beyond the salary which the law had annexed to his office. It had been usual for foreign princes who received the pay of England to give to the Paymaster of the Forces a small per centage on the subsidies. These ignominious vails Pitt resolutely declined.

Disinterestedness of this kind was, in his days, very rare. His conduct surprised and amused politicians. It excited the warmest admiration throughout the body of the people. In spite of the inconsistencies of which Pitt had been guilty, in spite of the strange contrast between his violence in Opposition and his tameness in office, he still possessed a large share of the public confidence. The motives which may lead a politician to change his connections or his general line of conduct are often obscure; but disinterestedness in pecuniary matters every body can understand. Pitt was thenceforth considered as a man who was proof to all sordid temptations. If he acted ill, it might be from an error in judgment; it might be from resentment; it might be from ambition. But poor as he was, he had vindicated himself from all suspicion of covetousness.

Eight quiet years followed, eight years during which the minority, which had been feeble ever since Lord Granville had been overthrown, continued to dwindle till it became almost invisible. Peace was made with France and Spain in 1748. Prince Frederick died in 1751; and with him died the very semblance of opposition. All the most distinguished survivors of the party which had supported Walpole and of the party which had opposed him were united under his successor. The fiery and vehement spirit of Pitt had for a time been laid to rest. He silently acquiesced in that very system of continental measures which he had lately condemned. He ceased to talk disrespectfully about Hanover. He did not object to the treaty with Spain, though that treaty left us exactly where we had been when he uttered his spirit-stirring harangues against the pacific policy of Walpole. Now and then glimpses of his former self appeared; but they were few and transient. Pelham knew with whom he had to deal, and felt that an ally, so little used to control, and so capable of inflicting injury, might well be indulged in an occasional fit of waywardness.

Two men, little, if at all, inferior to Pitt in powers of mind, held, like him, subordinate offices in the government. One of these, Murray, was successively Solicitor-General and Attorney-General. This distinguished person far surpassed Pitt in correctness of taste, in power of reasoning, in depth and variety of knowledge. His parliamentary eloquence never blazed into sudden flashes of dazzling brilliancy; but its clear, placid, and mellow splendour was never for an instant overclouded. Intellectually he was, we believe, fully equal to Pitt; but he was deficient in the moral qualities to which Pitt owed most of his success. Murray wanted the energy, the courage, the all-grasping and all-risking ambition, which make men great in stirring times. His heart was a little cold, his temper cautious even to timidity, his manners decorous even to formality. He never exposed his fortunes or his fame to any risk which he could avoid. At one time he might, in all probability, have been Prime Minister. But the object of his wishes was the judicial bench. The situation of Chief Justice might not be so splendid as that of First Lord of the Treasury; but it was dignified; it was quiet; it was secure; and therefore it was the favourite situation of Murray.

Fox, the father of the great man whose mighty efforts in the cause of peace, of truth, and of liberty, have made that name immortal, was Secretary-at-War. He was a favourite with the King, with the Duke of Cumberland, and with some of the most powerful members of the great Whig connection. His parliamentary talents were of the highest order. As a speaker he was in almost all respects the very opposite to Pitt. His figure was ungraceful; his face, as Reynolds and Nollekens have preserved it to us, indicated a strong understanding; but the features were coarse, and the general aspect dark and lowering. His manner was awkward; his delivery was hesitating; he was often at a stand for want of a word; but as a debater, as a master of that keen, weighty, manly logic, which is suited to the discussion of political questions, he has perhaps never been surpassed except by his son. In reply he was as decidedly superior to Pitt as in declamation he was Pitt's inferior. Intellectually the balance was nearly even between the rivals. But here, again, the moral qualities of Pitt turned the scale. Fox had undoubtedly many virtues. In natural disposition as well as in talents, he bore a great resemblance to his more celebrated son. He had the same sweetness of temper, the same strong passions, the same openness, boldness, and impetuosity, the same cordiality towards friends, the same placability towards enemies. No man was more warmly or justly beloved by his family or by his associates. But unhappily he had been trained in a bad political school, in a school, the doctrines of which were, that political virtue is the mere coquetry of political prostitution, that every patriot has his price, that Government can be carried on only by means of corruption, and that the state is given as a prey to statesmen. These maxims were too much in vogue throughout the lower ranks of Walpole's party, and were too much encouraged by Walpole himself, who, from contempt of what is in our day vulgarly called *humbug*, often ran extravagantly and offensively into the opposite extreme. The loose political morality of Fox presented a remarkable contrast to the ostentatious purity of Pitt. The nation distrusted the former, and placed implicit confidence in the latter. But almost all the statesmen of the age had still to learn that the confidence of the nation was worth having. While things went on quietly, while there was no opposition, while every thing was given by the favour of a small ruling junto, Fox had a decided advantage over Pitt; but when dangerous times came, when Europe was convulsed with war, when Parliament was broken up into factions, when the public mind was violently excited, the favourite of the people rose to supreme power, while his rival sank into insignificance.

Early in the year 1754 Henry Pelham died unexpectedly. "Now I shall have no more peace," said the old King, when he heard the news. He was in the right. Pelham had succeeded in bringing together and keeping together all the talents of the kingdom. By his death, the highest post to which an English subject can aspire was left vacant; and at the same moment, the influence which had yoked together and reined in so many turbulent and ambitious spirits was withdrawn.

Within a week after Pelham's death, it was determined that the Duke of Newcastle should be placed at the head of the Treasury; but the arrangement was still far from complete. Who was to be the leading Minister of the Crown in the House of Commons? Was the office to be intrusted to a man of eminent talents? And would not such a man in such a place demand and obtain a larger share of power and patronage than Newcastle would be disposed to concede? Was a mere drudge to be employed? And what probability was there that a mere drudge would be able to manage a large and stormy assembly, abounding with able and experienced men?

Pope has said of that wretched miser Sir John Cutler,

"Cutler saw tenants break and houses fall
For very want: he could not build a wall."

Newcastle's love of power resembled Cutler's love of money. It was an avarice which thwarted itself, a penny-wise and pound-foolish cupidity. An immediate outlay was so painful to him that he would not venture to make the most desirable improvement. If he could have found it in his heart to cede at once a portion of his authority, he might probably have ensured the continuance of what remained. But he thought it better to construct a weak and rotten government, which tottered at the smallest breath, and fell in the first storm, than to pay the necessary price for sound and durable materials. He wished to find some person who would be willing to accept the lead of the House of Commons on terms similar to those on which Secretary Craggs had acted under Sunderland, five and thirty years before. Craggs could hardly be called a minister. He was a mere agent for the Minister. He was not trusted with the higher secrets of state, but obeyed implicitly the directions of his superior, and was, to use Doddington's expression, merely Lord Sunderland's man. But times were changed. Since the days of Sunderland, the importance of the House of Commons had been constantly on the increase. During many years the person who conducted the business of the Government in that House had almost always been Prime Minister. Under these circumstances, it was not to be supposed that any person who possessed the talents necessary for the situation, would stoop to accept it on such terms as Newcastle was disposed to offer.

Pitt was ill at Bath; and, had he been well and in London, neither the King nor Newcastle would have been disposed to make any overtures to him. The cool and wary Murray had set his heart on professional objects. Negotiations were opened with Fox. Newcastle behaved like himself, that is to say, childishly and basely. The proposition which he made was, that Fox should be Secretary of State, with the lead of the House of Commons; that the disposal of the secret-service-money, or, in plain words, the business of buying members of Parliament, should be left to the First Lord of the Treasury; but that Fox should be exactly informed of the way in which this fund was employed.

To these conditions Fox assented. But the next day every thing was in confusion. Newcastle had changed his mind. The conversation which took place between Fox and the Duke is one of the most curious in English history. "My brother," said Newcastle, "when he was at the Treasury, never told anybody what he did with the secret-service-money. No more will I." The answer was obvious. Pelham had been, not only First Lord of the Treasury, but also manager of the House of Commons; and it was therefore
10 unneccessary for him to confide to any other person his dealings with the members of that House. "But how," said Fox, "can I lead in the Commons without information on this head? How can I talk to gentlemen when I do not know which of them have received gratifications and which have not? And who," he continued, "is to have the disposal of places?"—"I, myself," said the Duke.—"How then am I to manage the House of Commons?"—" Oh, let the members of the House of Commons come to me." Fox then mentioned the general election which was approaching, and asked how
20 the ministerial boroughs were to be filled up. "Do not trouble yourself," said Newcastle; "that is all settled." This was too much for human nature to bear. Fox refused to accept the Secretaryship of State on such terms; and the Duke confided the management of the House of Commons to a dull, harmless man, whose name is almost forgotten in our time, Sir Thomas Robinson.

When Pitt returned from Bath he affected great moderation, though his haughty soul was boiling with resentment. He did not complain of the manner in which he had been
30 passed by, but said openly that, in his opinion, Fox was the fittest man to lead the House of Commons. The rivals, reconciled by their common interest and their common enmities, concerted a plan of operations for the next session. "Sir Thomas Robinson lead us!" said Pitt to Fox. "The Duke might as well send his jack-boot to lead us!"

The elections of 1754 were favourable to the administration. But the aspect of foreign affairs was threatening. In India the English and the French had been employed, ever since the peace of Aix-la-Chapelle, in cutting each other's throats. They had lately taken to the same practice in America. It might have been foreseen that stirring times were at hand, times which would call for abilities very different from those of Newcastle and Robinson.

In November the Parliament met; and before the end of that month the new Secretary of State had been so unmercifully baited by the Paymaster of the Forces and the Secretary-at-War that he was thoroughly sick of his situation. Fox attacked him with great force and acrimony. Pitt affected a kind of contemptuous tenderness for Sir Thomas, and directed his attacks principally against Newcastle. On one occasion, he asked in tones of thunder whether Parliament sat only to register the edicts of one too-powerful subject? The Duke was scared out of his wits. He was afraid to dismiss the mutineers; he was afraid to promote them; but it was absolutely necessary to do something. Fox, as the less proud and intractable of the refractory pair, was preferred. A seat in the Cabinet was offered to him on condition that he would give efficient support to the ministry in Parliament. In an evil hour for his fame and his fortunes he accepted the offer, and abandoned his connection with Pitt, who never forgave this desertion.

Sir Thomas, assisted by Fox, contrived to get through the business of the year without much trouble. Pitt was waiting his time. The negotiations pending between France and England took every day a more unfavourable aspect. Towards the close of the session the King sent a message to inform the House of Commons that he had found it necessary to make preparations for war. The House returned an address of thanks, and passed a vote of credit. During the recess, the old animosity of both nations was inflamed by a series of disastrous events. An English force was cut off in America; and several French merchantmen were taken in the West Indian Seas. It was plain that an appeal to arms was at hand.

The first object of the King was to secure Hanover; and Newcastle was disposed to gratify his master. Treaties were concluded, after the fashion of those times, with several petty German princes, who bound themselves to find soldiers if England would find money; and, as it was suspected that Frederic the Second had set his heart on the electoral dominions of his uncle, Russia was hired to keep Prussia in
10 awe.

When the stipulations of these treaties were made known, there arose throughout the kingdom a murmur from which a judicious observer might easily prognosticate the approach of a tempest. Newcastle encountered strong opposition, even from those whom he had always considered as his tools. Legge, the Chancellor of the Exchequer, refused to sign the Treasury warrants which were necessary to give effect to the treaties. Those persons who were supposed to possess the confidence of the young Prince of Wales and of his mother
20 held very menacing language. In this perplexity Newcastle sent for Pitt, hugged him, patted him, smirked at him, wept over him, and lisped out the highest compliments and the most splendid promises. The King, who had hitherto been as sulky as possible, would be civil to him at the levee; he should be brought into the Cabinet; he should be consulted about every thing; if he would only be so good as to support the Hessian subsidy in the House of Commons. Pitt coldly declined the proffered seat in the Cabinet, expressed the highest love and reverence for the King, and said
30 that, if his Majesty felt a strong personal interest in the Hessian treaty he would so far deviate from the line which he had traced out for himself as to give that treaty his support. "Well, and the Russian subsidy," said Newcastle. "No," said Pitt, "not a system of subsidies." The Duke summoned Lord Hardwicke to his aid; but Pitt was inflexible. Murray would do nothing. Robinson could do nothing.

It was necessary to have recourse to Fox. He became Secretary of State, with the full authority of a leader in the House of Commons; and Sir Thomas was pensioned off on the Irish establishment.

In November, 1755, the Houses met. Public expectation was wound up to the height. After ten quiet years there was to be an Opposition, countenanced by the heir-apparent of the throne, and headed by the most brilliant orator of the age. The debate on the address was long remembered as one of the greatest parliamentary conflicts of that generation. It began at three in the afternoon, and lasted till five the next morning. It was on this night that Gerard Hamilton delivered that single speech from which his nickname was derived. His eloquence threw into the shade every orator except Pitt, who declaimed against the subsidies for an hour and a half with extraordinary energy and effect. These powers which had formerly spread terror through the majorities of Walpole and Carteret were now displayed in their highest perfection before an audience long unaccustomed to such exhibitions. One fragment of this celebrated oration remains in a state of tolerable preservation. It is the comparison between the coalition of Fox and Newcastle, and the junction of the Rhone and the Saone. "At Lyons," said Pitt, "I was taken to see the place where the two rivers meet, the one gentle, feeble, languid, and, though languid, yet of no depth, the other a boisterous and impetuous torrent; but different as they are, they meet at last." The amendment moved by the Opposition was rejected by a great majority; and Pitt and Legge were immediately dismissed from their offices.

During several months the contest in the House of Commons was extremely sharp. Warm debates took place on the estimates, debates still warmer on the subsidiary treaties. The Government succeeded in every division; but the fame of Pitt's eloquence, and the influence of his lofty and determined character, continued to increase through the

c

Session; and the events which followed the prorogation made it utterly impossible for any other person to manage the Parliament or the country.

The war began in every part of the world with events disastrous to England, and even more shameful than disastrous. But the most humiliating of these events was the loss of Minorca. The Duke of Richelieu, an old fop who had passed his life from sixteen to sixty in seducing women for whom he cared not one straw, landed on that island, and succeeded in reducing it. Admiral Byng was sent from Gibraltar to throw succours into Port-Mahon; but he did not think fit to engage the French squadron, and sailed back without having effected his purpose. The people were inflamed to madness. A storm broke forth, which appalled even those who remembered the days of Excise and of South-Sea. The shops were filled with labels and caricatures. The walls were covered with placards. The city of London called for vengeance, and the cry was echoed from every corner of the kingdom. Dorsetshire, Huntingdonshire, Bedfordshire, Buckinghamshire, Somersetshire, Lancashire, Suffolk, Shropshire, Surrey, sent up strong addresses to the throne, and instructed their representatives to vote for a strict inquiry into the causes of the late disasters. In the great towns the feeling was as strong as in the counties. In some of the instructions it was even recommended that the supplies should be stopped.

The nation was in a state of angry and sullen despondency, almost unparalleled in history. People have, in all ages, been in the habit of talking about the good old times of their ancestors, and the degeneracy of their contemporaries. This is in general merely a cant But in 1756 it was something more. At this time appeared Brown's Estimate, a book now remembered only by the allusions in Cowper's Table Talk and in Burke's Letters on a Regicide Peace. It was universally read, admired, and believed. The author fully convinced his readers that they were a race of cowards and scoundrels; that nothing could save them; that they were on the point of being enslaved by their enemies, and that they richly deserved their fate. Such were the speculations to which ready credence was given at the outset of the most glorious war in which England had ever been engaged.

Newcastle now began to tremble for his place, and for the only thing which was dearer to him than his place, his neck. The people were not in a mood to be trifled with. Their cry was for blood. For this once they might be contented with the sacrifice of Byng. But what if fresh disasters should take place? What if an unfriendly sovereign should ascend the throne? What if a hostile House of Commons should be chosen?

At length, in October, the decisive crisis came. The new Secretary of State had been long sick of the perfidy and levity of the First Lord of the Treasury, and began to fear that he might be made a scapegoat to save the old intriguer who, imbecile as he seemed, never wanted dexterity where danger was to be avoided. Fox threw up his office. Newcastle had recourse to Murray; but Murray had now within his reach the favourite object of his ambition. The situation of Chief-Justice of the King's Bench was vacant; and the Attorney-General was fully resolved to obtain it, or to go into Opposition. Newcastle offered him any terms, the Duchy of Lancaster for life, a tellership of the Exchequer, any amount of pension, two thousand a year, six thousand a year. When the Ministers found that Murray's mind was made up, they pressed for delay, the delay of a session, a month, a week, a day. Would he only make his appearance once more in the House of Commons? Would he only speak in favour of the address? He was inexorable, and peremptorily said that they might give or withhold the Chief-Justiceship, but that he would be Attorney-General no longer.

Newcastle now contrived to overcome the prejudices of the King, and overtures were made to Pitt, through Lord

Hardwicke. Pitt knew his power, and showed that he knew it. He demanded as an indispensable condition that Newcastle should be altogether excluded from the new arrangement.

The Duke was now in a state of ludicrous distress. He ran about chattering and crying, asking advice and listening to none. In the mean time, the Session drew near. The public excitement was unabated. Nobody could be found to face Pitt and Fox in the House of Commons. Newcastle's heart failed him, and he tendered his resignation.

10 The King sent for Fox, and directed him to form the plan of an administration in concert with Pitt. But Pitt had not forgotten old injuries, and positively refused to act with Fox.

The King now applied to the Duke of Devonshire, and this mediator succeeded in making an arrangement. He consented to take the Treasury. Pitt became Secretary of State, with the lead of the House of Commons. The Great Seal was put into commission. Legge returned to the Exchequer; and Lord Temple, whose sister Pitt had lately married, was placed at the head of the Admiralty.

20 It was clear from the first that this administration would last but a very short time. It lasted not quite five months; and, during those five months, Pitt and Lord Temple were treated with rudeness by the King, and found but feeble support in the House of Commons. It is a remarkable fact, that the Opposition prevented the re-election of some of the new Ministers. Pitt, who sat for one of the boroughs which were in the Pelham interest, found some difficulty in obtaining a seat after his acceptance of the seals. So destitute was the new Government of that sort of influence
30 without which no government could then be durable. One of the arguments most frequently urged against the Reform Bill was that, under a system of popular representation, men whose presence in the House of Commons was necessary to the conducting of public business might often find it impossible to find seats. Should this inconvenience ever be felt, there cannot be the slightest difficulty in devising and

applying a remedy. But those who threatened us with this evil ought to have remembered that, under the old system, a great man called to power at a great crisis by the voice of the whole nation was in danger of being excluded, by an aristocratical cabal, from that House of which he was the most distinguished ornament.

The most important event of this short administration was the trial of Byng. On that subject public opinion is still divided. We think the punishment of the Admiral altogether unjust and absurd. Treachery, cowardice, ignorance amounting to what lawyers have called *crassa ignorantia*, are fit objects of severe penal inflictions. But Byng was not found guilty of treachery, of cowardice, or of gross ignorance of his profession. He died for doing what the most loyal subject, the most intrepid warrior, the most experienced seaman, might have done. He died for an error in judgment, an error such as the greatest commanders, Frederic, Napoleon, Wellington, have often committed, and have often acknowledged. Such errors are not proper objects of punishment, for this reason, that the punishing of such errors tends not to prevent them, but to produce them. The dread of an ignominious death may stimulate sluggishness to exertion, may keep a traitor to his standard, may prevent a coward from running away, but it has no tendency to bring out those qualities which enable men to form prompt and judicious decisions in great emergencies. The best marksman may be expected to fail when the apple which is to be his mark is set on his child's head. We cannot conceive any thing more likely to deprive an officer of his self-possession at the time when he most needs it than the knowledge that, if the judgment of his superiors should not agree with his, he will be executed with every circumstance of shame. Queens, it has often been said, run far greater risk in childbed than private women, merely because their medical attendants are more anxious. The surgeon who attended Marie Louise was altogether unnerved by his emotions. "Compose yourself," said Bonaparte; "imagine that you are assisting a poor girl in the Faubourg St. Antoine." This was surely a far wiser course than that of the Eastern king in the Arabian Nights' Entertainments, who proclaimed that the physicians who failed to cure his daughter should have their heads chopped off. Bonaparte knew mankind well; and, as he acted towards this surgeon, he acted towards his officers. No sovereign was ever so indulgent to mere errors of judgment; and it is certain that no sovereign ever had in his service so many military men fit for the highest commands.

Pitt acted a brave and honest part on this occasion. He ventured to put both his power and his popularity to hazard, and spoke manfully for Byng, both in Parliament and in the royal presence. But the King was inexorable. "The House of Commons, Sir," said Pitt, "seems inclined to mercy." "Sir," answered the King, "you have taught me to look for the sense of my people in other places than the House of Commons." The saying has more point than most of those which are recorded of George the Second, and, though sarcastically meant, contains a high and just compliment to Pitt.

The King disliked Pitt, but absolutely hated Temple. The new Secretary of State, his Majesty said, had never read Vatel, and was tedious and pompous, but respectful. The First Lord of the Admiralty was grossly impertinent. Walpole tells one story, which, we fear, is much too good to be true. He assures us that Temple entertained his royal master with an elaborate parallel between Byng's behaviour at Minorca, and his Majesty's behaviour at Oudenarde, in which the advantage was all on the side of the Admiral.

This state of things could not last. Early in April, Pitt and all his friends were turned out, and Newcastle was summoned to St James's. But the public discontent was not extinguished. It had subsided when Pitt was called to power. But it still glowed under the embers; and it now burst at once into a flame. The stocks fell. The Common

Council met. The freedom of the city was voted to Pitt. All the greatest corporate towns followed the example. "For some weeks," says Walpole, "it rained gold boxes."

This was the turning point of Pitt's life. It might have been expected that a man of so haughty and vehement a nature, treated so ungraciously by the Court, and supported so enthusiastically by the people, would have eagerly taken the first opportunity of showing his power and gratifying his resentment; and an opportunity was not wanting. The members for many counties and large towns had been instructed to vote for an inquiry into the circumstances which had produced the miscarriage of the preceding year. A motion for inquiry had been carried in the House of Commons, without opposition; and, a few days after Pitt's dismissal, the investigation commenced. Newcastle and his colleagues obtained a vote of acquittal; but the minority were so strong that they could not venture to ask for a vote of approbation, as they had at first intended; and it was thought by some shrewd observers that, if Pitt had exerted himself to the utmost of his power, the inquiry might have ended in a censure, if not in an impeachment.

Pitt showed on this occasion a moderation and self-government which was not habitual to him. He had found by experience, that he could not stand alone. His eloquence and his popularity had done much, very much for him. Without rank, without fortune, without borough interest, hated by the King, hated by the aristocracy, he was a person of the first importance in the state. He had been suffered to form a ministry, and to pronounce sentence of exclusion on all his rivals, on the most powerful nobleman of the Whig party, on the ablest debater in the House of Commons. And he now found that he had gone too far. The English Constitution was not, indeed, without a popular element. But other elements generally predominated. The confidence and admiration of the nation might make a statesman formidable at the head of an Opposition, might load him with framed and glazed parchments and gold boxes, might possibly, under very peculiar circumstances, such as those of the preceding year, raise him for a time to power. But, constituted as Parliament then was, the favourite of the people could not depend on a majority in the people's own House. The Duke of Newcastle, however contemptible in morals, manners, and understanding, was a dangerous enemy. His rank, his wealth, his unrivalled parliamentary interest, would alone have made him important. But this was not all. The Whig aristocracy regarded him as their leader. His long possession of power had given him a kind of prescriptive right to possess it still. The House of Commons had been elected when he was at the head of affairs. The members for the ministerial boroughs had all been nominated by him. The public offices swarmed with his creatures.

Pitt desired power, and he desired it, we really believe, from high and generous motives. He was, in the strict sense of the word, a patriot. He had none of that philanthropy which the great French writers of his time preached to all the nations of Europe. He loved England as an Athenian loved the City of the Violet Crown, as a Roman loved the City of the Seven Hills. He saw his country insulted and defeated. He saw the national spirit sinking. Yet he knew what the resources of the empire, vigorously employed, could effect; and he felt that he was the man to employ them vigorously. "My Lord," he said to the Duke of Devonshire, "I am sure that I can save this country, and that nobody else can."

Desiring, then, to be in power, and feeling that his abilities and the public confidence were not alone sufficient to keep him in power against the wishes of the Court and of the aristocracy, he began to think of a coalition with Newcastle.

Newcastle was equally disposed to a reconciliation. He, too, had profited by his recent experience. He had found that the Court and the aristocracy, though powerful, were not every thing in the state. A strong oligarchical connection, a great borough interest, ample patronage, and secret-service-money, might, in quiet times, be all that a Minister needed; but it was unsafe to trust wholly to such support in time of war, of discontent, and of agitation. The composition of the House of Commons was not wholly aristocratical; and, whatever be the composition of large deliberative assemblies, their spirit is always in some degree popular. Where there are free debates, eloquence must have admirers, and reason must make converts. Where there is a free press, the governors must live in constant awe of the opinions of the governed.

Thus these two men, so unlike in character, so lately mortal enemies, were necessary to each other. Newcastle had fallen in November, for want of that public confidence which Pitt possessed, and of that parliamentary support which Pitt was better qualified than any man of his time to give. Pitt had fallen in April, for want of that species of influence which Newcastle had passed his whole life in acquiring and hoarding. Neither of them had power enough to support himself. Each of them had power enough to overturn the other. Their union would be irresistible. Neither the King nor any party in the state would be able to stand against them.

Under these circumstances, Pitt was not disposed to proceed to extremities against his predecessors in office. Something, however, was due to consistency; and something was necessary for the preservation of his popularity. He did little; but that little he did in such a manner as to produce great effect. He came down to the House in all the pomp of gout, his legs swathed in flannels, his arm dangling in a sling. He kept his seat through several fatiguing days, in spite of pain and languor. He uttered a few sharp and vehement sentences; but, during the greater part of the discussion, his language was unusually gentle.

When the inquiry had terminated without a vote either of approbation or of censure, the great obstacle to a coalition was removed. Many obstacles, however, remained. The

King was still rejoicing in his deliverance from the proud and aspiring Minister who had been forced on him by the cry of the nation. His Majesty's indignation was excited to the highest point when it appeared that Newcastle, who had, during thirty years, been loaded with marks of royal favour, and who had bound himself, by a solemn promise, never to coalesce with Pitt, was meditating a new perfidy. Of all the statesmen of that age, Fox had the largest share of royal favour. A coalition between Fox and Newcastle
10 was the arrangement which the King wished to bring about. But the Duke was too cunning to fall into such a snare. As a speaker in Parliament, Fox might perhaps be, on the whole, as useful to an administration as his great rival; but he was one of the most unpopular men in England. Then, again, Newcastle felt all that jealousy of Fox which, according to the proverb, generally exists between two of a trade. Fox would certainly intermeddle with that department which the Duke was most desirous to reserve entire to himself, the jobbing department. Pitt, on the other hand, was
20 quite willing to leave the drudgery of corruption to any who might be inclined to undertake it.

During eleven weeks England remained without a ministry; and in the mean time Parliament was sitting, and a war was raging. The prejudices of the King, the haughtiness of Pitt, the jealousy, levity, and treachery of Newcastle, delayed the settlement. Pitt knew the Duke too well to trust him without security. The Duke loved power too much to be inclined to give security. While they were haggling, the King was in vain attempting to produce a
30 final rupture between them, or to form a Government without them. At one time he applied to Lord Waldégrave, an honest and sensible man, but unpractised in affairs. Lord Waldégrave had the courage to accept the Treasury, but soon found that no administration formed by him had the smallest chance of standing a single week.

At length the King's pertinacity yielded to the necessity

of the case. After exclaiming with great bitterness, and with some justice, against the Whigs, who ought, he said, to be ashamed to talk about liberty while they submitted to be the footmen of the Duke of Newcastle, his Majesty submitted. The influence of Leicester House prevailed on Pitt to abate a little, and but a little, of his high demands; and all at once, out of the chaos in which parties had for some time been rising, falling, meeting, separating, arose a government as strong at home as that of Pelham, as successful abroad as that of Godolphin.

Newcastle took the Treasury. Pitt was Secretary of State, with the lead in the House of Commons, and with the supreme direction of the war and of foreign affairs. Fox, the only man who could have given much annoyance to the new government, was silenced with the office of Paymaster, which, during the continuance of that war, was probably the most lucrative place in the whole Government. He was poor, and the situation was tempting; yet it cannot but seem extraordinary that a man who had played a first part in politics, and whose abilities had been found not unequal to that part, who had sat in the Cabinet, who had led the House of Commons, who had been twice intrusted by the King with the office of forming a ministry, who was regarded as the rival of Pitt, and who at one time seemed likely to be a successful rival, should have consented, for the sake of emolument, to take a subordinate place, and to give silent votes for all the measures of a government to the deliberations of which he was not summoned.

The first measures of the new administration were characterized rather by vigour than by judgment. Expeditions were sent against different parts of the French coast with little success. The small island of Aix was taken, Rochefort threatened, a few ships burned in the harbour of St. Maloes, and a few guns and mortars brought home as trophies from the fortifications of Cherbourg. But soon conquests of a very different kind filled the kingdom with pride and rejoicing. A succession of victories undoubtedly brilliant, and, as it was thought, not barren, raised to the highest point the fame of the minister to whom the conduct of the war had been intrusted. In July, 1758, Louisburg fell. The whole island of Cape Breton was reduced. The fleet to which the Court of Versailles had confided the defence of French America was destroyed. The captured standards were borne in triumph from Kensington Palace to the city, and were suspended in St. Paul's Church, amidst the roar of guns and kettle-drums, and the shouts of an immense multitude. Addresses of congratulation came in from all the great towns of England. Parliament met only to decree thanks and monuments, and to bestow, without one murmur, supplies more than double of those which had been given during the war of the Grand Alliance.

The year 1759 opened with the conquest of Goree. Next fell Guadaloupe; then Ticonderoga; then Niagara. The Toulon squadron was completely defeated by Boscawen off Cape Lagos. But the greatest exploit of the year was the achievement of Wolfe on the heights of Abraham. The news of his glorious death and of the fall of Quebec reached London in the very week in which the Houses met. All was joy and triumph. Envy and faction were forced to join in the general applause. Whigs and Tories vied with each other in extolling the genius and energy of Pitt. His colleagues were never talked of or thought of. The House of Commons, the nation, the colonies, our allies, our enemies, had their eyes fixed on him alone.

Scarcely had Parliament voted a monument to Wolfe when another great event called for fresh rejoicings. The Brest fleet, under the command of Conflans, had put out to sea. It was overtaken by an English squadron under Hawke. Conflans attempted to take shelter close under the French coast. The shore was rocky: the night was black: the wind was furious: the waves of the Bay of Biscay ran high. But Pitt had infused into every branch of the service a spirit which had long been unknown. No British seaman was disposed to err on the same side with Byng. The pilot told Hawke that the attack could not be made without the greatest danger. "You have done your duty in remonstrating," answered Hawke; "I will answer for every thing. I command you to lay me alongside the French admiral." Two French ships of the line struck. Four were destroyed. The rest hid themselves in the rivers of Brittany.

The year 1760 came; and still triumph followed triumph. Montreal was taken; the whole province of Canada was subjugated; the French fleets underwent a succession of disasters in the seas of Europe and America.

In the mean time conquests equalling in rapidity, and far surpassing in magnitude, those of Cortes and Pizarro, had been achieved in the East. In the space of three years the English had founded a mighty empire. The French had been defeated in every part of India. Chandernagore had surrendered to Clive, Pondicherry to Coote. Throughout Bengal, Bahar, Orissa, and the Carnatic, the authority of the East India Company was more absolute than that of Acbar or Aurungzebe had ever been.

On the continent of Europe the odds were against England. We had but one important ally, the King of Prussia; and he was attacked, not only by France, but also by Russia and Austria. Yet even on the Continent the energy of Pitt triumphed over all difficulties. Vehemently as he had condemned the practice of subsidising foreign princes, he now carried that practice farther than Carteret himself would have ventured to do. The active and able Sovereign of Prussia received such pecuniary assistance as enabled him to maintain the conflict on equal terms against his powerful enemies. On no subject had Pitt ever spoken with so much eloquence and ardour as on the mischiefs of the Hanoverian connection. He now declared, not without much show of reason, that it would be unworthy of the English people to suffer their King to be deprived of his electoral dominions

in an English quarrel. He assured his countrymen that they should be no losers, and that he would conquer America for them in Germany. By taking this line he conciliated the King, and lost no part of his influence with the nation. In Parliament, such was the ascendency which his eloquence, his success, his high situation, his pride, and his intrepidity had obtained for him, that he took liberties with the House of which there had been no example, and which have never since been imitated. No orator could there venture to
10 reproach him with inconsistency. One unfortunate man made the attempt, and was so much disconcerted by the scornful demeanour of the Minister that he stammered, stopped, and sat down. Even the old Tory country gentlemen, to whom the very name of Hanover had been odious, gave their hearty Ayes to subsidy after subsidy. In a lively contemporary satire, much more lively indeed than delicate, this remarkable conversion is not unhappily described.

"No more they make a fiddle-faddle
About a Hessian horse or saddle.
20 No more of continental measures;
No more of wasting British treasures.
Ten millions, and a vote of credit,
'Tis right. He can't be wrong who did it."

The success of Pitt's continental measures was such as might have been expected from their vigour. When he came into power, Hanover was in imminent danger; and before he had been in office three months, the whole electorate was in the hands of France. But the face of affairs was speedily changed. The invaders were driven out. An army,
30 partly English partly Hanoverian, partly composed of soldiers furnished by the petty princes of Germany, was placed under the command of Prince Ferdinand of Brunswick. The French were beaten in 1758 at Crevelt. In 1759 they received a still more complete and humiliating defeat at Minden.

In the mean time, the nation exhibited all the signs of wealth and prosperity. The merchants of London had never been more thriving. The importance of several great commercial and manufacturing towns, of Glasgow in particular, dates from this period. The fine inscription on the monument of Lord Chatham in Guildhall records the general opinion of the citizens of London, that under his administration commerce had been "united with and made to flourish by war."

It must be owned that these signs of prosperity were in some degree delusive. It must be owned that some of our conquests were rather splendid than useful. It must be owned that the expense of the war never entered into Pitt's consideration. Perhaps it would be more correct to say that the cost of his victories increased the pleasure with which he contemplated them. Unlike other men in his situation, he loved to exaggerate the sums which the nation was laying out under his direction. He was proud of the sacrifices and efforts which his eloquence and his success had induced his countrymen to make. The price at which he purchased faithful service and complete victory, though far smaller than that which his son, the most profuse and incapable of war ministers, paid for treachery, defeat, and shame, was long and severely felt by the nation.

Even as a war minister, Pitt is scarcely entitled to all the praise which his contemporaries lavished on him. We, perhaps from ignorance, cannot discern in his arrangements any appearance of profound or dexterous combination. Several of his expeditions, particularly those which were sent to the coast of France, were at once costly and absurd. Our Indian conquests, though they add to the splendour of the period during which he was at the head of affairs, were not planned by him. He had undoubtedly great energy, great determination, great means at his command. His temper was enterprising; and, situated as he was, he had only to follow his temper. The wealth of a rich nation, the valour of a brave nation, were ready to support him in every attempt.

In one respect, however, he deserved all the praise that he has ever received. The success of our arms was perhaps owing less to the skill of his dispositions than to the national resources and the national spirit. But that the national spirit rose to the emergency, that the national resources were contributed with unexampled cheerfulness, this was undoubtedly his work. The ardour of his soul had set the whole kingdom on fire. It inflamed every soldier who dragged the cannon up the heights of Quebec, and every sailor who boarded the French ships among the rocks of Brittany. The Minister, before he had been long in office, had imparted to the commanders whom he employed his own impetuous, adventurous, and defying character. They, like him, were disposed to risk everything, to play double or quits to the last, to think nothing done while any thing remained undone, to fail rather than not to attempt. For the errors of rashness there might be indulgence. For over-caution, for faults like those of Lord George Sackville, there was no mercy. In other times, and against other enemies, this mode of warfare might have failed. But the state of the French government and of the French nation gave every advantage to Pitt. The fops and intriguers of Versailles were appalled and bewildered by his vigour. A panic spread through all ranks of society. Our enemies soon considered it as a settled thing that they were always to be beaten. Thus victory begot victory; till, at last, wherever the forces of the two nations met, they met with disdainful confidence on the one side, and with a craven fear on the other.

The situation which Pitt occupied at the close of the reign of George the Second was the most enviable ever occupied by any public man in English history. He had conciliated the King; he domineered over the House of Commons; he was adored by the people; he was admired by all Europe. He was the first Englishman of his time; and he had made England the first country in the world. The Great Commoner, the name by which he was often designated, might look down with scorn on coronets and garters. The nation was drunk with joy and pride. The Parliament was as quiet as it had been under Pelham. The old party distinctions were almost effaced; nor was their place yet supplied by distinctions of a still more important kind. A new generation of country squires and rectors had arisen who knew not the Stuarts. The Dissenters were tolerated; the Catholics not cruelly persecuted. The Church was drowsy and indulgent. The great civil and religious conflict which began at the Reformation seemed to have terminated in universal repose. Whigs and Tories, Churchmen and Puritans, spoke with equal reverence of the constitution, and with equal enthusiasm of the talents, virtues, and services of the Minister.

A few years sufficed to change the whole aspect of affairs. A nation convulsed by faction, a throne assailed by the fiercest invective, a House of Commons hated and despised by the nation, England set against Scotland, Britain set against America, a rival legislature sitting beyond the Atlantic, English blood shed by English bayonets, our armies capitulating, our conquests wrested from us, our enemies hastening to take vengeance for past humiliation, our flag scarcely able to maintain itself in our own seas, such was the spectacle which Pitt lived to see. But the history of this great revolution requires far more space than we can at present bestow. We leave the Great Commoner in the zenith of his glory. It is not impossible that we may take some other opportunity of tracing his life to its melancholy, yet not inglorious close.

THE EARL OF CHATHAM.

SECOND ESSAY, OCTOBER 1844.

1. Correspondence of William Pitt, Earl of Chatham. 4 vols. 8vo. London. 1840.
2. Letters of Horace Walpole, Earl of Orford, to Horace Mann. 4 vols. 8vo. London. 1843-4.

More than ten years ago we commenced a sketch of the political life of the great Lord Chatham. We then stopped at the death of George the Second, with the intention of speedily resuming our task. Circumstances, which it would be tedious to explain, long prevented us from carrying this intention into effect. Nor can we regret the delay. For the materials which were within our reach in 1834 were scanty and unsatisfactory, when compared with those which we at present possess. Even now, though we have had access to some valuable sources of information which have not yet been opened to the public, we cannot but feel that the history of the first ten years of the reign of George the Third is but imperfectly known to us. Nevertheless, we are inclined to think that we are in a condition to lay before our readers a narrative neither uninstructive nor uninteresting. We therefore return with pleasure to our long interrupted labour.

We left Pitt in the zenith of prosperity and glory, the idol of England, the terror of France, the admiration of the whole civilised world. The wind, from whatever quarter it blew, carried to England tidings of battles won, fortresses taken, provinces added to the empire. At home, factions had sunk into a lethargy, such as had never been known since the great religious schism of the sixteenth century had roused the public mind from repose.

In order that the events which we have to relate may be clearly understood, it may be desirable that we should advert to the causes which had for a time suspended the animation of both the great English parties.

If, rejecting all that is merely accidental, we look at the essential characteristics of the Whig and the Tory, we may consider each of them as the representative of a great principle, essential to the welfare of nations. One is, in an especial manner, the guardian of liberty, and the other, of order. One is the moving power, and the other the steadying power of the state. One is the sail, without which society would make no progress, the other the ballast, without which there would be small safety in a tempest. But, during the forty-six years which followed the accession of the House of Hanover, these distinctive peculiarities seemed to be effaced. The Whig conceived that he could not better serve the cause of civil and religious freedom than by strenuously supporting the Protestant dynasty. The Tory conceived that he could not better prove his hatred of revolutions than by attacking a government to which a revolution had given birth. Both came by degrees to attach more importance to the means than to the end. Both were thrown into unnatural situations ; and both, like animals transported to an uncongenial climate, languished and degenerated. The Tory, removed from the sunshine of the court, was as a camel in the snows of Lapland. The Whig, basking in the rays of royal favour, was as a reindeer in the sands of Arabia.

Dante tells us that he saw, in Malebolge, a strange encounter between a human form and a serpent. The enemies, after cruel wounds inflicted, stood for a time glaring on each other. A great cloud surrounded them, and then a wonderful metamorphosis began. Each creature was transfigured into the likeness of its antagonist. The serpent's tail divided itself into two legs ; the man's legs intertwined themselves into a tail. The body of the serpent put forth arms; the arms of the man shrank into his body. At length the serpent stood up a man, and spake; the man sank down a serpent, and glided hissing away. Something like this was the transformation which, during the reign of George the First, befel the two English parties. Each gradually took the shape and colour of its foe, till at length the Tory rose up erect the zealot of freedom, and the Whig crawled and licked the dust at the feet of power.

10 It is true that, when these degenerate politicians discussed questions merely speculative, and, above all, when they discussed questions relating to the conduct of their own grandfathers, they still seemed to differ as their grandfathers had differed. The Whig, who, during three Parliaments, had never given one vote against the court, and who was ready to sell his soul for the Comptroller's staff or for the Great Wardrobe, still professed to draw his political doctrines from Locke and Milton, still worshipped the memory of Pym and Hampden, and would still, on the thirtieth of
20 January, take his glass, first to the man in the mask, and then to the man who would do it without a mask. The Tory, on the other hand, while he reviled the mild and temperate Walpole, as a deadly enemy of liberty, could see nothing to reprobate in the iron tyranny of Strafford and Laud. But, whatever judgment the Whig or the Tory of that age might pronounce on transactions long past, there can be no doubt that, as respected the practical questions then pending, the Tory was a reformer, and indeed an intemperate and indiscreet reformer, while the Whig was conservative even to
30 bigotry. We have ourselves seen similar effects produced in a neighbouring country by similar causes. Who would have believed, fifteen years ago, that M. Guizot and M. Villemain would have to defend property and social order against the attacks of such enemies as M. Genoude and M. de La Roche Jaquelin?

Thus the successors of the old Cavaliers had turned demagogues; the successors of the old Roundheads had turned courtiers. Yet was it long before their mutual animosity began to abate; for it is the nature of parties to retain their original enmities far more firmly than their original principles. During many years, a generation of Whigs, whom Sidney would have spurned as slaves, continued to wage deadly war with a generation of Tories whom Jeffreys would have hanged for republicans.

Through the whole reign of George the First, and through nearly half of the reign of George the Second, a Tory was regarded as an enemy of the reigning house, and was excluded from all the favours of the crown. Though most of the country gentlemen were Tories, none but Whigs were created peers and baronets. Though most of the clergy were Tories, none but Whigs were appointed deans and bishops. In every county, opulent and well descended Tory squires complained that their names were left out of the commission of the peace, while men of small estate and mean birth, who were for toleration and excise, septennial parliaments and standing armies, presided at quarter sessions, and became deputy lieutenants.

By degrees some approaches were made towards a reconciliation. While Walpole was at the head of affairs, enmity to his power induced a large and powerful body of Whigs, headed by the heir apparent of the throne, to make an alliance with the Tories, and a truce even with the Jacobites. After Sir Robert's fall, the ban which lay on the Tory party was taken off. The chief places in the administration continued to be filled by Whigs, and, indeed, could scarcely have been filled otherwise; for the Tory nobility and gentry, though strong in numbers and in property, had among them scarcely a single man distinguished by talents, either for business or for debate. A few of them, however, were admitted to subordinate offices; and this indulgence produced a softening effect on the temper of the whole body. The first levee of George the Second after Walpole's resignation was a remarkable spectacle. Mingled with the constant supporters of the House of Brunswick, with the Russells, the Cavendishes, and the Pelhams, appeared a crowd of faces utterly unknown to the pages and gentlemen ushers, lords of rural manors, whose ale and foxhounds were renowned in the neighbourhood of the Mendip Hills, or round the Wrekin, but who had never crossed the threshold of the palace since the days when Oxford, with the white staff in his hand, stood behind Queen Anne.

During the eighteen years which followed this day, both factions were gradually sinking deeper and deeper into repose. The apathy of the public mind is partly to be ascribed to the unjust violence with which the administration of Walpole had been assailed. In the body politic, as in the natural body, morbid languor generally succeeds morbid excitement. The people had been maddened by sophistry, by calumny, by rhetoric, by stimulants applied to the national pride. In the fulness of bread, they had raved as if famine had been in the land. While enjoying such a measure of civil and religious freedom as, till then, no great society had ever known, they had cried out for a Timoleon or a Brutus to stab their oppressor to the heart. They were in this frame of mind when the change of administration took place; and they soon found that there was to be no change whatever in the system of government. The natural consequences followed. To frantic zeal succeeded sullen indifference. The cant of patriotism had not merely ceased to charm the public ear, but had become as nauseous as the cant of Puritanism after the downfall of the Rump. The hot fit was over: the cold fit had begun: and it was long before seditious arts, or even real grievances, could bring back the fiery paroxysm which had run its course and reached its termination.

Two attempts were made to disturb this tranquillity. The banished heir of the House of Stuart headed a rebellion; the discontented heir of the House of Brunswick headed an opposition. Both the rebellion and the opposition came to nothing. The battle of Culloden annihilated the Jacobite party. The death of Prince Frederic dissolved the faction which, under his guidance, had feebly striven to annoy his father's government. His chief followers hastened to make their peace with the ministry; and the political torpor became complete.

Five years after the death of Prince Frederic, the public mind was for a time violently excited. But this excitement had nothing to do with the old disputes between Whigs and Tories. England was at war with France. The war had been feebly conducted. Minorca had been torn from us. Our fleet had retired before the white flag of the House of Bourbon. A bitter sense of humiliation, new to the proudest and bravest of nations, superseded every other feeling. The cry of all the counties and great towns of the realm was for a government which would retrieve the honour of the English arms. The two most powerful men in the country were the Duke of Newcastle and Pitt. Alternate victories and defeats had made them sensible that neither of them could stand alone. The interest of the state, and the interest of their own ambition, impelled them to coalesce. By their coalition was formed the ministry which was in power when George the Third ascended the throne.

The more carefully the structure of this celebrated ministry is examined, the more shall we see reason to marvel at the skill or the luck which had combined in one harmonious whole such various and, as it seemed, incompatible elements of force. The influence which is derived from stainless integrity, the influence which is derived from the vilest arts of corruption, the strength of aristocratical connection, the strength of democratical enthusiasm, all these things were for the first time found together. Newcastle brought to the coalition a vast mass of power, which had descended to him from Walpole and Pelham. The public offices, the church, the courts of law, the army, the navy, the diplomatic service, swarmed with his creatures. The boroughs, which long afterwards made up the memorable schedules A and B, were represented by his nominees. The great Whig families, which, during several generations, had been trained in the discipline of party warfare, and were accustomed to stand together in a firm phalanx, acknowledged him as their captain. Pitt, on the other hand, had what Newcastle wanted, an eloquence which stirred the passions and charmed the imagination, a high reputation for purity, and the confidence and ardent love of millions.

10   The partition which the two ministers made of the powers of government was singularly happy. Each occupied a province for which he was well qualified; and neither had any inclination to intrude himself into the province of the other. Newcastle took the treasury, the civil and ecclesiastical patronage, and the disposal of that part of the secret service money which was then employed in bribing members of Parliament. Pitt was Secretary of State, with the direction of the war and of foreign affairs. Thus the filth of all the noisome and pestilential sewers of government was poured
20 into one channel. Through the other passed only what was bright and stainless. Mean and selfish politicians, pining for commissionerships, gold sticks, and ribands, flocked to the great house at the corner of Lincoln's Inn Fields. There, at every levee, appeared eighteen or twenty pair of lawn sleeves; for there was not, it was said, a single Prelate who had not owed either his first elevation or some subsequent translation to Newcastle. There appeared those members of the House of Commons in whose silent votes the main strength of the government lay. One wanted a place in the excise for his
30 butler. Another came about a prebend for his son. A third whispered that he had always stood by his Grace and the Protestant succession; that his last election had been very expensive; that potwallopers had now no conscience; that he had been forced to take up money on mortgage; and that he hardly knew where to turn for five hundred pounds. The Duke pressed all their hands, passed his arms round all their

shoulders, patted all their backs, and sent away some with wages, and some with promises. From this traffic Pitt stood haughtily aloof. Not only was he himself incorruptible, but he shrank from the loathsome drudgery of corrupting others. He had not, however, been twenty years in Parliament, and ten in office, without discovering how the government was carried on. He was perfectly aware that bribery was practised on a large scale by his colleagues. Hating the practice, yet despairing of putting it down, and doubting whether, in those times, any ministry could stand without it, he determined to be blind to it. He would see nothing, know nothing, believe nothing. People who came to talk to him about shares in lucrative contracts, or about the means of securing a Cornish corporation, were soon put out of countenance by his arrogant humility. They did him too much honour. Such matters were beyond his capacity. It was true that his poor advice about expeditions and treaties was listened to with indulgence by a gracious sovereign. If the question were, who should command in North America, or who should be ambassador at Berlin, his colleagues would probably condescend to take his opinion. But he had not the smallest influence with the Secretary of the Treasury, and could not venture to ask even for a tidewaiter's place.

It may be doubted whether he did not owe as much of his popularity to his ostentatious purity as to his eloquence, or to his talents for the administration of war. It was every where said with delight and admiration that the great Commoner, without any advantages of birth or fortune, had, in spite of the dislike of the Court and of the aristocracy, made himself the first man in England, and made England the first country in the world; that his name was mentioned with awe in every palace from Lisbon to Moscow ; that his trophies were in all the four quarters of the globe; yet that he was still plain William Pitt, without title or riband, without pension or sinecure place. Whenever he should retire, after saving the state, he must sell his coach horses and his silver candlesticks.

Widely as the taint of corruption had spread, his hands were clean. They had never received, they had never given, the price of infamy. Thus the coalition gathered to itself support from all the high and all the low parts of human nature, and was strong with the whole united strength of virtue and of Mammon.

Pitt and Newcastle were coordinate chief ministers. The subordinate places had been filled on the principle of including in the government every party and shade of party, the avowed Jacobites alone excepted, nay, every public man who, from his abilities or from his situation, seemed likely to be either useful in office or formidable in opposition.

The Whigs, according to what was then considered as their prescriptive right, held by far the largest share of power. The main support of the administration was what may be called the great Whig connection, a connection which, during near half a century, had generally had the chief sway in the country and which derived an immense authority from rank, wealth, borough interest, and firm union. To this connection, of which Newcastle was the head, belonged the houses of Cavendish, Lennox, Fitzroy, Bentinck, Manners, Conway, Wentworth, and many others of high note.

There were two other powerful Whig connections, either of which might have been a nucleus for a strong opposition. But room had been found in the government for both. They were known as the Grenvilles and the Bedfords.

The head of the Grenvilles was Richard Earl Temple. His talents for administration and debate were of no high order. But his great possessions, his turbulent and unscrupulous character, his restless activity, and his skill in the most ignoble tactics of faction, made him one of the most formidable enemies that a ministry could have. He was keeper of the privy seal. His brother George was treasurer of the navy. They were supposed to be on terms of close friendship with Pitt, who had married their sister, and was the most uxorious of husbands.

The Bedfords, or, as they were called by their enemies, the Bloomsbury gang, professed to be led by John Duke of Bedford, but in truth led him wherever they chose, and very often led him where he never would have gone of his own accord. He had many good qualities of head and heart, and would have been certainly a respectable, and possibly a distinguished man, if he had been less under the influence of his friends, or more fortunate in choosing them. Some of them were indeed, to do them justice, men of parts. But here, we are afraid, eulogy must end. Sandwich and Rigby were able debaters, pleasant boon companions, dexterous intriguers, masters of all the arts of jobbing and electioneering, and, both in public and private life, shamelessly immoral. Weymouth had a natural eloquence, which sometimes astonished those who knew how little he owed to study. But he was indolent and dissolute, and had early impaired a fine estate with the dicebox, and a fine constitution with the bottle. The wealth and power of the Duke, and the talents and audacity of some of his retainers, might have seriously annoyed the strongest ministry. But his assistance had been secured. He was Lord Lieutenant of Ireland; Rigby was his secretary; and the whole party dutifully supported the measures of the Government.

Two men had, a short time before, been thought likely to contest with Pitt the lead of the House of Commons, William Murray and Henry Fox. But Murray had been removed to the Lords, and was Chief Justice of the King's Bench. Fox was indeed still in the Commons: but means had been found to secure, if not his strenuous support, at least his silent acquiescence. He was a poor man; he was a doting father. The office of Paymaster-General during an expensive war was, in that age, perhaps the most lucrative situation in the gift of the government. This office was bestowed on Fox. The prospect of making a noble fortune in a few years, and of providing amply for his darling boy Charles, was irresistibly tempting. To hold a subordinate place, however profitable, after having led the House of Commons, and having been intrusted with the business of forming a ministry, was indeed a great descent. But a punctilious sense of personal dignity was no part of the character of Henry Fox.

We have not time to enumerate all the other men of weight who were, by some tie or other, attached to the government. We may mention Hardwicke, reputed the first lawyer of the age; Legge, reputed the first financier of the age; the acute and ready Oswald; the bold and humorous Nugent; Charles Townshend, the most brilliant and versatile of mankind; Elliot, Barrington, North, Pratt. Indeed, as far as we recollect, there were in the whole House of Commons only two men of distinguished abilities who were not connected with the government; and those two men stood so low in public estimation that the only service which they could have rendered to any government would have been to oppose it. We speak of Lord George Sackville and Bubb Doddington.

Though most of the official men, and all the members of the cabinet were reputed Whigs, the Tories were by no means excluded from employment. Pitt had gratified many of them with commands in the militia, which increased both their income and their importance in their own counties; and they were therefore in better humour than at any time since the death of Anne. Some of the party still continued to grumble over their punch at the Cocoa Tree; but in the House of Commons not a single one of the malcontents durst lift his eyes above the buckle of Pitt's shoe.

Thus there was absolutely no opposition. Nay, there was no sign from which it could be guessed in what quarter opposition was likely to arise. Several years passed, during which Parliament seemed to have abdicated its chief functions. The Journals of the House of Commons, during four sessions, contain no trace of a division on a party question. The supplies, though beyond precedent great, were voted without discussion. The most animated debates of that period were on road bills and inclosure bills.

The old King was content; and it mattered little whether he were content or not. It would have been impossible for him to emancipate himself from a ministry so powerful, even if he had been inclined to do so. But he had no such inclination. He had once, indeed, been strongly prejudiced against Pitt, and had repeatedly been ill used by Newcastle ; but the vigour and success with which the war had been waged in Germany, and the smoothness with which all public business was carried on, had produced a favourable change in the royal mind.

Such was the posture of affairs when, on the twenty-fifth of October, 1760, George the Second suddenly died, and George the Third, then twenty-two years old, became King. The situation of George the Third differed widely from that of his grandfather and that of his greatgrandfather. Many years had elapsed since a sovereign of England had been an object of affection to any part of his people. The first two Kings of the House of Hanover had neither those hereditary rights which have often supplied the defect of merit, nor those personal qualities which have often supplied the defect of title. A prince may be popular with little virtue or capacity, if he reigns by birthright derived from a long line of illustrious predecessors. An usurper may be popular, if his genius has saved or aggrandised the nation which he governs. Perhaps no rulers have in our time had a stronger hold on the affection of subjects than the Emperor Francis, and his son-in-law the Emperor Napoleon. But imagine a ruler with no better title than Napoleon, and no better understanding than Francis. Richard Cromwell was such a ruler; and, as soon as an arm was lifted up against him, he fell without a struggle, amidst universal derision. George the First and George the Second were in a situation which bore some resemblance to that of Richard Cromwell. They were saved from the fate of Richard Cromwell by the

strenuous and able exertions of the Whig party, and by the general conviction that the nation had no choice but between the House of Brunswick and Popery. But by no class were the Guelphs regarded with that devoted affection, of which Charles the First, Charles the Second, and James the Second, in spite of the greatest faults, and in the midst of the greatest misfortunes, received innumerable proofs. Those Whigs who stood by the new dynasty so manfully with purse and sword did so on principles independent of, and indeed almost
10 incompatible with, the sentiment of devoted loyalty. The moderate Tories regarded the foreign dynasty as a great evil, which must be endured for fear of a greater evil. In the eyes of the high Tories, the Elector was the most hateful of robbers and tyrants. The crown of another was on his head; the blood of the brave and loyal was on his hands. Thus, during many years, the Kings of England were objects of strong personal aversion to many of their subjects, and of strong personal attachment to none. They found, indeed, firm and cordial support against the pretender to their
20 throne; but this support was given, not at all for their sake, but for the sake of a religious and political system which would have been endangered by their fall. This support, too, they were compelled to purchase by perpetually sacrificing their private inclinations to the party which had set them on the throne, and which maintained them there.

At the close of the reign of George the Second, the feeling of aversion with which the House of Brunswick had long been regarded by half the nation had died away ; but no feeling of affection to that house had yet sprung up. There
30 was little, indeed, in the old King's character to inspire esteem or tenderness. He was not our countryman. He never set foot on our soil till he was more than thirty years old. His speech bewrayed his foreign origin and breeding. His love for his native land, though the most amiable part of his character, was not likely to endear him to his British subjects. He was never so happy

as when he could exchange St. James's for Hernhausen. Year after year, our fleets were employed to convoy him to the Continent, and the interests of his kingdom were as nothing to him when compared with the interests of his Electorate. As to the rest, he had neither the qualities which make dulness respectable, nor the qualities which make libertinism attractive. He had been a bad son and a worse father, an unfaithful husband and an ungraceful lover. Not one magnanimous or humane action is recorded of him; but many instances of meanness, and of a harshness which, but for the strong constitutional restraints under which he was placed, might have made the misery of his people.

He died; and at once a new world opened. The young King was a born Englishman. All his tastes and habits, good or bad, were English. No portion of his subjects had any thing to reproach him with. Even the remaining adherents of the House of Stuart could scarcely impute to him the guilt of usurpation. He was not responsible for the Revolution, for the Act of Settlement, for the suppression of the risings of 1715 and of 1745. He was innocent of the blood of Derwentwater and Kilmarnock, of Balmerino and Cameron. Born fifty years after the old line had been expelled, fourth in descent and third in succession of the Hanoverian dynasty, he might plead some show of hereditary right. His age, his appearance, and all that was known of his character, conciliated public favour. He was in the bloom of youth; his person and address were pleasing. Scandal imputed to him no vice; and flattery might, without any glaring absurdity, ascribe to him many princely virtues.

It is not strange, therefore, that the sentiment of loyalty, a sentiment which had lately seemed to be as much out of date as the belief in witches or the practice of pilgrimage, should, from the day of his accession, have begun to revive. The Tories in particular, who had always been inclined to King-worship, and who had long felt with pain the want of an idol before whom they could bow themselves down, were

as joyful as the priests of Apis, when, after a long interval, they had found a new calf to adore. It was soon clear that George the Third was regarded by a portion of the nation with a very different feeling from that which his two predecessors had inspired. They had been merely first Magistrates, Doges, Stadtholders; he was emphatically a King, the anointed of heaven, the breath of his people's nostrils. The years of the widowhood and mourning of the Tory party were over. Dido had kept faith long enough to
10 the cold ashes of a former lord; she had at last found a comforter, and recognised the vestiges of the old flame. The golden days of Harley would return. The Somersets, the Lees, and the Wyndhams would again surround the throne. The latitudinarian Prelates, who had not been ashamed to correspond with Doddridge and to shake hands with Whiston, would be succeeded by divines of the temper of South and Atterbury. The devotion which had been so signally shown to the House of Stuart, which had been proof against defeats, confiscations, and proscriptions, which
20 perfidy, oppression, ingratitude, could not weary out, was now transferred entire to the House of Brunswick. If George the Third would but accept the homage of the Cavaliers and High Churchmen, he should be to them all that Charles the First and Charles the Second had been.

The Prince, whose accession was thus hailed by a great party long estranged from his house, had received from nature a strong will, a firmness of temper to which a harsher name might perhaps be given, and an understanding not, indeed, acute or enlarged, but such as qualified him to be a
30 good man of business. But his character had not yet fully developed itself. He had been brought up in strict seclusion. The detractors of the Princess Dowager of Wales affirmed that she had kept her children from commerce with society, in order that she might hold an undivided empire over their minds. She gave a very different explanation of her conduct. She would gladly, she said, see her sons and

daughters mix in the world, if they could do so without risk to their morals. But the profligacy of the people of quality alarmed her. The young men were all rakes; the young women made love, instead of waiting till it was made to them. She could not bear to expose those whom she loved best to the contaminating influence of such society. The moral advantages of the system of education which formed the Duke of York, the Duke of Cumberland, and the Queen of Denmark, may perhaps be questioned. George the Third was indeed no libertine; but he brought to the throne a mind only half opened, and was for some time entirely under the influence of his mother and of his Groom of the Stole, John Stuart, Earl of Bute.

The Earl of Bute was scarcely known, even by name, to the country which he was soon to govern. He had indeed, a short time after he came of age, been chosen to fill a vacancy which, in the middle of a parliament, had taken place among the Scotch representative peers. He had disobliged the Whig ministers by giving some silent votes with the Tories, and consequently lost his seat at the next dissolution, and had never been reelected. Near twenty years had elapsed since he had borne any part in politics. He had passed some of those years at his seat in one of the Hebrides, and from that retirement he had emerged as one of the household of Prince Frederic. Lord Bute, excluded from public life, had found out many ways of amusing his leisure. He was a tolerable actor in private theatricals, and was particularly successful in the part of Lothario. A handsome leg, to which both painters and satirists took care to give prominence, was among his chief qualifications for the stage. He devised quaint dresses for masquerades. He dabbled in geometry, mechanics, and botany. He paid some attention to antiquities and works of art, and was considered in his own circle as a judge of painting, architecture, and poetry. It is said that his spelling was incorrect. But though, in our time, incorrect spelling is justly considered as

a proof of sordid ignorance, it would be unjust to apply the
same rule to people who lived a century ago. The novel of
Sir Charles Grandison was published about the time at
which Lord Bute made his appearance at Leicester House.
Our readers may perhaps remember the account which
Charlotte Grandison gives of her two lovers. One of them,
a fashionable baronet who talks French and Italian fluently,
cannot write a line in his own language without some sin
against orthography; the other, who is represented as a
10 most respectable specimen of the young aristocracy, and
something of a virtuoso, is described as spelling pretty well
for a lord. On the whole, the Earl of Bute might fairly be
called a man of cultivated mind. He was also a man of
undoubted honour. But his understanding was narrow, and
his manners cold and haughty. His qualifications for the
part of a statesman were best described by Frederic, who
often indulged in the unprincely luxury of sneering at his
dependents. "Bute," said his Royal Highness, "you are the
very man to be envoy at some small proud German court
20 where there is nothing to do."

Scandal represented the Groom of the Stole as the favoured
lover of the Princess Dowager. He was undoubtedly her
confidential friend. The influence which the two united
exercised over the mind of the King was for a time unbounded. The Princess, a woman and a foreigner, was not
likely to be a judicious adviser about affairs of state. The
Earl could scarcely be said to have served even a novitiate
in politics. His notions of government had been acquired in
the society which had been in the habit of assembling round
30 Frederic at Kew and Leicester House. That society consisted principally of Tories, who had been reconciled to the
House of Hanover by the civility with which the Prince had
treated them, and by the hope of obtaining high preferment
when he should come to the throne. Their political creed
was a peculiar modification of Toryism. It was the creed
neither of the Tories of the seventeenth nor of the Tories of

the nineteenth century; it was the creed, not of Filmer and Sacheverell, not of Perceval and Eldon, but of the sect of which Bolingbroke may be considered as the chief doctor. This sect deserves commendation for having pointed out and justly reprobated some great abuses which sprang up during the long domination of the Whigs. But it is far easier to point out and reprobate abuses than to propose beneficial reforms: and the reforms which Bolingbroke proposed would either have been utterly inefficient, or would have produced much more mischief than they would have removed.

The Revolution had saved the nation from one class of evils, but had at the same time—such is the imperfection of all things human—engendered or aggravated another class of evils which required new remedies. Liberty and property were secure from the attacks of prerogative. Conscience was respected. No government ventured to infringe any of the rights solemnly recognised by the instrument which had called William and Mary to the throne. But it cannot be denied that, under the new system, the public interests and the public morals were seriously endangered by corruption and faction. During the long struggle against the Stuarts, the chief object of the most enlightened statesmen had been to strengthen the House of Commons. The struggle was over; the victory was won; the House of Commons was supreme in the state; and all the vices which had till then been latent in the representative system were rapidly developed by prosperity and power. Scarcely had the executive government become really responsible to the House of Commons, when it began to appear that the House of Commons was not really responsible to the nation. Many of the constituent bodies were under the absolute control of individuals; many were notoriously at the command of the highest bidder. The debates were not published. It was very seldom known out of doors how a gentlemen had voted. Thus, while the ministry was accountable to the Parliament, the majority of the Parliament was accountable to nobody.

Under such circumstances, nothing could be more natural than that the members should insist on being paid for their votes, should form themselves into combinations for the purpose of raising the price of their votes, and should at critical conjunctures extort large wages by threatening a strike. Thus the Whig ministers of George the First and George the Second were compelled to reduce corruption to a system, and to practise it on a gigantic scale.

If we are right as to the cause of these abuses, we can
10 scarcely be wrong as to the remedy. The remedy was surely not to deprive the House of Commons of its weight in the state. Such a course would undoubtedly have put an end to parliamentary corruption and to parliamentary factions: for, when votes cease to be of importance, they will cease to be bought; and, when knaves can get nothing by combining, they will cease to combine. But to destroy corruption and faction by introducing despotism would have been to cure bad by worse. The proper remedy evidently was, to make the House of Commons responsible to the nation; and this
20 was to be effected in two ways; first, by giving publicity to parliamentary proceedings, and thus placing every member on his trial before the tribunal of public opinion; and secondly, by so reforming the constitution of the House that no man should be able to sit in it who had not been returned by a respectable and independent body of constituents.

Bolingbroke and Bolingbroke's disciples recommended a very different mode of treating the diseases of the state. Their doctrine was, that a vigorous use of the prerogative by a patriot King would at once break all factious combina-
30 tions, and supersede the pretended necessity of bribing members of Parliament. The King had only to resolve that he would be master, that he would not be held in thraldom by any set of men, that he would take for ministers any persons in whom he had confidence, without distinction of party, and that he would restrain his servants from influencing by immoral means, either the constituent bodies or the

representative body. This childish scheme proved that those who proposed it knew nothing of the nature of the evil with which they pretended to deal. The real cause of the prevalence of corruption and faction was that a House of Commons, not accountable to the people, was more powerful than the King. Bolingbroke's remedy could be applied only by a King more powerful than the House of Commons. How was the patriot Prince to govern in defiance of the body without whose consent he could not equip a sloop, keep a battalion under arms, send an embassy, or defray even the charges of his own household? Was he to dissolve the Parliament? And what was he likely to gain by appealing to Sudbury and Old Sarum against the venality of their representatives? Was he to send out privy seals? Was he to levy ship-money? If so, this boasted reform must commence in all probability by civil war, and, if consummated, must be consummated by the establishment of absolute monarchy. Or was the patriot King to carry the House of Commons with him in his upright designs? By what means? Interdicting himself from the use of corrupt influence, what motive was he to address to the Dodingtons and Winningtons? Was cupidity, strengthened by habit, to be laid asleep by a few fine sentences about virtue and union?

Absurd as this theory was, it had many admirers, particularly among men of letters. It was now to be reduced to practice; and the result was, as any man of sagacity must have foreseen, the most piteous and ridiculous of failures.

On the very day of the young King's accession, appeared some signs which indicated the approach of a great change. The speech which he made to his council was not submitted to the cabinet. It was drawn up by Bute, and contained some expressions which might be construed into reflections on the conduct of affairs during the late reign. Pitt remonstrated, and begged that these expressions might be softened down in the printed copy; but it was not till after some hours of altercation that Bute yielded; and, even after Bute had yielded, the King affected to hold out till the following afternoon. On the same day on which this singular contest took place, Bute was not only sworn of the privy council, but introduced into the cabinet.

Soon after this Lord Holdernesse, one of the Secretaries of State, in pursuance of a plan concerted with the court, resigned the seals. Bute was instantly appointed to the vacant place. A general election speedily followed, and the new Secretary entered parliament in the only way in which he then could enter it, as one of the sixteen representatives of Scotland.

Had the ministers been firmly united it can scarcely be doubted that they would have been able to withstand the court. The parliamentary influence of the Whig aristocracy, combined with the genius, the virtue, and the fame of Pitt, would have been irresistible. But there had been in the cabinet of George the Second latent jealousies and enmities, which now began to show themselves. Pitt had been estranged from his old ally Legge, the Chancellor of the Exchequer. Some of the ministers were envious of Pitt's popularity. Others were, not altogether without cause, disgusted by his imperious and haughty demeanour. Others, again, were honestly opposed to some parts of his policy. They admitted that he had found the country in the depths of humiliation, and had raised it to the height of glory; they admitted that he had conducted the war with energy, ability, and splendid success. But they began to hint that the drain on the resources of the state was unexampled, and that the public debt was increasing with a speed at which Montague or Godolphin would have stood aghast. Some of the acquisitions made by our fleets and armies were, it was acknowledged, profitable as well as honourable; but, now that George the Second was dead, a courtier might venture to ask why England was to become a party in a dispute between two German powers. What was it to her whether the House of Hapsburg or the House of Brandenburg ruled in Silesia? Why were the best English regiments fighting on the Main? Why were the Prussian battalions paid with English gold? The great minister seemed to think it beneath him to calculate the price of victory. As long as the Tower guns were fired, as the streets were illuminated, as French banners were carried in triumph through London, it was to him matter of indifference to what extent the public burdens were augmented. Nay, he seemed to glory in the magnitude of those sacrifices which the people, fascinated by his eloquence and success, had too readily made, and would long and bitterly regret. There was no check on waste or embezzlement. Our commissaries returned from the camp of Prince Ferdinand to buy boroughs, to rear palaces, to rival the magnificence of the old aristocracy of the realm. Already had we borrowed, in four years of war, more than the most skilful and economical government would pay in forty years of peace. But the prospect of peace was as remote as ever. It could not be doubted that France, smarting and prostrate, would consent to fair terms of accommodation; but this was not what Pitt wanted. War had made him powerful and popular; with war, all that was brightest in his life was associated; for war his talents were peculiarly fitted. He had at length begun to love war for its own sake, and was more disposed to quarrel with neutrals than to make peace with enemies.

Such were the views of the Duke of Bedford and of the Earl of Hardwicke; but no member of the government held these opinions so strongly as George Grenville, the treasurer of the navy. George Grenville was brother-in-law of Pitt, and had always been reckoned one of Pitt's personal and political friends. But it is difficult to conceive two men of talents and integrity more utterly unlike each other. Pitt, as his sister often said, knew nothing accurately except Spenser's Fairy Queen. He had never applied himself steadily to any branch of knowledge. He was a wretched financier. He never became familiar even with the rules of

that House of which he was the brightest ornament. He
had never studied public law as a system ; and was, indeed,
so ignorant of the whole subject, that George the Second, on
one occasion, complained bitterly that a man who had never
read Vattel should presume to undertake the direction of
foreign affairs. But these defects were more than redeemed
by high and rare gifts, by a strange power of inspiring great
masses of men with confidence and affection, by an eloquence
which not only delighted the ear, but stirred the blood, and
10 brought tears into the eyes, by originality in devising plans,
by vigour in executing them. Grenville, on the other hand,
was by nature and habit a man of details. He had been
bred a lawyer ; and he had brought the industry and acuteness of the Temple into official and parliamentary life. He
was supposed to be intimately acquainted with the whole
fiscal system of the country. He had paid especial attention
to the law of Parliament, and was so learned in all things
relating to the privileges and orders of the House of
Commons that those who loved him least pronounced him
20 the only person competent to succeed Onslow in the Chair.
His speeches were generally instructive, and sometimes, from
the gravity and earnestness with which he spoke, even
impressive, but never brilliant, and generally tedious.
Indeed, even when he was at the head of affairs, he sometimes found it difficult to obtain the ear of the House. In
disposition as well as in intellect, he differed widely from his
brother-in-law. Pitt was utterly regardless of money. He
would scarcely stretch out his hand to take it ; and, when it
came, he threw it away with childish profusion. Grenville,
30 though strictly upright, was grasping and parsimonious.
Pitt was a man of excitable nerves, sanguine in hope, easily
elated by success and popularity, keenly sensible of injury,
but prompt to forgive ; Grenville's character was stern,
melancholy, and pertinacious. Nothing was more remarkable
in him than his inclination always to look on the dark side of
things. He was the raven of the House of Commons, always

croaking defeat in the midst of triumphs, and bankruptcy with an overflowing exchequer. Burke, with general applause, compared him, in a time of quiet and plenty, to the evil spirit whom Ovid described looking down on the stately temples and wealthy haven of Athens, and scarce able to refrain from weeping because she could find nothing at which to weep. Such a man was not likely to be popular. But to unpopularity Grenville opposed a dogged determination, which sometimes forced even those who hated him to respect him.

It was natural that Pitt and Grenville, being such as they were, should take very different views of the situation of affairs. Pitt could see nothing but the trophies; Grenville could see nothing but the bill. Pitt boasted that England was victorious at once in America, in India, and in Germany, the umpire of the Continent, the mistress of the sea. Grenville cast up the subsidies, sighed over the army extraordinaries, and groaned in spirit to think that the nation had borrowed eight millions in one year.

With a ministry thus divided it was not difficult for Bute to deal. Legge was the first who fell. He had given offence to the young King in the late reign, by refusing to support a creature of Bute at a Hampshire election. He was now not only turned out, but in the closet, when he delivered up his seal of office, was treated with gross incivility.

Pitt, who did not love Legge, saw this event with indifference. But the danger was now fast approaching himself. Charles the Third of Spain had early conceived a deadly hatred of England. Twenty years before, when he was King of the Two Sicilies, he had been eager to join the coalition against Maria Theresa. But an English fleet had suddenly appeared in the Bay of Naples. An English captain had landed, had proceeded to the palace, had laid a watch on the table, and had told his majesty that, within an hour, a treaty of neutrality must be signed, or a bombardment would commence. The treaty was signed; the squadron sailed out

of the bay twenty-four hours after it had sailed in; and from
that day the ruling passion of the humbled Prince was
aversion to the English name. He was at length in a
situation in which he might hope to gratify that passion.
He had recently become King of Spain and the Indies. He
saw, with envy and apprehension, the triumphs of our navy,
and the rapid extension of our colonial Empire. He was a
Bourbon, and sympathised with the distress of the house
from which he sprung. He was a Spaniard; and no Spaniard
could bear to see Gibraltar and Minorca in the possession of
a foreign power. Impelled by such feelings, Charles concluded
a secret treaty with France. By this treaty, known as the
Family Compact, the two powers bound themselves, not in
express words, but by the clearest implication, to make war
on England in common. Spain postponed the declaration of
hostilities only till her fleet, laden with the treasures of
America, should have arrived.

The existence of the treaty could not be kept a secret from
Pitt. He acted as a man of his capacity and energy might
be expected to act. He at once proposed to declare war
against Spain, and to intercept the American fleet. He had
determined, it is said, to attack without delay both Havanna
and the Philippines.

His wise and resolute counsel was rejected. Bute was
foremost in opposing it, and was supported by almost the
whole cabinet. Some of the ministers doubted, or affected
to doubt, the correctness of Pitt's intelligence; some shrank
from the responsibility of advising a course so bold and
decided as that which he proposed; some were weary of his
ascendency, and were glad to be rid of him on any pretext.
One only of his colleagues agreed with him, his brother-in-
law, Earl Temple.

Pitt and Temple resigned their offices. To Pitt the young
King behaved at parting in the most gracious manner.
Pitt, who, proud and fiery every where else, was always meek
and humble in the closet, was moved even to tears. The

King and the favourite urged him to accept some substantial mark of royal gratitude. Would he like to be appointed governor of Canada? A salary of five thousand pounds a year should be annexed to the office. Residence would not be required. It was true that the governor of Canada, as the law then stood, could not be a member of the House of Commons. But a bill should be brought in, authorising Pitt to hold his government together with a seat in Parliament, and in the preamble should be set forth his claims to the gratitude of his country. Pitt answered, with all delicacy, that his anxieties were rather for his wife and family than for himself, and that nothing would be so acceptable to him as a mark of royal goodness which might be beneficial to those who were dearest to him. The hint was taken. The same Gazette which announced the retirement of the Secretary of State announced also that, in consideration of his great public services, his wife had been created a peeress in her own right, and that a pension of three thousand pounds a year, for three lives, had been bestowed on himself. It was doubtless thought that the rewards and honours conferred on the great minister would have a conciliatory effect on the public mind. Perhaps, too, it was thought that his popularity, which had partly arisen from the contempt which he had always shown for money, would be damaged by a pension; and, indeed, a crowd of libels instantly appeared, in which he was accused of having sold his country. Many of his true friends thought that he would have best consulted the dignity of his character by refusing to accept any pecuniary reward from the court. Nevertheless, the general opinion of his talents, virtues, and services, remained unaltered. Addresses were presented to him from several large towns. London showed its admiration and affection in a still more marked manner. Soon after his resignation came the Lord Mayor's day. The King and the royal family dined at Guildhall. Pitt was one of the guests. The young sovereign, seated by his bride in his state coach,

received a remarkable lesson. He was scarcely noticed. All eyes were fixed on the fallen minister; all acclamations directed to him. The streets, the balconies, the chimney tops, burst into a roar of delight as his chariot passed by. The ladies waved their handkerchiefs from the windows. The common people clung to the wheels, shook hands with the footmen, and even kissed the horses. Cries of "No Bute!" "No Newcastle salmon!" were mingled with the shouts of "Pitt for ever!" When Pitt entered Guildhall,
10 he was welcomed by loud huzzas and clapping of hands, in which the very magistrates of the city joined. Lord Bute, in the mean time, was hooted and pelted through Cheapside, and would, it was thought, have been in some danger, if he had not taken the precaution of surrounding his carriage with a strong body guard of boxers. Many persons blame the conduct of Pitt on this occasion as disrespectful to the King. Indeed, Pitt himself afterwards owned that he had done wrong. He was led into this error, as he was afterwards led into more serious errors, by the influence of his
20 turbulent and mischievous brother-in-law, Temple.

The events which immediately followed Pitt's retirement raised his fame higher than ever. War with Spain proved to be, as he had predicted, inevitable. News came from the West Indies that Martinique had been taken by an expedition which he had sent forth. Havanna fell; and it was known that he had planned an attack on Havanna. Manilla capitulated; and it was believed that he had meditated a blow against Manilla. The American fleet, which he had proposed to intercept, had unloaded an immense cargo of
30 bullion in the haven of Cadiz, before Bute could be convinced that the court of Madrid really entertained hostile intentions.

The session of Parliament which followed Pitt's retirement passed over without any violent storm. Lord Bute took on himself the most prominent part in the House of Lords. He had become Secretary of State, and indeed prime minister, without having once opened his lips in public except as an actor. There was, therefore, no small curiosity to know how he would acquit himself. Members of the House of Commons crowded the bar of the Lords, and covered the steps of the throne. It was generally expected that the orator would break down; but his most malicious hearers were forced to own that he had made a better figure than they expected. They, indeed, ridiculed his action as theatrical, and his style as tumid. They were especially amused by the long pauses which, not from hesitation, but from affectation, he made at all the emphatic words, and Charles Townshend cried out, "Minute guns!" The general opinion however was, that, if Bute had been early practised in debate, he might have become an impressive speaker.

In the Commons, George Grenville had been intrusted with the lead. The task was not, as yet, a very difficult one; for Pitt did not think fit to raise the standard of Opposition. His speeches at this time were distinguished, not only by that eloquence in which he excelled all his rivals, but also by a temperance and a modesty which had too often been wanting to his character. When war was declared against Spain, he justly laid claim to the merit of having foreseen what had at length become manifest to all, but he carefully abstained from arrogant and acrimonious expressions; and this abstinence was the more honourable to him, because his temper, never very placid, was now severely tried, both by gout and by calumny. The courtiers had adopted a mode of warfare, which was soon turned with far more formidable effect against themselves. Half the inhabitants of the Grub Street garrets paid their milk scores, and got their shirts out of pawn, by abusing Pitt. His German war, his subsidies, his pension, his wife's peerage, were shin of beef and gin, blankets and baskets of small coal, to the starving poetasters of the Fleet. Even in the House of Commons, he was, on one occasion during this session, assailed with an insolence and malice which called forth the indignation of men of all parties; but he endured the outrage with majestic patience. In his younger days he had been but too prompt to retaliate on those who attacked him; but now, conscious of his great services, and of the space which he filled in the eyes of all mankind, he would not stoop to personal squabbles. "This is no season," he said, in the debate on the Spanish war, "for altercation and recrimination. A day has arrived when every Englishman should stand forth for his country. Arm the whole; be one people; forget every thing but the public. I set you the example. Harassed by slanderers, sinking under pain and disease, for the public I forget both my wrongs and my infirmities!" On a general review of his life, we are inclined to think that his genius and virtue never shone with so pure an effulgence as during the session of 1762.

The session drew towards the close; and Bute, emboldened by the acquiescence of the Houses, resolved to strike another great blow, and to become first minister in name as well as in reality. That coalition, which a few months before had seemed all powerful, had been dissolved. The retreat of Pitt had deprived the government of popularity. Newcastle had exulted in the fall of the illustrious colleague whom he envied and dreaded, and had not foreseen that his own doom was at hand. He still tried to flatter himself that he was at the head of the government; but insults heaped on insults at length undeceived him. Places which had always been considered as in his gift, were bestowed without any reference to him. His expostulations only called forth significant hints that it was time for him to retire. One day he pressed on Bute the claims of a Whig Prelate to the Archbishopric of York. "If your grace thinks so highly of him," answered Bute, "I wonder that you did not promote him when you had the power." Still the old man clung with a desperate grasp to the wreck. Seldom, indeed, have Christian meekness and Christian humility equalled the meekness and humility of his patient and abject ambition. At length he was forced to understand that all was over. He quitted that court where he had held high office during forty-five years, and hid his shame and regret among the cedars of Claremont. Bute became first lord of the treasury.

The favourite had undoubtedly committed a great error. It is impossible to imagine a tool better suited to his purposes than that which he thus threw away, or rather put into the hands of his enemies. If Newcastle had been suffered to play at being first minister, Bute might securely and quietly have enjoyed the substance of power. The gradual introduction of Tories into all the departments of the government might have been effected without any violent clamour, if the chief of the great Whig connection had been ostensibly at the head of affairs. This was strongly represented to Bute by Lord Mansfield, a man who may justly be called the father of modern Toryism, of Toryism modified to suit an order of things under which the House of Commons is the most powerful body in the state. The theories which had dazzled Bute could not impose on the fine intellect of Mansfield. The temerity with which Bute provoked the hostility of powerful and deeply rooted interests was displeasing to Mansfield's cold and timid nature. Expostulation, however, was vain. Bute was impatient of advice, drunk with success, eager to be, in show as well as in reality, the head of the government. He had engaged in an undertaking in which a screen was absolutely necessary to his success, and even to his safety. He found an excellent screen ready in the very place where it was most needed; and he rudely pushed it away.

And now the new system of government came into full operation. For the first time since the accession of the House of Hanover, the Tory party was in the ascendant. The prime minister himself was a Tory. Lord Egremont, who had succeeded Pitt as Secretary of State, was a Tory, and the son of a Tory. Sir Francis Dashwood, a man of slender parts, of small experience, and of notoriously immoral character, was made Chancellor of the Exchequer, for no

reason that could be imagined, except that he was a Tory, and had been a Jacobite. The royal household was filled with men whose favourite toast, a few years before, had been the King over the water. The relative position of the two great national seats of learning was suddenly changed. The University of Oxford had long been the chief seat of disaffection. In troubled times, the High Street had been lined with bayonets; the colleges had been searched by the King's messengers. Grave doctors were in the habit of talking very
10 Ciceronian treason in the theatre; and the undergraduates drank bumpers to Jacobite toasts, and chanted Jacobite airs. Of four successive Chancellors of the University, one had notoriously been in the Pretender's service; the other three were fully believed to be in secret correspondence with the exiled family. Cambridge had therefore been especially favoured by the Hanoverian Princes, and had shown herself grateful for their patronage. George the First had enriched her library; George the Second had contributed munificently to her Senate House. Bishoprics and deaneries were showered
20 on her children. Her Chancellor was Newcastle, the chief of the Whig aristocracy; her High Steward was Hardwicke, the Whig head of the law. Both her burgesses had held office under the Whig ministry. Times had now changed. The University of Cambridge was received at St James's with comparative coldness. The answers to the addresses of Oxford were all graciousness and warmth.

The watchwords of the new government were prerogative and purity. The sovereign was no longer to be a puppet in the hands of any subject, or of any combination of subjects.
30 George the Third would not be forced to take ministers whom he disliked, as his grandfather had been forced to take Pitt. George the Third would not be forced to part with any whom he delighted to honour, as his grandfather had been forced to part with Carteret. At the same time, the system of bribery which had grown up during the late reigns was to cease. It was ostentatiously proclaimed that,

1844]   WILLIAM PITT, EARL OF CHATHAM.   81

since the accession of the young King, neither constituents nor representatives had been bought with the secret service money. To free Britain from corruption and oligarchical cabals, to detach her from continental connections, to bring the bloody and expensive war with France and Spain to a close, such were the specious objects which Bute professed to procure.

Some of these objects he attained. England withdrew, at the cost of a deep stain on her faith, from her German connections. The war with France and Spain was terminated by a peace, honourable indeed and advantageous to our country, yet less honourable and less advantageous than might have been expected from a long and almost unbroken series of victories, by land and sea, in every part of the world. But the only effect of Bute's domestic administration was to make faction wilder, and corruption fouler than ever.

The mutual animosity of the Whig and Tory parties had begun to languish after the fall of Walpole, and had seemed to be almost extinct at the close of the reign of George the Second. It now revived in all its force. Many Whigs, it is true, were still in office. The Duke of Bedford had signed the treaty with France. The Duke of Devonshire, though much out of humour, still continued to be Lord Chamberlain. Grenville, who led the House of Commons, and Fox, who still enjoyed in silence the immense gains of the Pay Office, had always been regarded as strong Whigs. But the bulk of the party throughout the country regarded the new minister with abhorrence. There was, indeed, no want of popular themes for invective against his character. He was a favourite; and favourites have always been odious in this country. No mere favourite had been at the head of the government since the dagger of Felton had reached the heart of the Duke of Buckingham. After that event the most arbitrary and the most frivolous of the Stuarts had felt the necessity of confiding the chief direction of affairs to

F

men who had given some proof of parliamentary or official talent. Strafford, Falkland, Clarendon, Clifford, Shaftesbury, Lauderdale, Danby, Temple, Halifax, Rochester, Sunderland, whatever their faults might be, were all men of acknowledged ability. They did not owe their eminence merely to the favour of the sovereign. On the contrary, they owed the favour of the sovereign to their eminence. Most of them, indeed, had first attracted the notice of the court by the capacity and vigour which they had shown in opposition.
10 The Revolution seemed to have for ever secured the state against the domination of a Carr or a Villiers. Now, however, the personal regard of the King had at once raised a man who had seen nothing of public business, who had never opened his lips in Parliament, over the heads of a crowd of eminent orators, financiers, diplomatists. From a private gentleman, this fortunate minion had at once been turned into a Secretary of State. He had made his maiden speech when at the head of the administration. The vulgar resorted to a simple explanation of the phenomenon, and the
20 coarsest ribaldry against the Princess Mother was scrawled on every wall and sung in every alley.

This was not all. The spirit of party, roused by impolitic provocation from its long sleep, roused in turn a still fiercer and more malignant Fury, the spirit of national animosity. The grudge of Whig against Tory was mingled with the grudge of Englishman against Scot. The two sections of the great British people had not yet been indissolubly blended together. The events of 1715 and of 1745 had left painful and enduring traces. The tradesmen of Cornhill had
30 been in dread of seeing their tills and warehouses plundered by barelegged mountaineers from the Grampians. They still recollected that Black Friday, when the news came that the rebels were at Derby, when all the shops in the city were closed, and when the Bank of England began to pay in sixpences. The Scots, on the other hand, remembered with natural resentment, the severity with which the insurgents

had been chastised, the military outrages, the humiliating laws, the heads fixed on Temple Bar, the fires and quartering blocks on Kennington Common. The favourite did not suffer the English to forget from what part of the island he came. The cry of all the south was that the public offices, the army, the navy, were filled with high-cheeked Drummonds and Erskines, Macdonalds and Macgillivrays, who could not talk a Christian tongue, and some of whom had but lately begun to wear Christian breeches. All the old jokes on hills without trees, girls without stockings, men eating the food of horses, pails emptied from the fourteenth storey, were pointed against these lucky adventurers. To the honour of the Scots it must be said, that their prudence and their pride restrained them from retaliation. Like the princess in the Arabian tale, they stopped their ears tight, and, unmoved by the shrillest notes of abuse, walked on, without once looking round, straight towards the Golden Fountain.

Bute, who had always been considered as a man of taste and reading, affected, from the moment of his elevation, the character of a Mæcenas. If he expected to conciliate the public by encouraging literature and art, he was grievously mistaken. Indeed, none of the objects of his munificence, with the single exception of Johnson, can be said to have been well selected; and the public, not unnaturally, ascribed the selection of Johnson rather to the Doctor's political prejudices than to his literary merits: for a wretched scribbler named Shebbeare, who had nothing in common with Johnson except violent Jacobitism, and who had stood in the pillory for a libel on the Revolution, was honoured with a mark of royal approbation, similar to that which was bestowed on the author of the English Dictionary, and of the Vanity of Human Wishes. It was remarked that Adam, a Scotchman, was the court architect, and that Ramsay, a Scotchman, was the court painter, and was preferred to Reynolds. Mallet, a Scotchman, of no high literary fame, and of infamous character, partook largely of the liberality of the government. John Home, a Scotchman, was rewarded for the tragedy of Douglas, both with a pension and with a sinecure place. But, when the author of the Bard, and of the Elegy in a Country Churchyard, ventured to ask for a Professorship, the emoluments of which he much needed, and for the duties of which he was, in many respects, better qualified than any man living, he was refused; and the post was bestowed on the pedagogue under whose care the favourite's son-in-law, Sir James Lowther, had made such signal proficiency in the graces and in the humane virtues.

Thus, the first lord of the treasury was detested by many as a Tory, by many as a favourite, and by many as a Scot. All the hatred which flowed from these various sources soon mingled, and was directed in one torrent of obloquy against the treaty of peace. The Duke of Bedford, who negotiated that treaty, was hooted through the streets. Bute was attacked in his chair, and was with difficulty rescued by a troop of guards. He could hardly walk the streets in safety without disguising himself. A gentleman who died not many years ago used to say that he once recognised the favourite Earl in the piazza of Covent Garden, muffled in a large coat, and with a hat and wig drawn down over his brows. His lordship's established type with the mob was a jack boot, a wretched pun on his Christian name and title. A jack boot, generally accompanied by a petticoat, was sometimes fastened on a gallows, and sometimes committed to the flames. Libels on the court, exceeding in audacity and rancour any that had been published for many years, now appeared daily both in prose and verse. Wilkes, with lively insolence, compared the mother of George the Third to the the mother of Edward the Third, and the Scotch minister to the gentle Mortimer. Churchill, with all the energy of hatred, deplored the fate of his country, invaded by a new race of savages, more cruel and ravenous than the Picts or the Danes, the poor, proud children of Leprosy and Hunger.

It is a slight circumstance, but deserves to be recorded, that in this year pamphleteers first ventured to print at length the names of the great men whom they lampooned. George the Second had always been the K——. His ministers had been Sir R—— W——, Mr. P——, and the Duke of N——. But the libellers of George the Third, of the Princess Mother, and of Lord Bute did not give quarter to a single vowel.

It was supposed that Lord Temple secretly encouraged the most scurrilous assailants of the government. In truth, those who knew his habits tracked him as men track a mole. It was his nature to grub underground. Whenever a heap of dirt was flung up, it might well be suspected that he was at work in some foul crooked labyrinth below. Pitt turned away from the filthy work of opposition, with the same scorn with which he had turned away from the filthy work of Government. He had the magnanimity to proclaim every where the disgust which he felt at the insults offered by his own adherents to the Scottish nation, and missed no opportunity of extolling the courage and fidelity which the Highland regiments had displayed through the whole war. But, though he disdained to use any but lawful and honourable weapons, it was well known that his fair blows were likely to be far more formidable than the privy thrusts of his brother-in-law's stiletto.

Bute's heart began to fail him. The Houses were about to meet. The treaty would instantly be the subject of discussion. It was probable that Pitt, the great Whig connection, and the multitude, would all be on the same side. The favourite had professed to hold in abhorrence those means by which preceding ministers had kept the House of Commons in good humour. He now began to think that he had been too scrupulous. His Utopian visions were at an end. It was necessary, not only to bribe, but to bribe more shamelessly and flagitiously than his predecessors, in order to make up for lost time. A majority must be secured, no matter by what means. Could Grenville do this? Would he do it? His firmness and ability had not yet been tried in any perilous crisis. He had been generally regarded as a humble follower of his brother Temple, and of his brother-in-law Pitt, and was supposed, though with little reason, to be still favourably inclined towards them. Other aid must be called in. And where was other aid to be found?

There was one man, whose sharp and manly logic had often in debate been found a match for the lofty and impassioned rhetoric of Pitt, whose talents for jobbing were
10 not inferior to his talents for debate, whose dauntless spirit shrank from no difficulty or danger, and who was as little troubled with scruples as with fears. Henry Fox, or nobody, could weather the storm which was about to burst. Yet was he a person to whom the court, even in that extremity, was unwilling to have recourse. He had always been regarded as a Whig of the Whigs. He had been the friend and disciple of Walpole. He had long been connected by close ties with William Duke of Cumberland. By the Tories he was more hated than any man living. So strong was their
20 aversion to him that when, in the late reign, he attempted to form a party against the Duke of Newcastle, they had thrown all their weight into Newcastle's scale. By the Scots, Fox was abhorred as the confidential friend of the conqueror of Culloden. He was, on personal grounds, most obnoxious to the Princess Mother. For he had, immediately after her husband's death, advised the late King to take the education of her son, the heir apparent, entirely out of her hands. He had recently given, if possible, still deeper offence; for he had indulged, not without some ground, the ambitious hope
30 that his beautiful sister-in-law, the Lady Sarah Lennox, might be queen of England. It had been observed that the King at one time rode every morning by the grounds of Holland House, and that, on such occasions, Lady Sarah, dressed like a shepherdess at a masquerade, was making hay close to the road, which was then separated by no wall from the lawn. On account of the part which Fox had taken in

this singular love affair, he was the only member of the Privy Council who was not summoned to the meeting at which his Majesty announced his intended marriage with the Princess of Mecklenburg. Of all the statesmen of the age, therefore, it seemed that Fox was the last with whom Bute, the Tory, the Scot, the favourite of the Princess Mother, could, under any circumstances, act. Yet to Fox Bute was now compelled to apply.

Fox had many noble and amiable qualities, which in private life shone forth in full lustre, and made him dear to his children, to his dependents, and to his friends; but as a public man he had no title to esteem. In him the vices which were common to the whole school of Walpole appeared, not perhaps in their worst, but certainly in their most prominent form; for his parliamentary and official talents made all his faults conspicuous. His courage, his vehement temper, his contempt for appearances, led him to display much that others, quite as unscrupulous as himself, covered with a decent veil. He was the most unpopular of the statesmen of his time, not because he sinned more than any of them, but because he canted less.

He felt his unpopularity; but he felt it after the fashion of strong minds. He became, not cautious, but reckless, and faced the rage of the whole nation with a scowl of inflexible defiance. He was born with a sweet and generous temper; but he had been goaded and baited into a savageness which was not natural to him, and which amazed and shocked those who knew him best. Such was the man to whom Bute, in extreme need, applied for succour.

That succour Fox was not unwilling to afford. Though by no means of an envious temper, he had undoubtedly contemplated the success and popularity of Pitt with bitter mortification. He thought himself Pitt's match as a debater, and Pitt's superior as a man of business. They had long been regarded as well-paired rivals. They had started fair in the career of ambition. They had long run side by side. At

length Fox had taken the lead, and Pitt had fallen behind.
Then had come a sudden turn of fortune, like that in Virgil's
foot-race. Fox had stumbled in the mire, and had not only
been defeated, but befouled. Pitt had reached the goal, and
received the prize. The emoluments of the Pay Office might
induce the defeated statesman to submit in silence to the
ascendancy of his competitor, but could not satisfy a mind
conscious of great powers, and sore from great vexations. As
soon, therefore, as a party arose adverse to the war and to the
supremacy of the great war minister, the hopes of Fox began
to revive. His feuds with the Princess Mother, with the
Scots, with the Tories, he was ready to forget, if, by the help
of his old enemies, he could now regain the importance which
he had lost, and confront Pitt on equal terms.

The alliance was, therefore, soon concluded. Fox was
assured that, if he would pilot the government out of its
embarrassing situation, he should be rewarded with a peerage,
of which he had long been desirous. He undertook on his
side to obtain, by fair or foul means, a vote in favour of the
peace. In consequence of this arrangement he became leader
of the House of Commons; and Grenville, stifling his vexation
as well as he could, sullenly acquiesced in the change.

Fox had expected that his influence would secure to the
court the cordial support of some eminent Whigs who were
his personal friends, particularly of the Duke of Cumberland
and of the Duke of Devonshire. He was disappointed, and
soon found that, in addition to all his other difficulties, he
must reckon on the opposition of the ablest prince of the
blood, and of the great house of Cavendish.

But he had pledged himself to win the battle ; and he was
not a man to go back. It was no time for squeamishness.
Bute was made to comprehend that the ministry could be
saved only by practising the tactics of Walpole to an extent
at which Walpole himself would have stared. The Pay Office
was turned into a mart for votes. Hundreds of members
were closeted there with Fox, and, as there is too much reason

to believe, departed carrying with them the wages of infamy. It was affirmed by persons who had the best opportunities of obtaining information, that twenty-five thousand pounds were thus paid away in a single morning. The lowest bribe given, it was said, was a bank-note for two hundred pounds.

Intimidation was joined with corruption. All ranks, from the highest to the lowest, were to be taught that the King would be obeyed. The Lords Lieutenants of several counties were dismissed. The Duke of Devonshire was especially singled out as the victim by whose fate the magnates of England were to take warning. His wealth, rank, and influence, his stainless private character, and the constant attachment of his family to the House of Hanover, did not secure him from gross personal indignity. It was known that he disapproved of the course which the government had taken; and it was accordingly determined to humble the Prince of the Whigs, as he had been nicknamed by the Princess Mother. He went to the palace to pay his duty. "Tell him," said the King to a page, "that I will not see him." The page hesitated. "Go to him," said the King, "and tell him those very words." The message was delivered. The Duke tore off his gold key, and went away boiling with anger. His relations who were in office instantly resigned. A few days later, the King called for the list of Privy Councillors, and with his own hand struck out the Duke's name.

In this step there was at least courage, though little wisdom or good nature. But, as nothing was too high for the revenge of the court, so also was nothing too low. A persecution, such as had never been known before and has never been known since, raged in every public department. Great numbers of humble and laborious clerks were deprived of their bread, not because they had neglected their duties, not because they had taken an active part against the ministry, but merely because they had owed their situations to the recommendation of some nobleman or gentleman who was against the peace. The proscription extended to tidewaiters, to gaugers, to doorkeepers. One poor man to whom a pension had been given for his gallantry in a fight with smugglers, was deprived of it because he had been befriended by the Duke of Grafton. An aged widow, who, on account of her husband's services in the navy, had, many years before, been made housekeeper to a public office, was dismissed from her situation, because it was imagined that she was distantly connected by marriage with the Cavendish family. The public clamour, as may well be supposed, grew daily louder and louder. But the louder it grew, the more resolutely did Fox go on with the work which he had begun. His old friends could not conceive what had possessed him. "I could forgive," said the Duke of Cumberland, "Fox's political vagaries, but I am quite confounded by his inhumanity. Surely he used to be the best-natured of men."

At last Fox went so far as to take a legal opinion on the question, whether the patents granted by George the Second were binding on George the Third. It is said that, if his colleagues had not flinched, he would at once have turned out the Tellers of the Exchequer and Justices in Eyre.

Meanwhile the Parliament met. The ministers, more hated by the people than ever, were secure of a majority, and they had also reason to hope that they would have the advantage in the debates as well as in the divisions; for Pitt was confined to his chamber by a severe attack of gout. His friends moved to defer the consideration of the treaty till he should be able to attend: but the motion was rejected. The great day arrived. The discussion had lasted some time, when a loud huzza was heard in Palace Yard. The noise came nearer and nearer, up the stairs, through the lobby. The door opened, and from the midst of a shouting multitude came forth Pitt, borne in the arms of his attendants. His face was thin and ghastly, his limbs swathed in flannel, his crutch in his hand. The bearers set him down within the bar. His friends instantly surrounded him, and with their help he crawled to his seat near the table. In this condition he spoke three hours and a half against the peace. During that time he was repeatedly forced to sit down and to use cordials. It may well be supposed that his voice was faint, that his action was languid, and that his speech, though occasionally brilliant and impressive, was feeble when compared with his best oratorical performances. But those who remembered what he had done, and who saw what he suffered, listened to him with emotions stronger than any that mere eloquence can produce. He was unable to stay for the division, and was carried away from the House amidst shouts as loud as those which had announced his arrival.

A large majority approved the peace. The exultation of the court was boundless. "Now," exclaimed the Princess Mother, "my son is really King." The young sovereign spoke of himself as freed from the bondage in which his grandfather had been held. On one point, it was announced, his mind was unalterably made up. Under no circumstances whatever should those Whig grandees, who had enslaved his predecessors and endeavoured to enslave himself, be restored to power.

This vaunting was premature. The real strength of the favourite was by no means proportioned to the number of votes which he had, on one particular division, been able to command. He was soon again in difficulties. The most important part of his budget was a tax on cider. This measure was opposed, not only by those who were generally hostile to his administration, but also by many of his supporters. The name of excise had always been hateful to the Tories. One of the chief crimes of Walpole, in their eyes, had been his partiality for this mode of raising money. The Tory Johnson had in his Dictionary given so scurrilous a definition of the word Excise, that the Commissioners of Excise had seriously thought of prosecuting him. The counties which the new impost particularly affected had always been Tory counties. It was the boast of John Philips, the poet of the English vintage, that the Cider-land had ever been faithful to the throne, and that all the pruning-hooks of her thousand orchards had been beaten into swords for the service of the ill-fated Stuarts. The effect of Bute's fiscal scheme was to produce an union between the gentry and yeomanry of the Cider-land and the Whigs of the capital. Herefordshire and Worcestershire were in a flame. The city of London, though not so directly interested, was, if possible, still more excited. The debates on this question irreparably damaged the government. Dashwood's financial statement had been confused and absurd beyond belief, and had been received by the House with roars of laughter. He had sense enough to be conscious of his unfitness for the high situation which he held, and exclaimed in a comical fit of despair, "What shall I do? The boys will point at me in the street, and cry, 'There goes the worst Chancellor of the Exchequer that ever was.'" George Grenville came to the rescue, and spoke strongly on his favourite theme, the profusion with which the late war had been carried on. That profusion, he said, had made taxes necessary. He called on the gentlemen opposite to him to say where they would have a tax laid, and dwelt on this topic with his usual prolixity. "Let them tell me where," he repeated in a monotonous and somewhat fretful tone. "I say, sir, let them tell me where. I repeat it, sir; I am entitled to say to them, Tell me where." Unluckily for him, Pitt had come down to the House that night, and had been bitterly provoked by the reflections thrown on the war. He revenged himself by murmuring, in a whine resembling Grenville's, a line of a well known song, "Gentle Shepherd, tell me where." "If," cried Grenville, "gentlemen are to be treated in this way——" Pitt, as was his fashion, when he meant to mark extreme contempt, rose deliberately, made his bow, and walked out of the House, leaving his brother-in-law in convulsions of rage, and everybody else in convulsions of laughter. It was long before Grenville lost the nickname of the Gentle Shepherd.

But the ministry had vexations still more serious to endure. The hatred which the Tories and Scots bore to Fox was unplacable. In a moment of extreme peril, they had consented to put themselves under his guidance. But the aversion with which they regarded him broke forth as soon as the crisis seemed to be over. Some of them attacked him about the accounts of the Pay Office. Some of them rudely interrupted him when speaking, by laughter and ironical cheers. He was naturally desirous to escape from so disagreeable a situation, and demanded the peerage which had been promised as the reward of his services.

It was clear that there must be some change in the composition of the ministry. But scarcely any, even of those who, from their situation, might be supposed to be in all the secrets of the government, anticipated what really took place. To the amazement of the Parliament and the nation, it was suddenly announced that Bute had resigned.

Twenty different explanations of this strange step were suggested. Some attributed it to profound design, and some to sudden panic. Some said that the lampoons of the opposition had driven the Earl from the field; some that he had taken office only in order to bring the war to a close, and had always meant to retire when that object had been accomplished. He publicly assigned ill health as his reason for quitting business, and privately complained that he was not cordially seconded by his colleagues, and that Lord Mansfield, in particular, whom he had himself brought into the cabinet, gave him no support in the House of Peers. Mansfield was, indeed, far too sagacious not to perceive that Bute's situation was one of great peril, and far too timorous to thrust himself into peril for the sake of another. The probability, however, is that Bute's conduct on this occasion, like the conduct of most men on most occasions, was determined by mixed motives. We suspect that he was sick of

office; for this is a feeling much more common among
ministers than persons who see public life from a distance
are disposed to believe; and nothing could be more natural
than that this feeling should take possession of the mind
of Bute. In general, a statesman climbs by slow degrees.
Many laborious years elapse before he reaches the topmost
pinnacle of preferment. In the earlier part of his career,
therefore, he is constantly lured on by seeing something
above him. During his ascent he gradually becomes inured
10 to the annoyances which belong to a life of ambition. By
the time that he has attained the highest point, he has
become patient of labour and callous to abuse. He is kept
constant to his vocation, in spite of all its discomforts, at
first by hope, and at last by habit. It was not so with Bute.
His whole public life lasted little more than two years. On
the day on which he became a politician he became a cabinet
minister. In a few months he was, both in name and in
show, chief of the administration. Greater than he had been
he could not be. If what he already possessed was vanity
20 and vexation of spirit, no delusion remained to entice him
onward. He had been cloyed with the pleasures of ambition
before he had been seasoned to its pains. His habits had
not been such as were likely to fortify his mind against
obloquy and public hatred. He had reached his forty-eighth
year in dignified ease, without knowing, by personal experience, what it was to be ridiculed and slandered. All at
once, without any previous initiation, he had found himself
exposed to such a storm of invective and satire as had never
burst on the head of any statesman. The emoluments of
30 office were now nothing to him; for he had just succeeded
to a princely property by the death of his father-in-law.
All the honours which could be bestowed on him he had
already secured. He had obtained the Garter for himself,
and a British peerage for his son. He seems also to have
imagined that by quitting the treasury he should escape
from danger and abuse without really resigning power, and

should still be able to exercise in private supreme influence over the royal mind.

Whatever may have been his motives, he retired. Fox at the same time took refuge in the House of Lords; and George Grenville became First Lord of the Treasury and Chancellor of the Exchequer.

We believe that those who made this arrangement fully intended that Grenville should be a mere puppet in the hands of Bute; for Grenville was as yet very imperfectly known even to those who had observed him long. He passed for a mere official drudge; and he had all the industry, the minute accuracy, the formality, the tediousness, which belong to the character. But he had other qualities which had not yet shown themselves, devouring ambition, dauntless courage, self-confidence amounting to presumption, and a temper which could not endure opposition. He was not disposed to be any body's tool; and he had no attachment, political or personal, to Bute. The two men had, indeed, nothing in common, except a strong propensity towards harsh and unpopular courses. Their principles were fundamentally different. Bute was a Tory. Grenville would have been very angry with any person who should have denied his claim to be a Whig. He was more prone to tyrannical measures than Bute; but he loved tyranny only when disguised under the forms of constitutional liberty. He mixed up, after a fashion then not very unusual, the theories of the republicans of the seventeenth century with the technical maxims of English law, and thus succeeded in combining anarchical speculation with arbitrary practice. The voice of the people was the voice of God; but the only legitimate organ through which the voice of the people could be uttered was the Parliament. All power was from the people; but to the Parliament the whole power of the people had been delegated. No Oxonian divine had ever, even in the years which immediately followed the Restoration, demanded for the king so abject, so unreasoning a homage, as Grenville, on what he considered as

the purest Whig principles, demanded for the Parliament.
As he wished to see the Parliament despotic over the nation,
so he wished to see it also despotic over the court. In his
view the prime minister, possessed of the confidence of the
House of Commons, ought to be Mayor of the Palace. The
King was a mere Childeric or Chilperic, who might well
think himself lucky in being permitted to enjoy such handsome apartments at Saint James's and so fine a park at
Windsor.

10   Thus the opinions of Bute and those of Grenville were
diametrically opposed. Nor was there any private friendship
between the two statesmen. Grenville's nature was not for-
giving; and he well remembered how, a few months before,
he had been compelled to yield the lead of the House of
Commons to Fox.

We are inclined to think, on the whole, that the worst
administration which has governed England since the Revolution was that of George Grenville. His public acts may
be classed under two heads, outrages on the liberty of the
20 people, and outrages on the dignity of the crown.

He began by making war on the press. John Wilkes,
member of Parliament for Aylesbury, was singled out for
persecution. Wilkes had, till very lately, been known chiefly
as one of the most profane, licentious, and agreeable rakes
about town. He was a man of taste, reading, and engaging
manners. His sprightly conversation was the delight of
green rooms and taverns, and pleased even grave hearers
when he was sufficiently under restraint to abstain from
detailing the particulars of his amours, and from breaking
30 jests on the New Testament. His expensive debaucheries
forced him to have recourse to the Jews. He was soon a
ruined man, and determined to try his chance as a political
adventurer. In parliament he did not succeed. His speaking, though pert, was feeble, and by no means interested his
hearers so much as to make them forget his face, which was
so hideous that the caricaturists were forced, in their own

despite, to flatter him. As a writer, he made a better figure. He set up a weekly paper called the North Briton. This journal, written with some pleasantry, and great audacity and impudence, had a considerable number of readers. Forty-four numbers had been published when Bute resigned; and, though almost every number had contained matter grossly libellous, no prosecution had been instituted. The forty-fifth number was innocent when compared with the majority of those which had preceded it, and indeed contained nothing so strong as may in our time be found daily in the leading articles of the Times and Morning Chronicle. But Grenville was now at the head of affairs. A new spirit had been infused into the administration. Authority was to be upheld. The government was no longer to be braved with impunity. Wilkes was arrested under a general warrant, conveyed to the Tower, and confined there with circumstances of unusual severity. His papers were seized, and carried to the Secretary of State. These harsh and illegal measures produced a violent outbreak of popular rage, which was soon changed to delight and exultation. The arrest was pronounced unlawful by the Court of Common Pleas, in which Chief Justice Pratt presided, and the prisoner was discharged. This victory over the government was celebrated with enthusiasm both in London and in the cider counties.

While the ministers were daily becoming more odious to the nation, they were doing their best to make themselves also odious to the court. They gave the King plainly to understand that they were determined not to be Lord Bute's creatures, and exacted a promise that no secret adviser should have access to the royal ear. They soon found reason to suspect that this promise had not been observed. They remonstrated in terms less respectful than their master had been accustomed to hear, and gave him a fortnight to make his choice between his favourite and his cabinet.

George the Third was greatly disturbed. He had but a few weeks before exulted in his deliverance from the yoke of

the great Whig connection. He had even declared that his
honour would not permit him ever again to admit the members of that connection into his service. He now found that
he had only exchanged one set of masters for another set
still harsher and more imperious. In his distress he thought
on Pitt. From Pitt it was possible that better terms might
be obtained than either from Grenville, or from the party of
which Newcastle was the head.

Grenville, on his return from an excursion into the country,
10 repaired to Buckingham House. He was astonished to find
at the entrance a chair, the shape of which was well known
to him, and indeed to all London. It was distinguished by
a large boot, made for the purpose of accommodating the
great Commoner's gouty leg. Grenville guessed the whole.
His brother-in-law was closeted with the King. Bute, provoked by what he considered as an unfriendly and ungrate-
ful conduct of his successors, had himself proposed that Pitt
should be summoned to the palace.

Pitt had two audiences on two successive days. What
20 passed at the first interview led him to expect that the
negotiation would be brought to a satisfactory close; but on
the morrow he found the King less complying. The best
account, indeed the only trustworthy account of the conference, is that which was taken from Pitt's own mouth by
Lord Hardwicke. It appears that Pitt strongly represented
the importance of conciliating those chiefs of the Whig party
who had been so unhappy as to incur the royal displeasure.
They had, he said, been the most constant friends of the
House of Hanover. Their power was great; they had been
30 long versed in public business. If they were to be under
sentence of exclusion, a solid administration could not be
formed. His Majesty could not bear to think of putting
himself into the hands of those whom he had recently chased
from his court with the strongest marks of anger. "I am
sorry, Mr. Pitt," he said, "but I see this will not do. My
honour is concerned. I must support my honour." How

His Majesty succeeded in supporting his honour, we shall soon see. Pitt retired, and the King was reduced to request the ministers, whom he had been on the point of discarding, to remain in office. During the two years which followed, Grenville, now closely leagued with the Bedfords, was the master of the court; and a hard master he proved. He knew that he was kept in place only because there was no choice except between himself and the Whigs. That, under any circumstances, the Whigs would be forgiven, he thought impossible. The late attempt to get rid of him had roused his resentment; the failure of that attempt had liberated him from all fear. He had never been very courtly. He now began to hold a language, to which, since the days of Cornet Joyce and President Bradshaw, no English King had been compelled to listen.

In one matter, indeed, Grenville, at the expense of justice and liberty, gratified the passions of the court while gratifying his own. The persecution of Wilkes was eagerly pressed. He had written a parody on Pope's Essay on Man, entitled the Essay on Woman, and had appended to it notes, in ridicule of Warburton's famous Commentary.

This composition was exceedingly profligate, but not more so, we think, than some of Pope's own works, the imitation of the second satire of the first book of Horace, for example; and, to do Wilkes justice, he had not, like Pope, given his ribaldry to the world. He had merely printed at a private press a very small number of copies, which he meant to present to some of his boon companions, whose morals were in no more danger of being corrupted by a loose book than a negro of being tanned by a warm sun. A tool of the government, by giving a bribe to the printer, procured a copy of this trash, and placed it in the hands of the ministers. The ministers resolved to visit Wilkes's offence against decorum with the utmost rigour of the law. What share piety and respect for morals had in dictating this resolution, our readers may judge from the fact that no person was more

eager for bringing the libertine poet to punishment than
Lord March, afterwards Duke of Queensberry. On the first
day of the session of Parliament, the book, thus disgrace-
fully obtained, was laid on the table of the Lords by the
Earl of Sandwich, whom the Duke of Bedford's interest had
made Secretary of State. The unfortunate author had not
the slightest suspicion that his licentious poem had ever
been seen, except by his printer and by a few of his dis-
sipated companions, till it was produced in full Parliament.
10 Though he was a man of easy temper, averse from danger,
and not very susceptible of shame, the surprise, the disgrace,
the prospect of utter ruin, put him beside himself. He
picked a quarrel with one of Lord Bute's dependents, fought
a duel, was seriously wounded, and, when half recovered,
fled to France. His enemies had now their own way both in
the Parliament and in the King's Bench. He was censured,
expelled from the House of Commons, outlawed. His works
were ordered to be burned by the common hangman. Yet
was the multitude still true to him. In the minds even of
20 many moral and religious men, his crime seemed light when
compared with the crime of his accusers. The conduct of
Sandwich, in particular, excited universal disgust. His own
vices were notorious ; and, only a fortnight before he laid
the Essay on Woman before the House of Lords, he had
been drinking and singing loose catches with Wilkes at one
of the most dissolute clubs in London. Shortly after the
meeting of Parliament, the Beggar's Opera was acted at
Covent Garden theatre. When Macheath uttered the words
—"That Jemmy Twitcher should peach me I own surprised
30 me,"—pit, boxes, and galleries, burst into a roar which
seemed likely to bring the roof down. From that day
Sandwich was universally known by the nickname of
Jemmy Twitcher. The ceremony of burning the North
Briton was interrupted by a riot. The constables were
beaten ; the paper was rescued ; and, instead of it, a jack-
boot and a petticoat were committed to the flames. Wilkes

had instituted an action for the seizure of his papers against the Under Secretary of State. The jury gave a thousand pounds damages. But neither these nor any other indications of public feeling had power to move Grenville. He had the Parliament with him: and, according to his political creed, the sense of the nation was to be collected from the Parliament alone.

Soon, however, he found reason to fear that even the Parliament might fail him. On the question of the legality of general warrants, the Opposition, having on its side all sound principles, all constitutional authorities, and the voice of the whole nation, mustered in great force, and was joined by many who did not ordinarily vote against the government. On one occasion the ministry, in a very full house, had a majority of only fourteen votes. The storm, however, blew over. The spirit of the Opposition, from whatever cause, began to flag at the moment when success seemed almost certain. The session ended without any change. Pitt, whose eloquence had shone with its usual lustre in all the principal debates, and whose popularity was greater than ever, was still a private man. Grenville, detested alike by the court and by the people, was still minister.

As soon as the Houses had risen, Grenville took a step which proved, even more signally than any of his past acts, how despotic, how acrimonious, and how fearless his nature was. Among the gentlemen not ordinarily opposed to the government, who, on the great constitutional question of general warrants, had voted with the minority, was Henry Conway, brother of the Earl of Hertford, a brave soldier, a tolerable speaker, and a well-meaning, though not a wise or vigorous politician. He was now deprived of his regiment, the merited reward of faithful and gallant service in two wars. It was confidently asserted that in this violent measure the King heartily concurred.

But whatever pleasure the persecution of Wilkes or the dismissal of Conway may have given to the royal mind, it is

certain that his Majesty's aversion to his ministers increased
day by day. Grenville was as frugal of the public money as
of his own, and morosely refused to accede to the King's
request, that a few thousand pounds might be expended in
buying some open fields to the west of the gardens of
Buckingham House. In consequence of this refusal, the
fields were soon covered with buildings, and the King and
Queen were overlooked in their most private walks by the
upper windows of a hundred houses. Nor was this the
worst. Grenville was as liberal of words as he was sparing
of guineas. Instead of explaining himself in that clear, con-
cise, and lively manner, which alone could win the attention
of a young mind new to business, he spoke in the closet
just as he spoke in the House of Commons. When he had
harangued two hours, he looked at his watch, as he had been
in the habit of looking at the clock opposite the Speaker's
chair, apologised for the length of his discourse, and then
went on for an hour more. The members of the House of
Commons can cough an orator down, or can walk away to
dinner; and they were by no means sparing in the use of
these privileges when Grenville was on his legs. But the
poor young King had to endure all this eloquence with
mournful civility. To the end of his life he continued to
talk with horror of Grenville's orations.

About this time took place one of the most singular events
in Pitt's life. There was a certain Sir William Pynsent, a
Somersetshire baronet of Whig politics, who had been a
member of the House of Commons in the days of Queen
Anne, and had retired to rural privacy when the Tory party
towards the end of her reign, obtained the ascendency in her
councils. His manners were eccentric. His morals lay
under very odious imputations. But his fidelity to his
political opinions was unalterable. During fifty years of
seclusion he continued to brood over the circumstances which
had driven him from public life, the dismissal of the Whigs,
the peace of Utrecht, the desertion of our allies. He now

thought that he perceived a close analogy between the well-remembered events of his youth and the events which he had witnessed in extreme old age ; between the disgrace of Marlborough and the disgrace of Pitt; between the elevation of Harley and the elevation of Bute ; between the treaty negotiated by St. John and the treaty negotiated by Bedford ; between the wrongs of the House of Austria in 1712 and the wrongs of the House of Brandenburg in 1762. This fancy took such possession of the old man's mind that he determined to leave his whole property to Pitt. In this way Pitt unexpectedly came into possession of near three thousand pounds a year. Nor could all the malice of his enemies find any ground for reproach in the transaction. Nobody could call him a legacy hunter. Nobody could accuse him of seizing that to which others had a better claim. For he had never in his life seen Sir William ; and Sir William had left no relation so near as to be entitled to form any expectations respecting the estate.

The fortunes of Pitt seemed to flourish ; but his health was worse than ever. We cannot find that during the session which began in January, 1765, he once appeared in parliament. He remained some months in profound retirement at Hayes, his favourite villa, scarcely moving except from his armchair to his bed, and from his bed to his armchair, and often employing his wife as his amanuensis in his most confidential correspondence. Some of his detractors whispered that his invisibility was to be ascribed quite as much to affectation as to gout. In truth his character, high and splendid as it was, wanted simplicity. With genius which did not need the aid of stage tricks, and with a spirit which should have been far above them, he had yet been, through life, in the habit of practising them. It was, therefore, now surmised that, having acquired all the consideration which could be derived from eloquence and from great services to the state, he had determined not to make himself cheap by often appearing in public, but, under the pretext of ill health, to surround himself with mystery, to emerge only at long intervals and on momentous occasions, and at other times to deliver his oracles only to a few favoured votaries, who were suffered to make pilgrimages to his shrine. If such were his object, it was for a time fully attained. Never was the magic of his name so powerful, never was he regarded by his country with such superstitious veneration, as during this year of silence and seclusion.

While Pitt was thus absent from Parliament, Grenville proposed a measure destined to produce a great revolution, the effects of which will long be felt by the whole human race. We speak of the act for imposing stamp duties on the North American colonies. The plan was eminently characteristic of its author. Every feature of the parent was found in the child. A timid statesman would have shrunk from a step, of which Walpole, at a time when the colonies were far less powerful, had said—"He who shall propose it, will be a much bolder man than I." But the nature of Grenville was insensible to fear. A statesman of large views would have felt that to lay taxes at Westminster on New England and New York, was a course opposed, not indeed to the letter of the Statute Book, or to any decision contained in the Term Reports, but to the principles of good government, and to the spirit of the constitution. A statesman of large views would also have felt that ten times the estimated produce of the American stamps would have been dearly purchased by even a transient quarrel between the mother country and the colonies. But Grenville knew of no spirit of the constitution distinct from the letter of the law, and of no national interests except those which are expressed by pounds, shillings, and pence. That his policy might give birth to deep discontents in all the provinces, from the shore of the Great Lakes to the Mexican Sea; that France and Spain might seize the opportunity of revenge; that the Empire might be dismembered; that the debt, that debt with the amount of which he perpetually reproached Pitt, might, in consequence of his own policy, be doubled ; these were possibilities which never occurred to that small, sharp mind.

The Stamp Act will be remembered as long as the globe lasts. But, at the time, it attracted much less notice in this country than another Act which is now almost utterly forgotten. The King fell ill, and was thought to be in a dangerous state. His complaint, we believe, was the same which, at a later period, repeatedly incapacitated him for the performance of his regal functions. The heir apparent was only two years old. It was clearly proper to make provision for the administration of the government, in case of a minority. The discussions on this point brought the quarrel between the court and the ministry to a crisis. The King wished to be intrusted with the power of naming a regent by will. The ministers feared, or affected to fear, that if this power were conceded to him, he would name the Princess Mother, nay, possibly the Earl of Bute. They, therefore, insisted on introducing into the bill words confining the King's choice to the royal family. Having thus excluded Bute, they urged the King to let them, in the most marked manner, exclude the Princess Dowager also. They assured him that the House of Commons would undoubtedly strike her name out, and by this threat they wrung from him a reluctant assent. In a few days, it appeared that the representations by which they had induced the King to put this gross and public affront on his mother were unfounded. The friends of the Princess in the House of Commons moved that her name should be inserted. The ministers could not decently attack the parent of their master. They hoped that the Opposition would come to their help, and put on them a force to which they would gladly have yielded. But the majority of the Opposition, though hating the Princess, hated Grenville more, beheld his embarrassment with delight, and would do nothing to extricate him from it. The Princess's name was accordingly placed in the list of persons qualified to hold the regency.

The King's resentment was now at the height. The present evil seemed to him more intolerable than any other. Even the junta of Whig grandees could not treat him worse than he had been treated by his present ministers. In his distress he poured out his whole heart to his uncle, the Duke of Cumberland. The Duke was not a man to be loved; but he was eminently a man to be trusted. He had an intrepid temper, a strong understanding, and a high sense of honour and duty. As a general, he belonged to a remarkable class of captains, captains, we mean, whose fate it has been to lose almost all the battles which they have fought, and yet to be reputed stout and skilful soldiers. Such captains were Coligni and William the Third. We might, perhaps, add Marshal Soult to the list. The bravery of the Duke of Cumberland was such as distinguished him even among the princes of his brave house. The indifference with which he rode about amidst musket balls and cannon balls was not the highest proof of his fortitude. Hopeless maladies, horrible surgical operations, far from unmanning him, did not even discompose him. With courage, he had the virtues which are akin to courage. He spoke the truth, was open in enmity and friendship, and upright in all his dealings. But his nature was hard; and what seemed to him justice was rarely tempered with mercy. He was, therefore, during many years one of the most unpopular men in England. The severity with which he had treated the rebels after the battle of Culloden, had gained for him the name of the Butcher. His attempts to introduce into the army of England, then in a most disorderly state, the rigorous discipline of Potsdam, had excited still stronger disgust. Nothing was too bad to be believed of him. Many honest people were so absurd as to fancy that, if he were left Regent during the minority of his nephews, there would be another smothering in the Tower. These feelings, however, had passed away. The Duke had been living, during some years, in retirement. The English, full of animosity against the Scots, now blamed his Royal Highness only for having left so many Camerons and Macphersons to be made gaugers and customhouse officers. He was, therefore, at present, a favourite with his countrymen, and especially with the inhabitants of London.

He had little reason to love the King, and had shown clearly, though not obtrusively, his dislike of the system which had lately been pursued. But he had high and almost romantic notions of the duty which, as a prince of the blood, he owed to the head of his house. He determined to extricate his nephew from bondage, and to effect a reconciliation between the Whig party and the throne, on terms honourable to both.

In this mind he set off for Hayes, and was admitted to Pitt's sick room; for Pitt would not leave his chamber, and would not communicate with any messenger of inferior dignity. And now began a long series of errors on the part of the illustrious statesman, errors which involved his country in difficulties and distresses more serious even than those from which his genius had formerly rescued her. His language was haughty, unreasonable, almost unintelligible. The only thing which could be discerned through a cloud of vague and not very gracious phrases, was that he would not at that moment take office. The truth, we believe, was this. Lord Temple, who was Pitt's evil genius, had just formed a new scheme of politics. Hatred of Bute and of the Princess had, it should seem, taken entire possession of Temple's soul. He had quarrelled with his brother George, because George had been connected with Bute and the Princess. Now that George appeared to be the enemy of Bute and of the Princess, Temple was eager to bring about a general family reconciliation. The three brothers, as Temple, Grenville, and Pitt, were popularly called, might make a ministry without leaning for aid either on Bute or on the Whig connection. With such views, Temple used all his influence to dissuade Pitt from acceding to the propositions of the Duke of Cumberland. Pitt was not convinced. But Temple had

an influence over him such as no other person had ever possessed. They were very old friends, very near relations. If Pitt's talents and fame had been useful to Temple, Temple's purse had formerly, in times of great need, been useful to Pitt. They had never been parted in politics. Twice they had come into the cabinet together; twice they had left it together. Pitt could not bear to think of taking office without his chief ally. Yet he felt that he was doing wrong, that he was throwing away a great opportunity of
10 serving his country. The obscure and unconciliatory style of the answers which he returned to the overtures of the Duke of Cumberland, may be ascribed to the embarrassment and vexation of a mind not at peace with itself. It is said that he mournfully exclaimed to Temple,

> "Extinxti te meque, soror, populumque, patresque
> Sidonios, urbemque tuam."

The prediction was but too just.

Finding Pitt impracticable, the Duke of Cumberland advised the King to submit to necessity, and to keep
20 Grenville and the Bedfords. It was, indeed, not a time at which offices could safely be left vacant. The unsettled state of the government had produced a general relaxation through all the departments of the public service. Meetings, which at another time would have been harmless, now turned to riots, and rapidly rose almost to the dignity of rebellions. The Houses of Parliament were blockaded by the Spitalfields weavers. Bedford House was assailed on all sides by a furious rabble, and was strongly garrisoned with horse and foot. Some people attributed these disturbances
30 to the friends of Bute, and some to the friends of Wilkes. But, whatever might be the cause, the effect was general insecurity. Under such circumstances the King had no choice. With bitter feelings of mortification, he informed the ministers that he meant to retain them.

They answered by demanding from him a promise on his

royal word never more to consult Lord Bute. The promise
was given. They then demanded something more. Lord
Bute's brother, Mr. Mackenzie, held a lucrative office in
Scotland. Mr. Mackenzie must be dismissed. The King
replied that the office had been given under very peculiar
circumstances, and that he had promised never to take it
away while he lived. Grenville was obstinate; and the
King, with a very bad grace, yielded.

The session of Parliament was over. The triumph of the
ministers was complete. The King was almost as much a
prisoner as Charles the First had been, when in the Isle of
Wight. Such were the fruits of the policy which, only a
few months before, was represented as having for ever
secured the throne against the dictation of insolent subjects.

His Majesty's natural resentment showed itself in every
look and word. In his extremity he looked wistfully
towards the Whig connection, once the object of his dread
and hatred. The Duke of Devonshire, who had been treated
with such unjustifiable harshness, had lately died, and had
been succeeded by his son, who was still a boy. The King
condescended to express his regret for what had passed, and
to invite the young Duke to court. The noble youth came,
attended by his uncles, and was received with marked
graciousness.

This and many other symptoms of the same kind irritated
the ministers. They had still in store for their sovereign an
insult which would have provoked his grandfather to kick
them out of the room. Grenville and Bedford demanded an
audience of him, and read him a remonstrance of many
pages, which they had drawn up with great care. His
Majesty was accused of breaking his word, and of treating
his advisers with gross unfairness. The Princess was mentioned in language by no means eulogistic. Hints were
thrown out that Bute's head was in danger. The King was
plainly told that he must not continue to show, as he had
done, that he disliked the situation in which he was placed,

that he must frown upon the Opposition, that he must carry
it fair towards his ministers in public. He several times
interrupted the reading, by declaring that he had ceased to
hold any communication with Bute. But the ministers, disregarding his denial, went on; and the King listened in
silence, almost choked by rage. When they ceased to read,
he merely made a gesture expressive of his wish to be left
alone. He afterwards owned that he thought he should
have gone into a fit.

10   Driven to despair, he again had recourse to the Duke of
Cumberland; and the Duke of Cumberland again had recourse to Pitt. Pitt was really desirous to undertake the
direction of affairs, and owned, with many dutiful expressions,
that the terms offered by the King were all that any subject
could desire. But Temple was impracticable; and Pitt, with
great regret, declared that he could not, without the concurrence of his brother-in-law, undertake the administration.

The Duke now saw only one way of delivering his nephew.
An administration must be formed of the Whigs in opposi-
20 tion, without Pitt's help. The difficulties seemed almost
insuperable. Death and desertion had grievously thinned
the ranks of the party lately supreme in the state. Those
among whom the Duke's choice lay might be divided into
two classes, men too old for important offices, and men who
had never been in any important office before. The cabinet
must be composed of broken invalids or of raw recruits.

This was an evil, yet not an unmixed evil. If the new
Whig statesmen had little experience in business and debate,
they were, on the other hand, pure from the taint of that
30 political immorality which had deeply infected their predecessors. Long prosperity had corrupted that great party
which had expelled the Stuarts, limited the prerogatives of
the Crown, and curbed the intolerance of the Hierarchy.
Adversity had already produced a salutary effect. On the
day of the accession of George the Third, the ascendency of
the Whig party terminated; and on that day the purification

of the Whig party began. The rising chiefs of that party were men of a very different sort from Sandys and Winnington, from Sir William Yonge and Henry Fox. They were men worthy to have charged by the side of Hampden at Chalgrove, or to have exchanged the last embrace with Russell on the scaffold in Lincoln's Inn Fields. They carried into politics the same high principles of virtue which regulated their private dealings, nor would they stoop to promote even the noblest and most salutary ends by means which honour and probity condemn. Such men were Lord John Cavendish, Sir George Savile, and others whom we hold in honour as the second founders of the Whig party, as the restorers of its pristine health and energy after half a century of degeneracy.

The chief of this respectable band was the Marquess of Rockingham, a man of splendid fortune, excellent sense, and stainless character. He was indeed nervous to such a degree that, to the very close of his life, he never rose without great reluctance and embarrassment to address the House of Lords. But, though not a great orator, he had in a high degree some of the qualities of a statesman. He chose his friends well; and he had, in an extraordinary degree, the art of attaching them to him by ties of the most honourable kind. The cheerful fidelity with which they adhered to him through many years of almost hopeless opposition was less admirable than the disinterestedness and delicacy which they showed when he rose to power.

We are inclined to think that the use and the abuse of party cannot be better illustrated than by a parallel between two powerful connections of that time, the Rockinghams and the Bedfords. The Rockingham party was, in our view, exactly what a party should be. It consisted of men bound together by common opinions, by common public objects, by mutual esteem. That they desired to obtain, by honest and constitutional means, the direction of affairs they openly avowed. But, though often invited to accept the honours and emoluments of office, they steadily refused to do so on any conditions inconsistent with their principles. The Bedford party, as a party, had, as far as we can discover, no principle whatever. Rigby and Sandwich wanted public money, and thought that they should fetch a higher price jointly than singly. They therefore acted in concert, and prevailed on a much more important and a much better man than themselves to act with them.

It was to Rockingham that the Duke of Cumberland now had recourse. The Marquess consented to take the treasury. Newcastle, so long the recognised chief of the Whigs, could not well be excluded from the ministry. He was appointed keeper of the privy seal. A very honest, clear-headed country gentleman, of the name of Dowdeswell, became Chancellor of the Exchequer. General Conway, who had served under the Duke of Cumberland, and was strongly attached to his royal highness, was made Secretary of State, with the lead in the House of Commons. A great Whig nobleman, in the prime of manhood, from whom much was at that time expected, Augustus Duke of Grafton, was the other Secretary.

The oldest man living could remember no government so weak in oratorical talents and in official experience. The general opinion was, that the ministers might hold office during the recess, but that the first day of debate in Parliament would be the last day of their power. Charles Townshend was asked what he thought of the new administration. "It is," said he, "mere lutestring; pretty summer wear. It will never do for the winter."

At this conjuncture Lord Rockingham had the wisdom to discern the value, and secure the aid, of an ally, who, to eloquence surpassing the eloquence of Pitt, and to industry which shamed the industry of Grenville, united an amplitude of comprehension to which neither Pitt nor Grenville could lay claim. A young Irishman had, some time before, come over to push his fortune in London. He had written much for the booksellers; but he was best known by a little treatise, in which the style and reasoning of Bolingbroke were mimicked with exquisite skill, and by a theory, of more ingenuity than soundness, touching the pleasures which we receive from the objects of taste. He had also attained a high reputation as a talker, and was regarded by the men of letters who supped together at the Turk's Head as the only match in conversation for Dr. Johnson. He now became private secretary to Lord Rockingham, and was brought into Parliament by his patron's influence. These arrangements, indeed, were not made without some difficulty. The Duke of Newcastle, who was always meddling and chattering, adjured the first lord of the treasury to be on his guard against this adventurer, whose real name was O'Bourke, and whom his grace knew to be a wild Irishman, a Jacobite, a Papist, a concealed Jesuit. Lord Rockingham treated the calumny as it deserved; and the Whig party was strengthened and adorned by the accession of Edmund Burke.

The party, indeed, stood in need of accessions; for it sustained about this time an almost irreparable loss. The Duke of Cumberland had formed the government, and was its main support. His exalted rank and great name in some degree balanced the fame of Pitt. As mediator between the Whigs and the Court, he held a place which no other person could fill. The strength of his character supplied that which was the chief defect of the new ministry. Conway, in particular, who, with excellent intentions and respectable talents, was the most dependent and irresolute of human beings, drew from the counsels of that masculine mind a determination not his own. Before the meeting of Parliament the Duke suddenly died. His death was generally regarded as a signal of great troubles, and on this account, as well as from respect for his personal qualities, was greatly lamented. It was remarked that the mourning in London was the most general ever known, and was both deeper and longer than the Gazette had prescribed.

In the mean time, every mail from America brought alarming tidings. The crop which Grenville had sown his successors had now to reap. The colonies were in a state bordering on rebellion. The stamps were burned. The revenue officers were tarred and feathered. All traffic between the discontented provinces and the mother country was interrupted. The Exchange of London was in dismay. Half the firms of Bristol and Liverpool were threatened with bankruptcy. In Leeds, Manchester, Nottingham, it was said that three artisans out of every ten had been turned adrift. Civil war seemed to be at hand; and it could not be doubted that, if once the British nation were divided against itself, France and Spain would soon take part in the quarrel.

Three courses were open to the ministers. The first was to enforce the Stamp Act by the sword. This was the course on which the King, and Grenville, whom the King hated beyond all living men, were alike bent. The natures of both were arbitrary and stubborn. They resembled each other so much that they could never be friends; but they resembled each other also so much that they saw almost all important practical questions in the same point of view. Neither of them would bear to be governed by the other; but they were perfectly agreed as to the best way of governing the people.

Another course was that which Pitt recommended. He held that the British Parliament was not constitutionally competent to pass a law for taxing the colonies. He therefore considered the Stamp Act as a nullity, as a document of no more validity than Charles's writ of shipmoney, or James's proclamation dispensing with the penal laws. This doctrine seems to us, we must own, to be altogether untenable.

Between these extreme courses lay a third way. The opinion of the most judicious and temperate statesman of those times was that the British constitution had set no limit whatever to the legislative power of the British King,

Lords, and Commons, over the whole British Empire. Parliament, they held, was legally competent to tax America, as Parliament was legally competent to commit any other act of folly or wickedness, to confiscate the property of all the merchants in Lombard Street, or to attaint any man in the kingdom of high treason, without examining witnesses against him, or hearing him in his own defence. The most atrocious act of confiscation or of attainder is just as valid an act as the Toleration Act or the Habeas Corpus Act. But from acts of confiscation and acts of attainder lawgivers are bound, by every obligation of morality, systematically to refrain. In the same manner ought the British legislature to refrain from taxing the American colonies. The Stamp Act was indefensible, not because it was beyond the constitutional competence of Parliament, but because it was unjust and impolitic, sterile of revenue, and fertile of discontents. These sound doctrines were adopted by Lord Rockingham and his colleagues, and were, during a long course of years, inculcated by Burke, in orations, some of which will last as long as the English language.

The winter came; the Parliament met; and the state of the colonies instantly became the subject of fierce contention. Pitt, whose health had been somewhat restored by the waters of Bath, reappeared in the House of Commons, and, with ardent and pathetic eloquence, not only condemned the Stamp Act, but applauded the resistance of Massachusetts and Virginia, and vehemently maintained, in defiance, we must say, of all reason and of all authority, that, according to the British constitution, the supreme legislative power does not include the power to tax. The language of Grenville, on the other hand, was such as Strafford might have used at the council table of Charles the First, when news came of the resistance to the liturgy at Edinburgh. The colonists were traitors; those who excused them were little better. Frigates, mortars, bayonets, sabres, were the proper remedies for such distempers.

The ministers occupied an intermediate position; they proposed to declare that the legislative authority of the British Parliament over the whole Empire was in all cases supreme; and they proposed, at the same time, to repeal the Stamp Act. To the former measure Pitt objected; but it was carried with scarcely a dissenting voice. The repeal of the Stamp Act Pitt strongly supported; but against the Government was arrayed a formidable assemblage of opponents. Grenville and the Bedfords were furious. Temple, who had now allied himself closely with his brother, and separated himself from Pitt, was no despicable enemy. This, however, was not the worst. The ministry was without its natural strength. It had a struggle, not only against its avowed enemies, but against the insidious hostility of the King, and of a set of persons who, about this time, began to be designated as the King's friends.

The character of this faction has been drawn by Burke with even more than his usual force and vivacity. Those who know how strongly, through his whole life, his judgment was biassed by his passions, may not unnaturally suspect that he has left us rather a caricature than a likeness; and yet there is scarcely, in the whole portrait, a single touch of which the fidelity is not proved by facts of unquestionable authenticity.

The public generally regarded the King's friends as a body of which Bute was the directing soul. It was to no purpose that the Earl professed to have done with politics, that he absented himself year after year from the levee and the drawing-room, that he went to the north, that he went to Rome. The notion that, in some inexplicable manner, he dictated all the measures of the court, was fixed in the minds, not only of the multitude, but of some who had good opportunities of obtaining information, and who ought to have been superior to vulgar prejudices. Our own belief is that these suspicions were unfounded, and that he ceased to have any communication with the King on political matters some time before the dismissal of George Grenville. The supposition of Bute's influence is, indeed, by no means necessary to explain the phænomena. The King, in 1765, was no longer the ignorant and inexperienced boy who had, in 1760, been managed by his mother and his Groom of the Stole. He had, during several years, observed the struggles of parties, and conferred daily on high questions of state with able and experienced politicians. His way of life had developed his understanding and character. He was now no longer a puppet, but had very decided opinions both of men and things. Nothing could be more natural than that he should have high notions of his own prerogatives, should be impatient of opposition, and should wish all public men to be detached from each other and dependent on himself alone; nor could anything be more natural than that, in the state in which the political world then was, he should find instruments fit for his purposes.

Thus sprang into existence and into note a reptile species of politicians never before and never since known in our country. These men disclaimed all political ties, except those which bound them to the throne. They were willing to coalesce with any party, to abandon any party, to undermine any party, to assault any party, at a moment's notice. To them, all administrations, and all oppositions were the same. They regarded Bute, Grenville, Rockingham, Pitt, without one sentiment either of predilection or of aversion. They were the King's friends. It is to be observed that this friendship implied no personal intimacy. These people had never lived with their master, as Dodington at one time lived with his father, or as Sheridan afterwards lived with his son. They never hunted with him in the morning, or played cards with him in the evening, never shared his mutton or walked with him among his turnips. Only one or two of them ever saw his face, except on public days. The whole band, however, always had early and accurate information as to his personal inclinations. None of these people were high in the administration. They were generally to be found in places of much emolument, little labour, and no responsibility; and these places they continued to occupy securely while the cabinet was six or seven times reconstructed. Their peculiar business was not to support the ministry against the opposition, but to support the King against the ministry. Whenever his Majesty was induced to give a reluctant assent to the introduction of some bill which his constitutional advisers regarded as necessary, his friends in the House of Commons were sure to speak against it, to vote against it, to throw in its way every obstruction compatible with the forms of Parliament. If his Majesty found it necessary to admit into his closet a Secretary of State or a First Lord of the Treasury whom he disliked, his friends were sure to miss no opportunity of thwarting and humbling the obnoxious minister. In return for these services, the King covered them with his protection. It was to no purpose that his responsible servants complained to him that they were daily betrayed and impeded by men who were eating the bread of the government. He sometimes justified the offenders, sometimes excused them, sometimes owned that they were to blame, but said that he must take time to consider whether he could part with them. He never would turn them out; and, while every thing else in the state was constantly changing, these sycophants seemed to have a life estate in their offices.

It was well known to the King's friends that, though his Majesty had consented to the repeal of the Stamp Act, he had consented with a very bad grace, and that though he had eagerly welcomed the Whigs, when, in his extreme need and at his earnest entreaty, they had undertaken to free him from an insupportable yoke, he had by no means got over his early prejudices against his deliverers. The ministers soon found that, while they were encountered in front by the whole force of a strong opposition, their rear was assailed by a large body of those whom they had regarded as auxiliaries.

Nevertheless, Lord Rockingham and his adherents went on resolutely with the bill for repealing the Stamp Act. They had on their side all the manufacturing and commercial interests of the realm. In the debates the government was powerfully supported. Two great orators and statesmen, belonging to two different generations, repeatedly put forth all their powers in defence of the bill. The House of Commons heard Pitt for the last time, and Burke for the first time, and was in doubt to which of them the palm of eloquence should be assigned. It was indeed a splendid sunset and a splendid dawn.

For a time the event seemed doubtful. In several divisions the ministers were hard pressed. On one occasion, not less than twelve of the King's friends, all men in office, voted against the government. It was to no purpose that Lord Rockingham remonstrated with the King. His Majesty confessed that there was ground for complaint, but hoped that gentle means would bring the mutineers to a better mind. If they persisted in their misconduct, he would dismiss them.

At length the decisive day arrived. The gallery, the lobby, the Court of Requests, the staircases, were crowded with merchants from all the great ports of the island. The debate lasted till long after midnight. On the division, the ministers had a great majority. The dread of civil war, and the outcry of all the trading towns of the kingdom, had been too strong for the combined strength of the court and the opposition.

It was in the first dim twilight of a February morning that the doors were thrown open, and that the chiefs of the hostile parties showed themselves to the multitude. Conway was received with loud applause. But, when Pitt appeared, all eyes were fixed on him alone. All hats were in the air. Loud and long huzzas accompanied him to his chair, and a train of admirers escorted him all the way to his home. Then came forth Grenville. As soon as he was recognised, a storm of hisses and curses broke forth. He turned fiercely on the crowd, and caught one man by the throat. The bystanders were in great alarm. If a scuffle began, none could say how it might end. Fortunately the person who had been collared only said, "If I may not hiss, sir, I hope I may laugh," and laughed in Grenville's face.

The majority had been so decisive, that all the opponents of the ministry, save one, were disposed to let the bill pass without any further contention. But solicitation and expos-
10 tulation were thrown away on Grenville. His indomitable spirit rose up stronger and stronger under the load of public hatred. He fought out the battle obstinately to the end. On the last reading he had a sharp altercation with his brother-in-law, the last of their many sharp altercations. Pitt thundered in his loftiest tones against the man who had wished to dip the ermine of a British King in the blood of the British people. Grenville replied with his wonted intrepidity and asperity. "If the tax," he said, "were still to be laid on, I would lay it on. For the evils which it may
20 produce my accuser is answerable. His profusion made it necessary. His declarations against the constitutional powers of King, Lords, and Commons, have made it doubly necessary. I do not envy him the huzza. I glory in the hiss. If it were to be done again, I would do it."

The repeal of the Stamp Act was the chief measure of Lord Rockingham's government. But that government is entitled to the praise of having put a stop to two oppressive practices, which, in Wilkes's case, had attracted the notice and excited the just indignation of the public. The House
30 of Commons was induced by the ministers to pass a resolution condemning the use of general warrants, and another resolution, condemning the seizure of papers in cases of libel.

It must be added, to the lasting honour of Lord Rockingham, that his administration was the first which, during a long course of years, had the courage and the virtue to refrain from bribing members of Parliament. His enemies accused him and his friends of weakness, of haughtiness, of party spirit; but calumny itself never dared to couple his name with corruption.

Unhappily his government, though one of the best that has ever existed in our country, was also one of the weakest. The King's friends assailed and obstructed the ministers at every turn. To appeal to the King was only to draw forth new promises and new evasions. His Majesty was sure that there must be some misunderstanding. Lord Rockingham had better speak to the gentlemen. They should be dismissed on the next fault. The next fault was soon committed, and his Majesty still continued to shuffle. It was too bad. It was quite abominable; but it mattered less as the prorogation was at hand. He would give the delinquents one more chance. If they did not alter their conduct next session, he should not have one word to say for them. He had already resolved that, long before the commencement of the next session, Lord Rockingham should cease to be minister.

We have now come to a part of our story which, admiring as we do the genius and the many noble qualities of Pitt, we cannot relate without much pain. We believe that, at this conjuncture, he had it in his power to give the victory either to the Whigs or to the King's friends. If he had allied himself closely with Lord Rockingham, what could the court have done? There would have been only one alternative, the Whigs or Grenville; and there could be no doubt what the King's choice would be. He still remembered, as well he might, with the utmost bitterness, the thraldom from which his uncle had freed him, and said about this time, with great vehemence, that he would sooner see the Devil come into his closet than Grenville.

And what was there to prevent Pitt from allying himself with Lord Rockingham? On all the most important questions their views were the same. They had agreed in condemning the peace, the Stamp Act, the general warrants, the seizure of papers. The points on which they differed were few and unimportant. In integrity, in disinterestedness, in hatred of corruption, they resembled each other. Their personal interests could not clash. They sat in different houses, and Pitt had always declared that nothing should induce him to be first lord of the treasury.

If the opportunity of forming a coalition beneficial to the state, and honourable to all concerned, was suffered to escape, the fault was not with the Whig ministers. They behaved towards Pitt with an obsequiousness which, had it not been the effect of sincere admiration and of anxiety for the public interests, might have been justly called servile. They repeatedly gave him to understand that, if he chose to join their ranks, they were ready to receive him, not as an associate, but as a leader. They had proved their respect for him by bestowing a peerage on the person who, at that time, enjoyed the largest share of his confidence, Chief Justice Pratt. What then was there to divide Pitt from the Whigs? What, on the other hand, was there in common between him and the King's friends, that he should lend himself to their purposes, he who had never owed any thing to flattery or intrigue, he whose eloquence and independent spirit had overawed two generations of slaves and jobbers, he who had twice been forced by the enthusiasm of an admiring nation on a reluctant Prince?

Unhappily the court had gained Pitt, not, it is true, by those ignoble means which were employed when such men as Rigby and Wedderburn were to be won, but by allurements suited to a nature noble even in its aberrations. The King set himself to seduce the one man who could turn the Whigs out without letting Grenville in. Praise, caresses, promises, were lavished on the idol of the nation. He, and he alone, could put an end to faction, could bid defiance to all the powerful connections in the land united, Whigs and Tories, Rockinghams, Bedfords, and Grenvilles. These blandishments produced a great effect. For though Pitt's spirit was high and manly, though his eloquence was often exerted with formidable effect against the court, and though his theory of government had been learned in the school of Locke and Sidney, he had always regarded the person of the sovereign with profound veneration. As soon as he was brought face to face with royalty, his imagination and sensibility were too strong for his principles. His Whiggism thawed and disappeared; and he became, for the time, a Tory of the old Ormond pattern. Nor was he by any means unwilling to assist in the work of dissolving all political connections. His own weight in the state was wholly independent of such connections. He was therefore inclined to look on them with dislike, and made far too little distinction between gangs of knaves associated for the mere purpose of robbing the public, and confederacies of honourable men for the promotion of great public objects. Nor had he the sagacity to perceive that the strenuous efforts which he made to annihilate all parties tended only to establish the ascendency of one party, and that the basest and most hateful of all.

It may be doubted whether he would have been thus misled, if his mind had been in full health and vigour. But the truth is that he had for some time been in an unnatural state of excitement. No suspicion of this sort had yet got abroad. His eloquence had never shone with more splendour than during the recent debates. But people afterwards called to mind many things which ought to have roused their apprehensions. His habits were gradually becoming more and more eccentric. A horror of all loud sounds, such as is said to have been one of the many oddities of Wallenstein, grew upon him. Though the most affectionate of fathers, he could not at this time bear to hear the voices of his own children, and laid out great sums at Hayes in buying up houses contiguous to his own, merely that he might have no neighbours to disturb him with their noise. He then sold Hayes, and took possession of a villa at Hamp-

stead, where he again began to purchase houses to right and
left. In expense, indeed, he vied, during this part of his
life, with the wealthiest of the conquerors of Bengal and
Tanjore. At Burton Pynsent, he ordered a great extent of
ground to be planted with cedars. Cedars enough for the
purpose were not to be found in Somersetshire. They were
therefore collected in London, and sent down by land carriage. Relays of labourers were hired; and the work went
on all night by torchlight. No man could be more abstemious
10 than Pitt; yet the profusion of his kitchen was a wonder
even to epicures. Several dinners were always dressing; for
his appetite was capricious and fanciful; and at whatever
moment he felt inclined to eat, he expected a meal to be
instantly on the table. Other circumstances might be mentioned, such as separately are of little moment, but such as,
when taken together, and when viewed in connection with
the strange events which followed, justify us in believing
that his mind was already in a morbid state.

Soon after the close of the session of Parliament, Lord
20 Rockingham received his dismissal. He retired, accompanied
by a firm body of friends, whose consistency and uprightness
enmity itself was forced to admit. None of them had asked
or obtained any pension or any sinecure, either in possession
or in reversion. Such disinterestedness was then rare among
politicians. Their chief, though not a man of brilliant
talents, had won for himself an honourable fame, which he
kept pure to the last. He had, in spite of difficulties which
seemed almost insurmountable, removed great abuses and
averted a civil war. Sixteen years later, in a dark and
30 terrible day, he was again called upon to save the state,
brought to the very brink of ruin by the same perfidy and
obstinacy which had embarrassed, and at length overthrown,
his first administration.

Pitt was planting in Somersetshire when he was summoned to court by a letter written by the royal hand. He
instantly hastened to London. The irritability of his mind

and body were increased by the rapidity with which he travelled; and when he reached his journey's end he was suffering from fever. Ill as he was, he saw the King at Richmond, and undertook to form an administration.

Pitt was scarcely in the state in which a man should be who has to conduct delicate and arduous negotiations. In his letters to his wife, he complained that the conferences in which it was necessary for him to bear a part heated his blood and accelerated his pulse. From other sources of information we learn, that his language, even to those whose cooperation he wished to engage, was strangely peremptory and despotic. Some of his notes written at this time have been preserved, and are in a style which Lewis the Fourteenth would have been too well bred to employ in addressing any French gentleman.

In the attempt to dissolve all parties, Pitt met with some difficulties. Some Whigs, whom the court would gladly have detached from Lord Rockingham, rejected all offers. The Bedfords were perfectly willing to break with Grenville; but Pitt would not come up to their terms. Temple, whom Pitt at first meant to place at the head of the treasury, proved intractable. A coldness indeed had, during some months, been fast growing between the brothers-in-law, so long and so closely allied in politics. Pitt was angry with Temple for opposing the repeal of the Stamp Act. Temple was angry with Pitt for refusing to accede to that family league which was now the favourite plan at Stowe. At length the Earl proposed an equal partition of power and patronage, and offered, on this condition, to give up his brother George. Pitt thought the demand exorbitant, and positively refused compliance. A bitter quarrel followed. Each of the kinsmen was true to his character. Temple's soul festered with spite, and Pitt's swelled into contempt. Temple represented Pitt as the most odious of hypocrites and traitors. Pitt held a different and perhaps a more provoking tone. Temple was a good sort of man enough, whose single title to distinction was, that he had a large garden, with a large piece of water, and a great many pavilions and summer-houses. To his fortunate connection with a great orator and statesman he was indebted for an importance in the state which his own talents could never have gained for him. That importance had turned his head. He had begun to fancy that he could form administrations, and govern empires. It was piteous to see a well-meaning man under such a delusion.

10   In spite of all these difficulties, a ministry was made such as the King wished to see, a ministry in which all his Majesty's friends were comfortably accommodated, and which, with the exception of his Majesty's friends, contained no four persons who had ever in their lives been in the habit of acting together. Men who had never concurred in a single vote found themselves seated at the same board. The office of paymaster was divided between two persons who had never exchanged a word. Most of the chief posts were filled either by personal adherents of Pitt, or by members of
20 the late ministry, who had been induced to remain in place after the dismissal of Lord Rockingham. To the former class belonged Pratt, now Lord Camden, who accepted the great seal, and Lord Shelburne, who was made one of the Secretaries of State. To the latter class belonged the Duke of Grafton, who became First Lord of the Treasury, and Conway, who kept his old position both in the government and in the House of Commons. Charles Townshend, who had belonged to every party, and cared for none, was Chancellor of the Exchequer. Pitt himself was declared prime
30 minister, but refused to take any laborious office. He was created Earl of Chatham, and the privy seal was delivered to him.

It is scarcely necessary to say, that the failure, the complete and disgraceful failure, of this arrangement, is not to be ascribed to any want of capacity in the persons whom we have named. None of them were deficient in abilities;

and four of them, Pitt himself, Shelburne, Camden, and Townshend, were men of high intellectual eminence. The fault was not in the materials, but in the principle on which the materials were put together. Pitt had mixed up these conflicting elements, in the full confidence that he should be able to keep them all in perfect subordination to himself, and in perfect harmony with each other. We shall soon see how the experiment succeeded.

On the very day on which the new prime minister kissed hands, three fourths of that popularity which he had long enjoyed without a rival, and to which he owed the greater part of his authority, departed from him. A violent outcry was raised, not against that part of his conduct which really deserved severe condemnation, but against a step in which we can see nothing to censure. His acceptance of a peerage produced a general burst of indignation. Yet surely no peerage had ever been better earned; nor was there ever a statesman who more needed the repose of the Upper House. Pitt was now growing old. He was much older in constitution than in years. It was with imminent risk to his life that he had, on some important occasions, attended his duty in Parliament. During the session of 1764, he had not been able to take part in a single debate. It was impossible that he should go through the nightly labour of conducting the business of the government in the House of Commons. His wish to be transferred, under such circumstances, to a less busy and a less turbulent assembly, was natural and reasonable. The nation, however, overlooked all these considerations. Those who had most loved and honoured the great Commoner were loudest in invective against the new made Lord. London had hitherto been true to him through every vicissitude. When the citizens learned that he had been sent for from Somersetshire, that he had been closeted with the King at Richmond, and that he was to be first minister, they had been in transports of joy. Preparations were made for a grand entertainment and for a general illumination. The lamps had actually been placed round the Monument, when the Gazette announced that the object of all this enthusiasm was an Earl. Instantly the feast was countermanded. The lamps were taken down. The newspapers raised the roar of obloquy. Pamphlets, made up of calumny and scurrility, filled the shops of all the booksellers; and of those pamphlets, the most galling were written under the direction of the malignant Temple. It was now the fashion to compare the two Williams, William Pulteney and William Pitt. Both, it was said, had, by eloquence and simulated patriotism, acquired a great ascendency in the House of Commons and in the country. Both had been intrusted with the office of reforming the government. Both had, when at the height of power and popularity, been seduced by the splendour of the coronet. Both had been made earls, and both had at once become objects of aversion and scorn to the nation which a few hours before had regarded them with affection and veneration.

The clamour against Pitt appears to have had a serious effect on the foreign relations of the country. His name had till now acted like a spell at Versailles and St. Ildefonso. English travellers on the Continent had remarked that nothing more was necessary to silence a whole room full of boasting Frenchmen than to drop a hint of the probability that Mr. Pitt would return to power. In an instant there was deep silence: all shoulders rose, and all faces were lengthened. Now, unhappily, every foreign court, in learning that he was recalled to office, learned also that he no longer possessed the hearts of his countrymen. Ceasing to be loved at home, he ceased to be feared abroad. The name of Pitt had been a charmed name. Our envoys tried in vain to conjure with the name of Chatham.

The difficulties which beset Chatham were daily increased by the despotic manner in which he treated all around him. Lord Rockingham had, at the time of the change of ministry, acted with great moderation, had expressed a hope that the new government would act on the principles of the late government, and had even interfered to prevent many of his friends from quitting office. Thus Saunders and Keppel, two naval commanders of great eminence, had been induced to remain at the Admiralty, where their services were much needed. The Duke of Portland was still Lord Chamberlain, and Lord Besborough Postmaster. But within a quarter of a year, Lord Chatham had so deeply affronted these men, that they all retired in disgust. In truth, his tone, submissive in the closet, was at this time insupportably tyrannical in the cabinet. His colleagues were merely his clerks for naval, financial, and diplomatic business. Conway, meek as he was, was on one occasion provoked into declaring that such language as Lord Chatham's had never been heard west of Constantinople, and was with difficulty prevented by Horace Walpole from resigning, and rejoining the standard of Lord Rockingham.

The breach which had been made in the government by the defection of so many of the Rockinghams, Chatham hoped to supply by the help of the Bedfords. But with the Bedfords he could not deal as he had dealt with other parties. It was to no purpose that he bade high for one or two members of the faction, in the hope of detaching them from the rest. They were to be had; but they were to be had only in the lot. There was indeed for a moment some wavering and some disputing among them. But at length the counsels of the shrewd and resolute Rigby prevailed. They determined to stand firmly together, and plainly intimated to Chatham that he must take them all, or that he should get none of them. The event proved that they were wiser in their generation than any other connection in the state. In a few months they were able to dictate their own terms.

The most important public measure of Lord Chatham's administration was his celebrated interference with the corn trade. The harvest had been bad; the price of food was

I

high ; and he thought it necessary to take on himself the
responsibility of laying an embargo on the exportation of
grain. When Parliament met, this proceeding was attacked
by the Opposition as unconstitutional, and defended by the
ministers as indispensably necessary. At last an act was
passed to indemnify all who had been concerned in the
embargo.

The first words uttered by Chatham, in the House of
Lords, were in defence of his conduct on this occasion. He
10 spoke with a calmness, sobriety, and dignity, well suited to
the audience which he was addressing. A subsequent speech
which he made on the same subject was less successful. He
bade defiance to aristocratical connections, with a supercili-
ousness to which the Peers were not accustomed, and with
tones and gestures better suited to a large and stormy
assembly than to the body of which he was now a member.
A short altercation followed, and he was told very plainly
that he should not be suffered to browbeat the old nobility
of England.

20 It gradually became clearer and clearer that he was in a
distempered state of mind. His attention had been drawn
to the territorial acquisitions of the East India Company,
and he determined to bring the whole of that great subject
before Parliament. He would not, however, confer on the
subject with any of his colleagues. It was in vain that
Conway, who was charged with the conduct of business in
the House of Commons, and Charles Townshend, who was
responsible for the direction of the finances, begged for some
glimpse of light as to what was in contemplation. Chat-
30 ham's answers were sullen and mysterious. He must decline
any discussion with them ; he did not want their assistance ;
he had fixed on a person to take charge of his measure in the
House of Commons. This person was a member who was
not connected with the government, and who neither had,
nor deserved to have, the ear of the House, a noisy, purse-
proud, illiterate demagogue, whose Cockney English and

scraps of mispronounced Latin were the jest of the newspapers, Alderman Beckford. It may well be supposed that these strange proceedings produced a ferment through the whole political world. The city was in commotion. The East India Company invoked the faith of charters. Burke thundered against the ministers. The ministers looked at each other and knew not what to say. In the midst of the confusion, Lord Chatham proclaimed himself gouty, and retired to Bath. It was announced, after some time, that he was better, that he would shortly return, that he would soon put every thing in order. A day was fixed for his arrival in London. But when he reached the Castle inn at Marlborough, he stopped, shut himself up in his room, and remained there some weeks. Every body who travelled that road was amazed by the number of his attendants. Footmen and grooms, dressed in his family livery, filled the whole inn, though one of the largest in England, and swarmed in the streets of the little town. The truth was that the invalid had insisted that, during his stay, all the waiters and stable-boys of the Castle should wear his livery.

His colleagues were in despair. The Duke of Grafton proposed to go down to Marlborough in order to consult the oracle. But he was informed that Lord Chatham must decline all conversation on business. In the mean time, all the parties which were out of office, Bedfords, Grenvilles, and Rockinghams, joined to oppose the distracted government on the vote for the land tax. They were reinforced by almost all the county members, and had a considerable majority. This was the first time that a ministry had been beaten on an important division in the House of Commons since the fall of Sir Robert Walpole. The administration, thus furiously assailed from without, was torn by internal dissensions. It had been formed on no principle whatever. From the very first, nothing but Chatham's authority had prevented the hostile contingents which made up his ranks from going to blows with each other. That authority was now withdrawn, and every thing was in commotion. Conway, a brave soldier, but in civil affairs the most timid and irresolute of men, afraid of disobliging the King, afraid of being abused in the newspapers, afraid of being thought factious if he went out, afraid of being thought interested if he stayed in, afraid of every thing, and afraid of being known to be afraid of any thing, was beaten backwards and forwards like a shuttlecock between Horace Walpole who wished to make him prime minister, and Lord John Cavendish who wished to draw him into opposition. Charles Townshend, a man of splendid talents, of lax principles, and of boundless vanity and presumption, would submit to no control. The full extent of his parts, of his ambition, and of his arrogance, had not yet been made manifest; for he had always quailed before the genius and the lofty character of Pitt. But now that Pitt had quitted the House of Commons, and seemed to have abdicated the part of chief minister, Townshend broke loose from all restraint.

While things were in this state, Chatham at length returned to London. He might as well have remained at Marlborough. He would see nobody. He would give no opinion on any public matter. The Duke of Grafton begged piteously for an interview, for an hour, for half an hour, for five minutes. The answer was, that it was impossible. The King himself repeatedly condescended to expostulate and implore. "Your duty," he wrote, "your own honour, require you to make an effort." The answers to these appeals were commonly written in Lady Chatham's hand, from her lord's dictation; for he had not energy even to use a pen. He flings himself at the King's feet. He is penetrated by the royal goodness, so signally shown to the most unhappy of men. He implores a little more indulgence. He cannot as yet transact business. He cannot see his colleagues. Least of all can he bear the excitement of an interview with majesty.

Some were half inclined to suspect that he was, to use a

military phrase, malingering. He had made, they said, a great blunder, and had found it out. His immense popularity, his high reputation for statesmanship, were gone for ever. Intoxicated by pride, he had undertaken a task beyond his abilities. He now saw nothing before him but distresses and humiliations; and he had therefore simulated illness, in order to escape from vexations which he had not fortitude to meet. This suspicion, though it derived some colour from that weakness which was the most striking blemish of his character, was certainly unfounded. His mind, before he became first minister, had been, as we have said, in an unsound state; and physical and moral causes now concurred to make the derangement of his faculties complete. The gout, which had been the torment of his whole life, had been suppressed by strong remedies. For the first time since he was a boy at Oxford, he passed several months without a twinge. But his hand and foot had been relieved at the expense of his nerves. He became melancholy, fanciful, irritable. The embarrassing state of public affairs, the grave responsibility which lay on him, the consciousness of his errors, the disputes of his colleagues, the savage clamours raised by his detractors, bewildered his enfeebled mind. One thing alone, he said, could save him. He must repurchase Hayes. The unwilling consent of the new occupant was extorted by Lady Chatham's entreaties and tears; and her lord was somewhat easier. But if business were mentioned to him, he, once the proudest and boldest of mankind, behaved like a hysterical girl, trembled from head to foot, and burst into a flood of tears.

His colleagues for a time continued to entertain the expectation that his health would soon be restored, and that he would emerge from his retirement. But month followed month, and still he remained hidden in mysterious seclusion, and sunk, as far as they could learn, in the deepest dejection of spirits. They at length ceased to hope or to fear any thing from him; and, though he was still nominally Prime

Minister, took without scruple steps which they knew to be diametrically opposed to all his opinions and feelings, allied themselves with those whom he had proscribed, disgraced those whom he most esteemed, and laid taxes on the colonies, in the face of the strong declarations which he had recently made.

When he had passed about a year and three quarters in gloomy privacy, the King received a few lines in Lady Chatham's hand. They contained a request, dictated by her lord, that he might be permitted to resign the Privy Seal. After some civil show of reluctance, the resignation was accepted. Indeed Chatham was, by this time, almost as much forgotten as if he had already been lying in Westminster Abbey.

At length the clouds which had gathered over his mind broke and passed away. His gout returned, and freed him from a more cruel malady. His nerves were newly braced. His spirits became buoyant. He woke as from a sickly dream. It was a strange recovery. Men had been in the habit of talking of him as of one dead, and when he first showed himself at the King's levee, started as if they had seen a ghost. It was more than two years and a half since he had appeared in public.

He too, had cause for wonder. The world which he now entered was not the world which he had quitted. The administration which he had formed had never been, at any one moment, entirely changed. But there had been so many losses and so many accessions, that he could scarcely recognise his own work. Charles Townshend was dead. Lord Shelburne had been dismissed. Conway had sunk into utter insignificance. The Duke of Grafton had fallen into the hands of the Bedfords. The Bedfords had deserted Grenville, had made their peace with the King and the King's friends, and had been admitted to office. Lord North was Chancellor of the Exchequer, and was rising fast in importance. Corsica had been given up to France without a struggle. The disputes with the American colonies had been revived. A general election had taken place. Wilkes had returned from exile, and, outlaw as he was, had been chosen knight of the shire for Middlesex. The multitude was on his side. The court was obstinately bent on ruining him, and was prepared to shake the very foundations of the constitution for the sake of a paltry revenge. The House of Commons, assuming to itself an authority which of right belongs only to the whole legislature, had declared Wilkes incapable of sitting in Parliament. Nor had it been thought sufficient to keep him out. Another must be brought in. Since the freeholders of Middlesex had obstinately refused to choose a member acceptable to the Court, the House had chosen a member for them. This was not the only instance, perhaps not the most disgraceful instance, of the inveterate malignity of the Court. Exasperated by the steady opposition of the Rockingham party, the King's friends had tried to rob a distinguished Whig nobleman of his private estate, and had persisted in their mean wickedness till their own servile majority had revolted from mere disgust and shame. Discontent had spread throughout the nation, and was kept up by stimulants such as had rarely been applied to the public mind. Junius had taken the field, had trampled Sir William Draper in the dust, had well-nigh broken the heart of Blackstone, and had so mangled the reputation of the Duke of Grafton, that his grace had become sick of office, and was beginning to look wistfully towards the shades of Euston. Every principle of foreign, domestic, and colonial policy which was dear to the heart of Chatham had, during the eclipse of his genius, been violated by the government which he had formed.

The remaining years of his life were spent in vainly struggling against that fatal policy which, at the moment when he might have given it a death blow, he had been induced to take under his protection. His exertions redeemed his own fame, but they effected little for his country.

He found two parties arrayed against the government, the party of his own brothers-in-law, the Grenvilles, and the party of Lord Rockingham. On the question of the Middlesex election these parties were agreed. But on many other important questions they differed widely; and they were, in truth, not less hostile to each other than to the Court. The Grenvilles had, during several years, annoyed the Rockinghams with a succession of acrimonious pamphlets. It was long before the Rockinghams could be induced to retaliate.
10 But an ill-natured tract, written under Grenville's direction, and entitled, a State of the Nation, was too much for their patience. Burke undertook to defend and avenge his friends, and executed the task with admirable skill and vigour. On every point he was victorious, and nowhere more completely victorious than when he joined issue on those dry and minute questions of statistical and financial detail in which the main strength of Grenville lay. The official drudge, even on his own chosen ground, was utterly unable to maintain the fight against the great orator and philosopher.
20 When Chatham reappeared, Grenville was still writhing with the recent shame and smart of this well-merited chastisement. Cordial cooperation between the two sections of the Opposition was impossible. Nor could Chatham easily connect himself with either. His feelings, in spite of many affronts given and received, drew him towards the Grenvilles. For he had strong domestic affections; and his nature, which, though haughty, was by no means obdurate, had been softened by affliction. But from his kinsmen he was separated by a wide difference of opinion on the question of colonial taxation.
30 A reconciliation, however, took place. He visited Stowe: he shook hands with George Grenville; and the Whig freeholders of Buckinghamshire, at their public dinners, drank many bumpers to the union of the three brothers.

In opinions, Chatham was much nearer to the Rockinghams than to his own relatives. But between him and the Rockinghams there was a gulf not easily to be passed. He had deeply injured them, and in injuring them, had deeply injured his country. When the balance was trembling between them and the Court, he had thrown the whole weight of his genius, of his renown, of his popularity, into the scale of misgovernment. It must be added, that many eminent members of the party still retained a bitter recollection of the asperity and disdain with which they had been treated by him at the time when he assumed the direction of affairs. It is clear from Burke's pamphlets and speeches, and still more clear from his private letters, and from the language which he held in conversation, that he regarded Chatham with a feeling not far removed from dislike. Chatham was undoubtedly conscious of his error, and desirous to atone for it. But his overtures of frendship, though made with earnestness, and even with unwonted humility, were at first received by Lord Rockingham with cold and austere reserve. Gradually the intercourse of the two statesmen became courteous and even amicable. But the past was never wholly forgotten.

Chatham did not, however, stand alone. Round him gathered a party, small in number, but strong in great and various talents. Lord Camden, Lord Shelburne, Colonel Barré, and Dunning, afterwards Lord Ashburton, were the principal members of this connection.

There is no reason to believe that, from this time till within a few weeks of Chatham's death, his intellect suffered any decay. His eloquence was almost to the last heard with delight. But it was not exactly the eloquence of the House of Lords. That lofty and passionate, but somewhat desultory declamation, in which he excelled all men, and which was set off by looks, tones, and gestures, worthy of Garrick or Talma, was out of place in a small apartment where the audience often consisted of three or four drowsy prelates, three or four old judges, accustomed during many years to disregard rhetoric, and to look only at facts and arguments, and three or four listless and supercilious men of fashion, whom any thing like enthusiasm moved to a sneer. In the House of Commons, a flash of his eye, a wave of his arm, had sometimes cowed Murray. But, in the House of Peers, his utmost vehemence and pathos produced a less effect than the moderation, the reasonableness, the luminous order, and the serene dignity, which characterised the speeches of Lord Mansfield.

On the question of the Middlesex election, all the three divisions of the Opposition acted in concert. No orator in either House defended what is now universally admitted to have been the constitutional cause with more ardour or eloquence than Chatham. Before this subject had ceased to occupy the public mind, George Grenville died. His party rapidly melted away; and in a short time most of his adherents appeared on the ministerial benches.

Had George Grenville lived many months longer, the friendly ties which, after years of estrangement and hostility, had been renewed between him and his brother-in-law, would, in all probability, have been a second time violently dissolved. For now the quarrel between England and the North American colonies took a gloomy and terrible aspect. Oppression provoked resistance; resistance was made the pretext for fresh oppression. The warnings of all the greatest statesmen of the age were lost on an imperious court and a deluded nation. Soon a colonial senate confronted the British Parliaments. Then the colonial militia crossed bayonets with the British regiments. At length the commonwealth was torn asunder. Two millions of Englishmen, who, fifteen years before, had been as loyal to their prince and as proud of their country as the people of Kent or Yorkshire, separated themselves by a solemn act from the Empire. For a time it seemed that the insurgents would struggle to small purpose against the vast financial and military means of the mother country. But disasters, following one another in rapid succession, rapidly dispelled the illusions of national vanity. At length a great British force, exhausted, famished, harassed on every side by a hostile peasantry, was compelled to deliver up its arms. Those governments which England had, in the late war, so signally humbled, and which had during many years been sullenly brooding over the recollections of Quebec, of Minden, and of the Moro, now saw with exultation that the day of revenge was at hand. France recognised the independence of the United States ; and there could be little doubt that the example would soon be followed by Spain.

Chatham and Rockingham had cordially concurred in opposing every part of the fatal policy which had brought the state into this dangerous situation. But their paths now diverged. Lord Rockingham thought, and, as the event proved, thought most justly, that the revolted colonies were separated from the Empire for ever, and that the only effect of prolonging the war on the American continent would be to divide resources which it was desirable to concentrate. If the hopeless attempt to subjugate Pennsylvania and Virginia were abandoned, war against the House of Bourbon might possibly be avoided, or, if inevitable, might be carried on with success and glory. We might even indemnify ourselves for part of what we had lost, at the expense of those foreign enemies who had hoped to profit by our domestic dissensions. Lord Rockingham, therefore, and those who acted with him, conceived that the wisest course now opened to England was to acknowledge the independence of the United States, and to turn her whole force against her European enemies.

Chatham, it should seem, ought to have taken the same side. Before France had taken any part in our quarrel with the colonies, he had repeatedly, and with great energy of language, declared that it was impossible to conquer America; and he could not without absurdity maintain that it was easier to conquer France and America together than America alone. But his passions overpowered his judgment, and made him blind to his own inconsistency. The very circumstances which made the separation of the colonies inevitable made it to him altogether insupportable.

The dismemberment of the Empire seemed to him less ruinous and humiliating, when produced by domestic dissensions, than when produced by foreign interference. His blood boiled at the degradation of his country. Whatever lowered her among the nations of the earth, he felt as a personal outrage to himself. And the feeling was natural. He had made her so great. He had been so proud of her; and she had been so proud of him. He remembered how, more than twenty years before, in a day of gloom and dismay, when her possessions were torn from her, when her flag was dishonoured, she had called on him to save her. He remembered the sudden and glorious change which his energy had wrought, the long series of triumphs, the days of thanksgiving, the nights of illumination. Fired by such recollections, he determined to separate himself from those who advised that the independence of the colonies should be acknowledged. That he was in error will scarcely, we think, be disputed by his warmest admirers. Indeed, the treaty, by which, a few years later, the republic of the United States was recognised, was the work of his most attached adherents and of his favourite son.

The Duke of Richmond had given notice of an address to the throne, against the further prosecution of hostilities with America. Chatham had, during some time, absented himself from Parliament, in consequence of his growing infirmities. He determined to appear in his place on this occasion, and to declare that his opinions were decidedly at variance with those of the Rockingham party. He was in a state of great excitement. His medical attendants were uneasy, and strongly advised him to calm himself, and to remain at home. But he was not to be controlled. His son William, and his son-in-law Lord Mahon, accompanied him to Westminster. He rested himself in the Chancellor's room till the debate commenced, and then, leaning on his two young relations, limped to his seat. The slightest particulars of that day were remembered, and have been carefully recorded.

He bowed, it was remarked, with great courtliness to those peers who rose to make way for him and his supporters. His crutch was in his hand. He wore, as was his fashion, a rich velvet coat. His legs were swathed in flannel. His wig was so large, and his face so emaciated, that none of his features could be discerned, except the high curve of his nose, and his eyes, which still retained a gleam of the old fire.

When the Duke of Richmond had spoken, Chatham rose. For some time his voice was inaudible. At length his tones became distinct and his action animated. Here and there his hearers caught a thought or an expression which reminded them of William Pitt. But it was clear that he was not himself. He lost the thread of his discourse, hesitated, repeated the same words several times, and was so confused that, in speaking of the Act of Settlement, he could not recall the name of the Electress Sophia. The House listened in solemn silence, and with the aspect of profound respect and compassion. The stillness was so deep that the dropping of a handkerchief would have been heard. The Duke of Richmond replied with great tenderness and courtesy; but while he spoke the old man was observed to be restless and irritable. The Duke sat down. Chatham stood up again, pressed his hand on his breast, and sank down in an apoplectic fit. Three or four lords who sat near him caught him in his fall. The House broke up in confusion. The dying man was carried to the residence of one of the officers of Parliament, and was so far restored as to be able to bear a journey to Hayes. At Hayes, after lingering a few weeks, he expired in his seventieth year. His bed was watched to the last, with anxious tenderness, by his wife and children; and he well deserved their care. Too often haughty and wayward to others, to them he had been almost effeminately kind. He had through life been dreaded by his political opponents, and regarded with more awe than love even by his political associates. But no fear seems to have mingled with the affection which his fondness, constantly overflowing in a thousand endearing forms, had inspired in the little circle at Hayes.

Chatham, at the time of his decease, had not, in both Houses of Parliament, ten personal adherents. Half the public men of the age had been estranged from him by his errors, and the other half by the exertions which he had made to repair his errors. His last speech had been an attack at once on the policy pursued by the government, and on the policy recommended by the opposition. But death restored him to his old place in the affection of his country. Who could hear unmoved of the fall of that which had been so great, and which had stood so long? The circumstances, too, seemed rather to belong to the tragic stage than to real life. A great statesman, full of years and honours, led forth to the Senate House by a son of rare hopes, and stricken down in full council while straining his feeble voice to rouse the drooping spirit of his country, could not but be remembered with peculiar veneration and tenderness. Detraction was overawed. The voice even of just and temperate censure was mute. Nothing was remembered but the lofty genius, the unsullied probity, the undisputed services, of him who was no more. For once, all parties were agreed. A public funeral, a public monument, were eagerly voted. The debts of the deceased were paid. A provision was made for his family. The City of London requested that the remains of the great man whom she had so long loved and honoured might rest under the dome of her magnificent cathedral. But the petition came too late. Every thing was already prepared for the interment in Westminster Abbey.

Though men of all parties had concurred in decreeing posthumous honours to Chatham, his corpse was attended to the grave almost exclusively by opponents of the government. The banner of the lordship of Chatham was borne by Colonel Barré, attended by the Duke of Richmond and Lord Rockingham. Burke, Savile, and Dunning upheld the pall.

Lord Camden was conspicuous in the procession. The chief mourner was young William Pitt. After the lapse of more than twenty-seven years, in a season as dark and perilous, his own shattered frame and broken heart were laid, with the same pomp, in the same consecrated mould.

Chatham sleeps near the northern door of the Church, in a spot which has ever since been appropriated to statesmen, as the other end of the same transept has long been to poets. Mansfield rests there, and the second William Pitt, and Fox, and Grattan, and Canning, and Wilberforce. In no other cemetery do so many great citizens lie within so narrow a space. High over those venerable graves towers the stately monument of Chatham, and from above, his effigy, graven by a cunning hand, seems still, with eagle face and outstretched arm, to bid England be of good cheer, and to hurl defiance at her foes. The generation which reared that memorial of him has disappeared. The time has come when the rash and indiscriminate judgments which his contemporaries passed on his character may be calmly revised by history. And, history, while, for the warning of vehement, high, and daring natures, she notes his many errors, will yet deliberately pronounce, that, among the eminent men whose bones lie near his, scarcely one has left a more stainless, and none a more splendid name.

NOTES.

WILLIAM PITT, EARL OF CHATHAM.

Page 1, l. 4. **Mr. Thackeray,** etc. Macaulay seems to be somewhat severe upon the author of the *Life of Pitt*; for this work is frequently quoted and referred to by historians like Lecky and Green.

l. 5. **the State Paper Office.** The State Papers run from Henry VIII. to the present time. When they first began to be preserved they were locked up in chests, then confined in the larder of the Privy Seal, then lodged in the tower over the gateway of Whitehall Palace, then transferred to the upper floor of the Lord Chamberlain's lodgings, then despatched to an old house in Scotland Yard; and it was not till 1833 that the State Paper Office in St. James's Park was specially erected for their accommodation. Twenty years later it was deemed advisable by the Government of the day to amalgamate the State Papers with the Public Records: the State Paper Office was therefore pulled down and its contents transferred to the present Record Repository in Fetter Lane. The amalgamation of the State Paper Office in 1854 with the Record Office has been the means of rendering the series of English national archives an almost complete collection. With the exception of certain MSS. in the British Museum and in a few public libraries, most of the public muniments of the realm are now placed in one repository under the supervision of the Master of the Rolls. Sir Francis Palgrave, under whose auspices as deputy keeper the public muniments were brought together under one roof, has given a sketch of the history both of the Public Records and of the State Papers; most of the above facts are drawn from that account; he writes also as follows, "Whether we consider them in relation to antiquity, to continuity, to variety, to extent, or to amplitude of facts and details they have no equals in the civilised world. For the archives of France, the most perfect and complete in continental Europe, do not ascend higher than the reign of St. Louis, and compared with ours are stinted and jejune: whereas in England, taking up our title (so to speak) from Doomsday, the documents placed under the custody of the Master of the Rolls contain the whole of the materials for the history of this country, in every branch and under every aspect, civil, religious, political, social, moral, or material, from the Norman Conquest to the present day."

l. 7. **Gifford's or Tomline's Life of the second Pitt.** *The Political Life of Pitt,* by John Gifford, was published in 1809. John Gifford was an assumed name of John Richards Green (b. 1758, d. 1818); he was the publisher of *The Anti-Jacobin Review* (1798) and of *The British Review.* He was also the author of a *History of France to the Death of Louis XVI.*, and of a number of pamphlets against Paine and Priestley.

George Pretyman Tomline, Bishop of Winchester (b. 1750, d. 1827), wrote *Elements of Christian Theology, A Refutation of the Charge of Calvinism against the Church of England,* and *The Life of the Right Hon. William Pitt.* Bishop Tomline was for a time tutor to the younger Pitt. Lord Rosebery writes of these two lives of the second Pitt as follows : " That by Richards Green, who wrote under the name of Gifford, need scarcely be mentioned. That by Tomline has been severely judged, more perhaps with reference to what it might have been than to what it is; for there are worse books."

l. 9. **the Parliamentary History,** by Corbett, 1066-1803, precedes the collection of *Hansard's Parliamentary Debates,* which begin in 1803. The History is in thirty-six volumes.

l. 10. **the Annual Register** begins with 1758: the earlier portions are attributed to Burke. It is published still by Longmans & Co.

l. 14. **blear-eyed,** (1) having blear eyes, (2) having the mental vision dimmed; dull of perception, short-sighted. The origin of the word, M.E. *blere,* as an epithet of the eyes is uncertain. "There are no corresponding words in O.E., and the only cognates in other Teutonic langs. are the mod. G. *blerr,* soreness of the eyes, L.G. *blarr-oged, blerr-oged,* blear-eyed. S.W. *plira, daplire,* to blink, leer, can hardly be connected " (Murray).

l. 19. **lues Boswelliana,** the disease of admiration, to which we are indebted for James Boswell's *Life of Dr. Samuel Johnson.* See Macaulay's *Essay on Boswell's Life of Johnson,* pp. 21, etc., in this series.

Page 2, l. 3. **In spite of Gods, men, and columns.** Cf. Horace, *A.P.* 373:

" Mediocribus esse poetis,
Non homines, non di, non concessere columnae,"

where *columnae* is used as equivalent to the booksellers' shops. At Rome the shops (*tabernae*) were sometimes under a *porticus,* and the titles of books for sale were then hung on the *columnae* outside.

l. 13. **cornet** (Fr. *cornette*, dim. of *corne*; Rom. *corna*, f. sing., horn; Lat. *cornua*, n. pl., horns) has many meanings:
  (1) A kind of head-dress formerly worn by ladies.
  (2) A scarf anciently worn by doctors as part of their academical costume.
  (3) The standard of a troop of cavalry, originally a long pennon narrowing gradually to a point.
  (4) A company of cavalry, so called from the standard carried at its head (no longer in use).
  (5) The fifth commissioned officer in a troop of cavalry, who carried the colours; corresponding to the *ensign* in infantry (no longer in use).—See Murray.

l. 16. **in esse**, in reality, at the present, already.

in posse, in possibility, possibly, in the future.

l. 19. **to give bounties for perjury, in order to get Walpole's head.** Pitt insisted with vindictive malice on the prosecution of Walpole, and supported the bill of indemnity to witnesses against the fallen minister.

l. 21. **when, being in opposition, he maintained that no peace ought to be made with Spain**, etc. Pitt made an effective speech against the Spanish Convention in 1739; but when in office (during the administration of 1746-1754) he supported measures such as the Spanish Treaty and the Continental Subsidies, which he had denounced when in opposition. Mr. Thackeray takes the trouble to offer an elaborate defence of such conduct; but the vindication is in part unnecessary and in part unsatisfactory. Within certain limits, not indeed very well defined, inconsistency has never been counted a vice in an English statesman. The times change, and he is not blamed for changing with the times. Pitt in office, looking back on the commencement of his public life, might have used the plea, "A good deal has happened since then," at least as justly as some others have done. Allowance must always be made for the restraints and responsibilities of office. In Pitt's case, too, it is to be borne in mind that the opposition with which he had acted gradually dwindled away, and that it ceased to have any organised existence after the death of the Prince of Wales in 1751. Then in regard to the important question with Spain, as to the right of search, Pitt has disarmed criticism by acknowledgment that the course he followed during Walpole's administration was indefensible. All due weight being given to these various considerations, it must be admitted nevertheless that Pitt did overstep the limits within which inconsistency is usually regarded as venial. His one great object was first to gain office, and then to make his tenure of office secure by conciliating the King. The entire revolution which much of his policy underwent in order to effect this object bears too close a resemblance to the endless and inexplicable changes of front habitual to the placemen of the Tadpole stamp to be altogether pleasant to contemplate in a politician of pure aims and lofty ambition. Humiliating is not too strong a term to apply to a letter in which he expresses his desire to "efface the past by every action of his life," in order that he may stand well with the King. (*Encyclopædia Britannica.*)

l. 26. **When he left the Duke of Newcastle**, etc. After the failure of Admiral Byng against the French fleet in 1756, Fox resigned office and Pitt refused his aid to the King unless Newcastle quitted power. In November Newcastle resigned office, and was succeeded by the Duke of Devonshire as First Lord of the Treasury, with Pitt as Secretary of State and Leader of the Commons. But this lasted for only a year, and in April, 1757, Pitt was dismissed from office on account of his opposition to the King's favourite continental policy. So strong, however, was the confidence and admiration of the public for the Great Commoner that any arrangement that excluded him was impracticable. At length a coalition was arranged between Newcastle and Pitt on such terms that while Newcastle was nominal, Pitt was the virtual head of the Government.

l. 27. **when he thundered against subsidies.** In 1743 the two Bourbon powers—France and Spain—made their second "Family Compact," binding them to make common cause against each other's enemies in every quarter. George II. became anxious for Hanover, and treaties were concluded for the payment of subsidies, in return for a supply of troops, to Hesse-Cassel, and other petty German States. Pitt, who was Paymaster of the Forces, declaimed against these subsidies with great power and effect in 1755.

l. 36. **Hampden**, John, was the head of a wealthy Buckinghamshire family; he was born in London in 1594, was educated at Oxford and at the Inner Temple. In 1624 he was returned to Parliament for the Borough of Grampound. His sympathies were with the popular party. In 1626 he refused to contribute to the general loan required by the King and was imprisoned for a time, but was afterwards set free unconditionally. He was several times returned member for Wendover, and finally for his own County of Buckinghamshire, for which he sat in the Long Parliament. In 1636 he refused to pay the Shipmoney. Proceedings were instituted against him, and after a trial of thirteen days the decision was given against him. He now became more than ever the favourite of the people. The Civil War broke out soon after this trial; and Hampden levied a body of troops and served under Essex, and met his death in a skirmish with Prince Rupert at Chalgrove in 1643. For a longer account of Hampden see Macaulay's *Essays*, p. 192, etc., etc.

Page 3, l. 1. **Somers**, Lord John, a distinguished statesman and lawyer, was born at Worcester about 1652; he was called to the bar and was one of the Counsels for the Seven Bishops: he was opposed to all the tyrannical measures of Charles II. and James II.: he promoted the Revolution and was Chairman of the Committee which framed the Declaration of Rights. He became successively Solicitor-General, Attorney-General, Lord-Keeper, and in 1697 Lord High Chancellor of England, with the title of Lord Somers, Baron Evesham. In 1706 he drew up the plan for the Union between England and Scotland, and was chosen by Anne as one of the Commissioners to carry it into execution. He died in 1716, having earned a high character for political purity and legal ability. In fact his purity of character, commanding genius, unaffected modesty, calm courage, and habitual courtesy not only gave him the lead of the Liberal party, but also won the respect of most of his opponents.

l. 22. **till the light was thrown with Rembrandt-like effect.** Rembrandt Harmens van Rijn (1607-1699) was the chief of the Dutch School of painting and one of the greatest painters the world has seen. One of the characteristics of his work is the boldness of his system of light and shade. His favourite mode of arresting attention is to concentrate the light on the principal figure in the picture, and where the light falls on the drapery to give full play to the magical effect of his subtle colour, while the background is left dark and full of mystery.

l. 25. **Belisarius** was the great General of Justinian. He was a native of Illyria. His first campaign was in 530, when he made an expedition against the King of Persia; he subsequently drove the Vandals out of Africa, was successful against the Goths in Italy, and took Rome in 537: he was then recalled, but was afterwards sent against the Huns. He died in 565.
The story that he was deprived of sight and reduced to beggary appears to be a fable of late invention.

l. 26. **Lear**, King of Britain, who is represented by Shakespeare as worn out with age and fatigues of government, and determined to part his kingdom between his three daughters:
"Only we still retain
The name and all the addition to a King."
Probably Macaulay recalls Macready's representation of Lear.

l. 31. **tergiversation** (Lat. *tergiversari*, to turn one's back), evasive conduct of any kind; shifting; shuffling; inconsistency; "ratting."

l. 33. **Wordsworth**, etc. This quotation is from the *Excursion*, Bk. ii., l. 300 (*circiter*).

Page 4, l. 2. **Doddington**, George Bubb, Lord Melcombe Regis, statesman, remarkable for his political versatility, was born in

1691 in Dorsetshire and educated at Oxford. In 1715 he entered Parliament for Winchelsea, was soon after appointed Envoy to Spain, became a Lord of the Treasury during Walpole's administration, and after years of political intrigue, in which the most shameless dereliction of principle was manifest, he was made a peer by the title of Lord Melcombe. Though servile as a politician, he was generous, witty, and hospitable in private life.

Sandys, Samuel, was first returned for Worcester in 1717, but did not become prominent till 1741, when he was chosen to bring forward a motion for the removal of Sir R. Walpole from the King's Council. On the fall of Walpole he became Chancellor of the Exchequer under Wilmington, but soon afterwards resigned, being raised to the peerage and receiving a place in the King's household.

l. 18. **not, like the Pelhams, to a strong aristocratical connection.** Sir Henry Pelham, in conjunction with his brother the Duke of Newcastle, was supported by a vast amount of family and borough influence, and succeeded in overthrowing the Ministry of Walpole, and in 1743 became the first Lord of the Treasury. The same year he was also named Chancellor of the Exchequer: in 1744 he resigned, but was recalled to office in a few days, and continued to be Prime Minister till his death in 1754.

l. 19. **not, like Bute, to the personal favour of the sovereign.** John Stuart, Earl of Bute, was descended from an ancient Scotch family; he was born early in the 18th century. In 1738 he was appointed one of the Lords of the Bed-chamber to Frederick, Prince of Wales. On the accession of George III., the son of Frederick, he was made Secretary of State: his influence over George III. was unbounded, and in 1762 he was appointed First Lord of the Treasury.

l. 31. **which the Regent Orleans, by the advice of Saint Simon,** etc. On the death of Louis XIV. in 1715, Philip, Duke of Orleans, was appointed Regent: he retained this office till Louis XV. attained his legal majority in 1723. One of the principal members of the Council of Regency was the Duke of Saint Simon, who advised the purchase of the diamond known as the Pitt or Regent Diamond. This stone was discovered in 1702; it weighed 410 carats (uncut), $136\frac{7}{8}$ carats (cut). The Braganza diamond, now among the Portuguese State Jewels, is the largest diamond of note, being as large as a hen's egg; that of the Rajah of Mattan (Borneo) is the second largest, the Pitt Diamond is the seventh largest, the Koh-i-Noor is the ninth largest. The Pitt Diamond is now in the possession of the King of Prussia.

l. 36. **Old Sarum** is generally regarded as the Roman Sorbiodunum. The Saxons captured it from the Britons in 552, and named it Searesbyrig. In 960 a Witanagemot was held at Old Sarum, and the barons were assembled here by William I. in 1086. From the reign of William I. till the 13th century it was the seat of a bishop; but the town (Salisbury) then followed the church, which was rebuilt in the plain, and hereafter Old Sarum has been almost deserted. Nevertheless it continued to send two members to Parliament until 1832, when it was disenfranchised by the Reform Bill.

Page 5, l. 1. **Oakhampton,** or Okehampton, a market town in Devonshire, 26 miles west of Exeter, in the middle of Dartmoor.

l. 19. **Mars,** the Latin god of war; his name means the crusher or grinder.

Themis, the goddess of law and order, Justice personified.

Neptune, the god of the sea.

Cocytus, one of the five rivers of Hades; the others were named Acheron, Styx, Phlegethon (or Pyriphlegethon), and Lethe. Milton describes them thus, giving the meaning of each name:
"Abhorrèd Styx, the flood of deadly hate;
Sad Acheron of sorrow, black and deep;
Cocytus, nam'd of lamentation loud
Heard on the rueful stream; fierce Phlegethon,
Whose waves of torrent fire inflame with rage.
Far off from these, a slow and silent stream,
Lethe, the river of oblivion, rolls." (*P.L.* ii. 577, etc.)

l. 20. **The Muses,** goddesses of music, poetry, art, and science, originally three in number, afterwards increased to nine. Their names were Clio (the proclaimer), Euterpe (the charmer), Erato (the lovely), Thalia (the joyous), Melpomene (the singer), Terpsichore (the enjoyer of dances), Polymnia (the lover of songs), Urania (the heavenly), and Calliope (the beautiful voiced).

urn. The Latin *urna* is often applied to a vessel for holding the ashes of the dead, and is thus synonymous with tomb. Cf. Ovid, *Amorum,* III. ix.:
"Ossa quieta, precor, tuta requiescite in urna;
Et sit humus cineri non onerosa tuo."

l. 21. **Caesar,** the cognomen of the Roman dictator Caius Julius Caesar, transferred as a title to the emperors from Augustus to Hadrian, and applied here by the poet to George II.

l. 24. **Pitt...gout.** Pitt had suffered from the gout before leaving Eton: his son, the younger Pitt, was also a martyr to this disease, which was then (as Lord Rosebery expresses it in his life of the second Pitt) "an appanage of Statesmanship."

l. 34. **the Blues,** the Royal Horse Guards, named in 1690 "The Oxford Blues," from their commander the Earl of Oxford, to distinguish them from the Dutch troops of William III., who likewise wore blue.

Page 6, 1. 7. Walpole, Sir Robert, etc., was Prime Minister of England twice, first from 1715 to 1717; and, when Sunderland was forced to resign after the bursting of the South Sea Bubble, Walpole was again made Premier (April, 1721), and held that office practically without a break for 21 years. His detractors dwell upon his inordinate love of power and his systematic corruption; while his admirers describe him as an able financier, a clever tactician in debate, a most serviceable minister to the House of Brunswick, and a firm friend of the Protestant succession.

1. 14. **the South Sea Act** of 1720 was a measure for enabling the South Sea Company to absorb in their stock a quantity of irredeemable annuities (amounting to £800,000), to reduce all the different public securities into one uniform fund, to reduce the rate of interest from 5 to 4 per cent., and to pay off the national debt (amounting to upwards of £36,000,000 and costing the country over 3 millions a year) within 26 years. The Bank regarded this scheme with great jealousy, and the Company was induced, through the competition of the Bank, to offer the Government a bonus of no less than £7,567,000, if all the debts were subscribed.

1. 17. **Sunderland's administration.** In 1717 Sunderland became First Lord of the Treasury. Stanhope received an earldom, and became Secretary of State; Addison was the other Secretary of State; Aislabie was made Chancellor of the Exchequer, and James Craggs the Secretary of War. Sunderland resigned in 1721, and Walpole returned to power.

1. 36. **parricides in ancient Rome** were tied up in bags along with an ape and a snake. Cf. Juvenal, viii. 214:

"Quis tam
Perditus, ut dubitet Senecam praeferre Neroni;
Cujus supplicio non debuit una parari
Simia nec serpens unus, nec culeus unus."

Page 7, 1. 6. Stanhope was no more. Lord Stanhope died in February, 1721, and was replaced, as Secretary of State, by Lord Townshend. Stanhope was almost the only member of Sunderland's ministry upon whose integrity no aspersions were cast regarding the South Sea scheme. His death was sudden. In the course of a debate the Duke of Wharton compared him to Sejanus, the odious minister of Tiberius. Stanhope was roused to so great a fury at this gibe, that he was seized with a fit when trying to reply, and died the next day.

Aislabie was expelled, etc. He is said to have acquired fraudulently a fortune of nearly £800,000.

l. 8. **Craggs was saved by a timely death**, etc. "Craggs, the Secretary of State, and his father, the Postmaster General, were both implicated in the receipt of enormous sums, as the difference in transactions in fictitious stock created to buy the passing of the South Sea Bill. The son died of small-pox, and the father quickly followed, leaving a fortune of a million and a half." (*Walpole*, by John Morley.)

This does not quite agree with the statements in the epitaph by Pope inscribed on Craggs' tomb in Westminster Abbey:

"Statesman, yet Friend to Truth! of Soul sincere,
In Action faithful, and in Honour clear!
Who broke no promise, serv'd no private End;
Who gain'd no Title, and who lost no Friend;
Ennobled by Himself, by All approv'd;
Prais'd, wept, and honour'd by the Muse he lov'd."

l. 22. **the course which Pelham afterwards took**, etc. This alludes to the formation of the so-called "Broad-bottomed Ministry." See p. 23, l. 16 *infra*, and note.

l. 33. **Pulteney**, William, was born in 1682, and educated at Westminster School and Christ Church, Oxford. He began parliamentary life as a zealous Whig, but he was bitterly offended when, on the resignation of Carteret, Walpole neglected his claims and made Newcastle Secretary of State. He then went into violent opposition, and joined Bolingbroke in conducting a paper called the *Craftsman*, which for years contained the bitterest and ablest attacks on Walpole. On the resignation of Walpole in 1742 Pulteney was created Earl of Bath, but from that time his popularity and influence ceased. He became Prime Minister in February, 1746, but was in office only two days. He is said to have shortened his life by drinking, but we must remember that hard drinking was the fashion of the day, and that he nevertheless reached the good old age of 82 before he died in 1764.

Page 8, l. 15. **Carteret**, John, was born in 1690. He entered the House of Lords in 1711, joined the Sunderland section of the Whigs in 1717, was appointed Ambassador to Sweden in the following year, and had afterwards accepted several brief diplomatic missions in Germany and France: he was Secretary of State in 1721, but, disagreeing with Lord Townshend, he was compelled to relinquish this post in 1724, when he became Lord-Lieutenant of Ireland. Although he gave some offence by prosecuting the publisher of the Drapier's (Swift's) letters, he was on the whole a popular viceroy. He resigned this appointment in 1730, and from that time became a leader of Opposition, and a close ally of Pulteney.

Horace Walpole and Chesterfield have pronounced him the ablest man of his time; Swift and Smollett admired his genius, and Chatham declared that in the upper departments of Government he had no equal. The singular versatility of his intellect made him almost equally conspicuous as an orator, a linguist, a statesman and a wit (see Lecky, vol. i., p. 440, etc.).

l. 25. **Townshend, Charles,** was born in 1676. He succeeded to the peerage on the death of his father in 1686; after taking his seat in the House of Lords he joined the Whig party; he was one of the Commissioners for the Union with Scotland in 1706, and plenipotentiary with Marlborough at the conferences for peace held at Gertruydenberg in 1710. He remained at the Hague as Ambassador to the States General, and negotiated the "Barrier Treaty." On the accession of George I. Lord Townshend was made principal Secretary of State. Walpole was Paymaster of the Forces and also of Chelsea Hospital. Townshend married Walpole's sister; and these two friends and brothers-in-law offended the King's Hanoverian favourites, incurred the enmity of Sunderland, lost the King's favour, and were compelled to resign office in 1716, and joined the ranks of the Opposition. In 1720 Townshend was received into favour again, and was made President of the Council; in 1721 Walpole was Prime Minister and Townshend Secretary of State. An unhappy breach afterwards took place between the two friends, with the result described here by Macaulay.

l. 29. **Godolphin** was First Lord of the Treasury in 1684 under Charles II.; he was retained in office by James II., but not as First Lord. In November, 1690, he became First Lord of the Treasury for the second time, and held that office for more than six years. In 1702 he became Prime Minister to Queen Anne, but after a long struggle with Harley he was dismissed from the office by the Queen in 1710.

l. 30. **Harley** was made Chancellor of the Exchequer and Commissioner of the Treasury in 1710; he afterwards became Lord High Treasurer, but resigned that office in 1714.

Page 9, l. 23. **Rainham Hall** is in Norfolk, about four miles from Fakenham; it is only six miles from Houghton, the seat of Sir Robert Walpole: Townshend and Walpole were therefore neighbours and "friends from childhood."

l. 24. **Chesterfield.** Philip Dormer Stanhope was born in 1694, educated at Trinity College, Cambridge. He sat in Parliament as member for Lostwithiel, and in 1726, on his father's death, succeeded to the earldom of Chesterfield. He was a favourite of George II., and was made by him a privy councillor; he was twice ambassador to Holland; in 1730 he was made a Knight of the Garter and Steward of the Household. He was dismissed from office soon after the Excise Bill, and from that time became the strenuous opponent of Walpole, and distinguished himself by his writings in the *Craftsman* and by his eloquence in the House. As a man of letters he wrote *Letters to his Son, Miscellaneous Pieces* and *Characters, Letters to his Friends, The Art of Pleasing, Free Thoughts and Bold Truths,* etc., etc., and *Poems*.

l. 26. **ton**, tone, style, taste, fashion: *donner le ton* means to set the fashion. Chesterfield's letters "furnish ample evidence of his delicate but fastidious taste, of his low moral principle, and of his hard, keen, and worldly wisdom" (Lecky).

l. 30. **the Excise Bill.** In 1643 the Long Parliament had taxed wines, beer, spirits, etc.; these duties were continued under Charles II. and in the two following reigns. Such duties had been very productive, but were nevertheless greatly diminished by fraud. A committee of the Commons reported in 1732 that in tobacco alone the Government lost a third of the duties through perjury, forgery, and collusion; that 250 custom-house officers had been severely injured, and six had been killed by armed gangs of smugglers. Walpole therefore proposed in 1733 his Excise Bill, which was to readjust the duties on wine, spirits, and tobacco, and to exact the tax from the manufacturer or retailer instead of from the importer of these commodities, that is to say, to change the tax from a custom-house duty to an excise.

The Bill met with fierce opposition; it was said that a host of new excise officers would thus be raised to vote for the Government at elections, and that tradesmen would be the victims of an odious inquisition; the feeling indeed was so strong that Walpole bowed before the storm and withdrew the Bill; this battle was "the beginning of the end," and led to Walpole's fall.

Page 10, l. 8. **John Campbell, Duke of Argyle,** was born in 1678. He served in the campaigns of Marlborough, and won distinction at Ramilies, Oudenarde, and Malplaquet. In 1711 he commanded the English forces in Spain; and in 1715 was sent to quell the Jacobite rebellion in Scotland; he defeated the Earl of Mar at Sheriffmuir and compelled the Pretender to quit the kingdom. He supported the Union with Scotland, and was rewarded with the Garter and the English dukedom of Greenwich; but "his great name, his talents and his paramount influence in his native country" made him distasteful to Walpole, and he was accordingly dismissed from office.

l. 10. **the Act of Settlement** was passed in 1702: by this statute the succession to the Crown, after the death of William III. and Queen Anne, without issue, was limited to Sophia, Electress of Hanover, grand-daughter of James I., and her heirs, being Protestants.

l. 25. **his son.** Horace Walpole, Earl of Orford, the youngest son of Sir Robert Walpole, was an antiquary and prolific writer; his chief works are *The Castle of Otranto, The Mysterious Mother,*

Historic Doubts on the Life and Reign of Richard III., *Memoirs of the Last Ten Years* (1751-60) *of the Reign of George II.*, *Memoirs of the Reign of George III.*, etc., etc., and also *Letters.* For a criticism of his *Letters*, etc., see Macaulay's *Essays*, p. 267, etc.

l. 26. **Hume**, David, historian and philosopher (b. 1711, d. 1776), wrote a *Treatise on Human Nature*, an *Enquiry concerning Human Understanding*, *The History of England*, etc., etc.

l. 35. **his brother Horace.** Lord Horatio Walpole, brother of Sir Robert, was born in 1678. He held various offices under Government, and must not be confused with Horace Walpole, Earl of Orford, son of Sir Robert, described above.

Henry Pelham, the younger brother of the Duke of Newcastle, "had been first brought into office chiefly by the recommendation of Walpole, had supported his patron faithfully in the contest about the Excise and in the disastrous struggle of 1740 and 1741, and was looked upon as the natural heir of his policy. Like Walpole, he had none of the talents that are necessary for the successful conduct of war, and was, perhaps for that very reason, warmly in favour of peace. Like Walpole, too, he was thoroughly conversant with questions of finance, and almost uniformly successful in dealing with them. A timid, desponding, and somewhat fretful man, with little energy either of character or intellect, he possessed at least, to a high degree, good sense, industry, knowledge of business, and parliamentary experience; his manners were conciliatory and decorous, and he was content to hold the reins of power very loosely, freely admitting competitors to office and allowing much divergence of opinion" (Lecky).

Page 11, l. 3. Fox, Henry, the first Lord Holland, was born in 1705. After filling lower offices he was, in 1746, made Secretary at War and Paymaster of the Forces. Lecky sketches his character as that of "a bold, bad man, educated in the school of Walpole, but almost destitute of principle, patriotism, and consistency—who possessed rare talents for business and for intrigue, and social qualities which gave him great influence and won for him much affection, without any of the higher imaginative qualities or any of the lighter graces of oratory, his clear, strong sense, his indomitable courage, and his admirable tact, readiness, and memory, made him one of the most formidable of debaters.... He was known to be ambitious and unscrupulous, and it did not yet appear that he cared more for money than for power."

l. 4. **Sir William Yonge** was Secretary at War during Walpole's administration, and characterised by Johnson as the best speaker in the House of Commons. He wrote the epilogue to Johnson's *Irene*.

l. 7. **Winnington** was a member of the Government of the time. We may draw attention to Macaulay's accuracy of detail which extends to the characterisation of such obscure statesmen as these.

l. 18. **Squire Western**, a jovial fox-hunting country gentleman in Fielding's novel of *Tom Jones*, described by Sir Walter Scott as "an inimitable picture of ignorance, prejudice, irascibility, and rusticity, united with natural shrewdness, constitutional good humour, and an instinctive affection for his daughter."

l. 21. **October Club** consisted of 150 Tory squires, members of Parliament, who met at the Bell Tavern in King Street, Westminster, and nourished their patriotism with October ale. Cf. *Spectator*, No. 9, "Our modern celebrated clubs are founded on eating and drinking. ... The Kit-Cat itself is said to have taken its original from a mutton-pie. The Beef-Steak and October Clubs are neither of them averse to eating and drinking, if we may form a judgment from their respective titles."

l. 25. **Sir William Wyndham** was born in Somersetshire in 1687. He was educated at Eton and Oxford. He represented his own county in Parliament, and was distinguished as one of the best speakers in the House. He was Chancellor of the Exchequer in 1713, but on the death of Queen Anne was dismissed from office and joined the Opposition : he defended the Duke of Ormond and the Earls of Oxford and Strafford when they were impeached. In 1715 he was committed to the Tower on the charge of being concerned in the rebellion of the Earl of Mar, but was never brought to trial. He died at Wells in 1740.

l. 29. **the patriots**. This was the name assumed by some of the Whigs in opposition. The party was organised by Bolingbroke and Pulteney against Sir Robert Walpole. They started the *Craftsman* as a journal in which to promulgate their opinions. Lecky writes thus : "The ranks of the opponents of Walpole contained a small group of young men who did not altogether coalesce with either party, and who were much ridiculed under the name of Boy Patriots, but who reckoned in their number several men of credit and ability and one man of the most splendid and majestic genius. The principal members of this party were Lord Cobham, Lyttleton, George Grenville, and, above all, William Pitt."

Page 12, l. 1. Pulteney. See p. 7, l. 33 *supra*, and note.

l. 6. **Hampden.** See p. 2, l. 36 *supra*, and note.

Russell, Lord William. A distinguished supporter of constitutional liberty. In 1671, when Charles II. found it necessary to ingratiate himself with the Whigs, Russell was appointed a member of the Privy Council. He soon learned, however, that his party was not in the King's confidence, and on the recall of the Duke of York without their concurrence he resigned. In 1680 he supported the Exclusion Bill, and at the head of two hundred other members of Parliament carried it up to the House of Lords. When the King dissolved Parliament and determined to govern without it, Russell, along with the other Whig leaders, Monmouth, Argyle, Essex, Howard, Algernon Sidney, and

Hampden (grandson of the great Hampden), were resolved to resist such arbitrary measures; but they held different views as to the best plan of action. Russell looked only to the exclusion of the Duke of York; he was, however, accused of being engaged in the "Rye House Plot," which had for its object the assassination of the King on his return from Newmarket: he was arrested, condemned, and executed in 1683. After the Revolution the proceedings against him were annulled.

l. 9. **the Revolution** of 1688, when William and Mary were called to the throne of England by the nation to deliver it from the tyranny of James II. "The principles of the Revolution" are embodied in the Declaration and Bill of Rights.

l. 16. **The Prince of Wales**, Frederick, the son of George II., (b. 1707, d. 1751) and father of George III. In the Opposition there were really four separate elements: (1) The Jacobites, (2) the Tories, (3) the adherents of the Prince of Wales, (4) the discontented Whigs for whom Walpole could find no room.

Page 13, l. 2. **Lord Granville.** See p. 8, l. 15, **Carteret,** *supra,* and note, and p. 23, l. 14 *infra.*

l. 10. **Since the accession of George the First... Opposition.** George II. opposed his father; Frederick, Prince of Wales, hated his parents, and they hated him; George IV. (as Prince of Wales) was allied with the chiefs of the Opposition against his father, George III. On this fact Lecky remarks: "The bitter hatred, both personal and political, that subsisted between the first three Hanoverian Sovereigns and their eldest sons, though it threw great scandal and discredit on the royal family, and added largely to the difficulties of Parliamentary Government, was probably on the whole rather beneficial to the dynasty than otherwise, as it led the most prominent opponents to the existing Governments to place their chief hopes in the heir-apparent to the Crown."

l. 21. **Tories who had impeached Somers.** Towards the end of William III.'s reign Somers was assailed with false accusations of corrupt conduct. It was discovered that he had lent money to a sea captain who became a pirate, and was well known as Captain Kidd. It was not proved that Somers knew of any evil intentions on the part of the sailor. But the storm against him raged so furiously that, when William made him a grant of Crown lands, the feeling was renewed, and, as the easiest way of quieting the storm, Lord Somers was dismissed from office. (For further account of Somers, see p. 3, l. 1, note.)

l. 22. **who had murmured against Harley and St. John.** In 1708 Robert Harley was Secretary of State and Henry St. John Secretary at War. At the representations of Marlborough and Godolphin they were compelled to resign office.

Page 14, l. 27. Henry the Fourth, King of France from 1589 to 1610, caused great dissatisfaction and anxiety to his country through his unbridled passions. He was married to Marguerite of Valois, from whom he tried to get a divorce in order that he might be married to his mistress, Gabrielle d'Estrées; he afterwards became enamoured of Henriette d'Etragnes. On the death of Marguerite of Valois he married Mary de Medici; this second marriage was not happy, and in his old age he became desperately enamoured of the Princess of Condé. The Prince of Condé fled with his wife to Brussels to save her from the unprincipled pursuit of the King.

the Regent Orleans (see p. 4, l. 31, note) possessed superior abilities, eager ambition, great personal courage, and a warm, amiable, generous temper; but at the same time he was totally destitute of religious and moral principle, and his habits of life were shamelessly dissolute. His example had a most pernicious and deplorable effect upon the tone of society in France.

Page 15, l. 3. Tindal, probably Nicholas Tindal, clergyman and author (b. 1687, d. 1774), wrote *A History of Essex* (1726); a continuation of Rapin's *History of England* (1757); some translations, and various other miscellaneous works.

l. 10. **Archdeacon Coxe.** William Coxe, historian and traveller, was born in 1747. He acted as travelling tutor to several young noblemen. He became Canon Residentiary of Salisbury and Archdeacon of Wilts. He wrote several books of travels; also *Memoirs of the Life and Administration of Sir Robert Walpole* (1798), *A History of the House of Austria* (1807), etc., etc.

l. 14. **Lord Brougham** (b. 1779, d. 1868) was distinguished as an advocate, politician, author, law reformer, educational reformer, man of science, and Lord Chancellor. "Macaulay, who knew his own range and kept within it, and who gave the world nothing except his best and most finished work, was fretted by the slovenly omniscience of Brougham, who affected to be a walking encyclopædia, 'a kind of semi-Solomon, half-knowing everything from the cedar to the hyssop.' The student, who in his later years never left his library for the House of Commons without regret, had little in common with one who, like Napoleon, held that a great reputation was a great noise: who could not change horses without making a speech, see the Tories come in without offering to take a Judgeship, or allow the French to make a revolution without proposing to naturalise himself as a citizen of the new Republic. The statesman who never deserted an ally, or distrusted a friend, could have no fellowship with a freelance, ignorant of the very meaning of loyalty: who, if the surfeited pen of the reporter had not declined its task, would have enriched our collection of British oratory by at least one Philippic against every colleague with whom he had ever acted." (*Lord Macaulay's Life and Letters,* by Trevelyan, vol. i., pp. 193, 4.

l. 15. **Mr. Hunt** (b. 1773, d. 1835), better known as "Orator Hunt," was born in Widdington, Wiltshire, and was a farmer in well-to-do circumstances. In 1812 he stood for Bristol, but was beaten in this and in many subsequent attempts to enter Parliament. He then took to stump oratory, held reform meetings at Westminster, and was especially conspicuous at Spa Fields and Manchester. During the excitement of the Reform Bill he defeated Lord Stanley at Preston, and entered the House of Commons; but his oratory produced little effect in the House.

l. 17. **the Polish Count**, a celebrated dwarf named Bornlwaski, 3 feet 2 inches in height (b. 1739, d. 1837).

l. 18. **Giant O'Brien**, Patrick Cotter O'Brien, native of Kinsale, 8 feet 7¾ inches (b. 1780).

l. 19. **Anatomie Vivante**, living skeleton, a nickname of Voltaire, who in old age was a mere skeleton with a long nose and eyes of preternatural brilliancy peering out of his wig.

Daniel Lambert, noted for his extraordinary corpulence, was born at Leicester in 1770. Up to his nineteenth year he gave no indication of the remarkable stoutness which he afterwards attained, for he was an enthusiastic follower of field sports and athletic exercises. He succeeded his father as keeper of Leicester prison, and through changing an active for a sedentary life he rapidly increased in size. In course of time he determined to turn his obesity to account, and exhibited himself in Piccadilly, London, and in the principal provincial towns. He died at Stamford in 1809. He was 5 feet 11 inches high, weighed 739 lbs., measured 9 feet 4 inches round the body, and 3 feet 1 inch round the leg. His clothes may be seen at a public-house in St. John's Street, Stamford; his stocking will hold a bushel of wheat. He was buried in the churchyard of St. Martin's, Stamford.

Page 16, l. 12. **Brutus or Coriolanus**, characters in Shakespeare's *Julius Cæsar* and *Coriolanus*.

l. 30. **Court of Requests** was first instituted in the reign of Henry VII. in 1493, and remodelled by Henry VIII. in 1517. It was established for the summary recovery of small debts under forty shillings, but in the City of London the jurisdiction extended to debts of five pounds. This Court was superseded in 1847 by the County Courts. (See Appendix.)

l. 31. **Westminster Hall**, the old Hall of the Palace of our Kings at Westminster incorporated by Mr. Barry into his new Houses of Parliament, to serve as their vestibule.

The old House of Lords was formed out of the building known as the Court of Requests; but it did not occupy the whole of this old Court, part of the north end being formed into a lobby by which the Commons passed to the Upper House. Macaulay therefore means that Pitt's voice reached in one direction to the

House of Lords, in the other direction to Westminster Hall. Both Houses of Parliament were destroyed by fire in October, 1834, a few months after Macaulay's essay was published. (See Appendix.)

l. 34. **Garrick**, David, actor, tragedian, and dramatist (b. 1716, d. 1779). As an actor Garrick seems never to have been equalled for truth, nature, variety, and facility of expression, though perhaps surpassed by some of his contemporaries in the enunciation of calm sentimental eloquence. He wrote or adapted for the stage nearly forty pieces; the chief of these are *The Lying Valet*, *Miss in her Teens*, and *The Clandestine Marriage*.

Page 17, l. 17. **General Wolfe** was present at Dettingen, Fontenoy, Falkirk, Culloden, and the siege of Maestricht; but he won most renown for his successful expedition against Quebec in 1759, when on the heights of Abraham he defeated the French, and in the moment of victory lost his own life.

l. 25. **Lord Shelburne**, and first Marquis of Lansdowne, entered Parliament as member for Wycombe in 1761. He was opposed to the taxation of the American Colonies, and became a supporter of Pitt, and in 1766 took office under him as Secretary of State. Subsequently, on the death of Rockingham in 1781, he became Prime Minister; during his ministry he concluded peace with the American colonies and recognised their independence.

l. 32. **Mr. Fox**, Charles James Fox. See p. 143, l. 9 *infra*.

Page 18, l. 2. **Mr. Stanley**, better known as the 14th Earl of Derby. His speeches are distinguished for their fire and eloquence, and he has been called the "Rupert of Debate."

l. 29. **apophthegms**, Gr. ἀπόφθεγμα, a terse, pointed saying, embodying an important truth in few words; a pithy or sententious maxim.

Page 19, l. 22. **Mr. Burke truly says, in the Appeal to the Old Whigs** (see vol. iii., p. 50), "Mr. Walpole was an honourable man and a sound Whig. He was not as the Jacobites and discontented Whigs of his time have represented him, and as ill-informed people still represent him, a prodigal and corrupt minister. They charged him, in their libels and seditious conversations, with having first reduced corruption to a system. Such was their cant. But he was far from governing by corruption. He governed by party attachments. The charge of systematic corruption is less applicable to him, perhaps, than to any minister who ever served the Crown for so great a length of time. He gained over very few from the Opposition. Without being a genius of the first class, he was an intelligent, prudent, and safe minister. He loved peace, and he helped to communicate the same disposition to nations at least as warlike and restless as that in which he had the chief direction of affairs. Though he served a master who was fond of martial fame he kept all the establishments very low. The land tax continued at two shillings in the pound for the greater part of his administration. The other impositions were moderate. The profound repose, the equal liberty, the firm protection of just laws, during the long period of his power, were the principal causes of that prosperity which afterwards took such rapid strides towards perfection, and which furnished to this nation ability to acquire the military glory which it has since obtained, as well as to bear the burthens, the cause and consequence of that warlike reputation. With many virtues, public and private, he had his faults, but his faults were superficial. A careless, coarse, and over-familiar style of discourse, without sufficient regard to persons or occasions, and an almost total want of political decorum, were the errors by which he was most hurt in the public opinion, and those through which his enemies obtained the greatest advantage over him. But justice must be done. The prudence, steadiness, and vigilance of that man, joined to the greatest possible lenity in his character and his politics, preserved the crown to this royal family, and with it, their laws and liberties to this country."

l. 31. **Pepys learned them, as he tells us, from the counsellors of Charles the Second** (see Pepys' *Diary*, vol. ii., p. 413, 6th October, 1666). "Sir W. Coventry told me that it is always observed that by bringing over one discontented man you raise up three in his room; which is a state lesson I never knew before. But, when others discover your fear, and that discontent produces fear, they will be discontented too, and impose on you."

l. 36. **The question of maritime right,** *i.e.* the right of search. It is admitted by all, that within the waters which may be called the territory of nations, the vessel of a friendly state may be boarded and searched on suspicion of being engaged in unlawful commerce, or of violating the laws concerning revenue. And further than this, on account of the ease with which a criminal may escape beyond the proper sea-line of a country, it is allowable to chase a vessel into the high sea and then execute the arrest and search which flight had prevented before. Furthermore, suspicion of offences against the laws taking their commencement in the neighbouring waters beyond the sea-line, will authorise the detention and examination of the supposed criminal.

Now, by one of the stipulations of the Treaty of Utrecht (1713) the Assiento (or contract for supplying the Spanish colonies with negro slaves) was surrendered to England. England was to furnish 4800 slaves annually, and had the right of sending two ships a year, each of 500 tons burden, to America with negroes. This traffic was so profitable that the terms of the contract were frequently violated, and the Spaniards were justified in exercising their right of search upon English ships.

Page 20, l. 10. Buccaneers. Fr. *boucanier*, orig., one who hunts wild oxen.

1. Orig., one who dries and smokes flesh on a *boucan* (a wooden framework or hurdle on which meat was roasted or smoked over a fire) after the manner of the Indians. The name was first given to the French hunters of St. Domingo, who prepared the flesh of the wild oxen and boars in this way.

2. (From the habits which these subsequently assumed) a name given to piratical rovers who infested the Spanish coast in America. (Murray.)

l. 15. "**I have seen**," **says Burke**, etc. The passage occurs in vol. v., p. 193, *Letters on a Regicide Peace*. The paragraph begins thus: "In stating that Walpole was driven by a popular clamour into a measure not to be justified, I do not mean wholly to excuse his conduct," etc.

l. 34. **Duke of Newcastle** (b. 1693, d. 1768) at an early age joined the Whigs: in 1710 he displayed great zeal in suppressing the Jacobite rebellion. When the schism took place in the Whig ministry he joined Sunderland and Stanhope, but on their deaths, in 1720, he joined Townshend and Walpole. In 1724, on the dismissal of Carteret, he became Secretary of State. For many years he continued to be a follower of Walpole. At length, in 1738, seeing that Walpole was deprived of the friendship of Queen Caroline, and that the King was opposed to his peace policy, Newcastle began to intrigue against him. The King was encouraged in his wish for war; angry despatches were sent to the English ambassador in Spain. In 1742 his intrigues were successful; Walpole resigned. Wilmington was made Premier, and on his death (1743), Newcastle's brother, Henry Pelham, became leader of the ministry. On the death of Henry Pelham (1754), Newcastle became First Lord of the Treasury. (The rest of his career is sketched here by Macaulay.)

Lord Hardwicke. Philip Yorke, the son of an attorney, was born at Dover in 1690. His political rise was due to Newcastle and Stanhope. After serving as Solicitor-General and Attorney-General, he became Lord Chief Justice and Lord Hardwicke (1733) and Lord Chancellor in 1737. He supported Walpole through his long administration, but towards the close of it he was induced to join the war party. On the fall of Walpole he continued to hold office under Wilmington, and subsequently under the Pelhams. In 1753 he introduced the Marriage Act, which put a stop to those Fleet Marriages which had become one of the strangest scandals in English life.

Page 21, l. 8. the Boys. See p. 11, l. 29, the **Patriots**, and note.

l. 16. **Coxe's Life of Walpole.** See p. 15, l. 10, **Archdeacon Coxe**, and note.

l. 19. **placeman**, a man holding an office under a Government.

l. 33. **a bill of indemnity to witnesses.** Cf. p. 2, l. 19, **bounties for perjury,** and note.

Page 22, l. 19. **The chief topic of Pitt's invective. ... House of Brunswick.** Cf. p. 2, l. 27, when he thundered against subsidies, and note.

l. 29. **the Duchess of Marlborough** is described as follows in Pope's *Moral Essays*, Epistle ii., under the name of Atossa:

"But what are these to great Atossa's mind?
Scarce once herself, by turns all Womankind!
Who with herself, or others, from her birth
Finds all her life one warfare upon earth:
Shines in exposing Knaves, and painting Fools,
Yet is, whate'er she hates and ridicules.
No Thought advances, but her Eddy Brain
Whisks it about, and down it goes again.
Full sixty years the World has been her Trade,
The wisest fool much time has ever made.
From loveless youth to unrespected age,
No Passion gratified except her Rage.
So much the Fury still out-ran the Wit,
The Pleasure miss'd her and the Scandal hit.
Who breaks with her provokes Revenge from Hell,
But he's a bolder man who dares be well.
Her ev'ry turn with Violence pursued,
Nor more a storm her Hate than Gratitude:
To that each Passion turns or soon or late:
Love, if it makes her yield, must make her hate;
Superiors? death! and Equals? what a curse!
But an inferior not dependant? worse!
Offend her, and she knows not to forgive;
Oblige her, and she'll hate you while you live:
But die, and she'll adore you—Then the bust
And Temple rise—then fall again to dust.
Last night her lord was all that's good and great;
A Knave this morning, and his Will a Cheat.
Strange! by the Means defeated of the Ends,
By Spirit robb'd of Power, by Warmth of Friends,
By Wealth of Followers! without one distress
Sick of herself thro' very selfishness!
Atossa, cursed with every granted prayer,
Childless with all her Children, wants an Heir.
To Heirs unknown descends the unguarded store,
Or wanders, Heav'n directed, to the Poor."

l. 31. **Yet her love ... whom she adored.** After Queen Anne's accession the influence of Marlborough became for a time absolute, and his wife exercised an almost absolute empire over the Queen. The intimacy of the Queen and the Duchess was very close indeed:

they even corresponded with each other under assumed names; the Queen was Mrs. Morley and the Duchess Mrs. Freeman: their husbands, Prince George and the Duke, were Mr. Morley and Mr. Freeman respectively. But this warm personal friendship was at length cut. The furious, domineering, and insolent temper of the Duchess at last wore out a patience and an affection of no common strength, and Abigail Hill, who as Mrs. Masham played so great a part during the rest of the reign, rose rapidly into favour. Abigail Hill was in close alliance with Harley, and they two gradually undermined the influence of the Marlboroughs, with the result that the Duke of Marlborough was dismissed from all his employments.

Page 23, l. 16. the broad bottom (1744-1754). This administration was so called because it professed to admit to office the heads of Opposition, both Whig and Tory, except Carteret and Bath. Various posts were assigned to the Pelhams, Lord Hardwicke, Chesterfield, Pitt, the Dukes of Devonshire and Bedford, Lords Cobham, Lyttleton, Hobart, Gower, Bubb Doddington, and others.

Page 24, l. 10. the Pretender was master of the northern extremity of the island. In the last week of July, 1745, Charles Edward Stuart landed on the west coast of Inverness. The Highlanders flocked to his standard. He marched southwards, entered the palace of Holyrood, was proclaimed as "King James VIII." at the High Cross, Edinburgh; he then continued his march southwards, he routed Sir John Cope at Prestonpans, on the Firth of Forth, and then returned in triumph to Edinburgh.

Page 25, l. 12. vails (perhaps an abbreviation of avails), (1) money given to servants, gratuities; (2) windfalls, slices of luck (cf. Gr. Ἑρμαῖον); (3) avails, proceeds.

l. 31. Peace was made with France and Spain in 1748, *i.e.* the Peace of Aix-la-Chapelle.

Page 26, l. 14. Murray, William, Earl of Mansfield, was the fourth son of Lord Stormont. He became Solicitor-General in Lord Wilmington's cabinet (1742). In 1754 he became Attorney-General, and ultimately rose to the Chief Justiceship and was created a peer. He was a very able judge. Lecky describes him as "the silver-tongued Murray—the most graceful, luminous, and subtle of all legal speakers." He presided over the case of Wilkes, and was assailed with much bitterness by Junius in his letters; he presided also at the trial of Horne Tooke. His house was burned with his books and manuscripts by the "Protestant" rioters in 1780. He died in 1793, leaving behind a high reputation, tempered by the memory of the humour for which he is praised by Pope. (See *Imitations of Horace*, Epistle vi.)

l. 34. Fox, Henry, the first Lord Holland (b. 1705, d. 1774), was appointed Secretary at War in 1746: he retired in 1757 to make way for Mr. Pitt, but returned to office the following year as Paymaster of the Forces; his opinion was that the Government of the country could be carried on only by corruption, and he acted accordingly. (See p. 11, l. 3 *supra*, and note.)

Page 27, l. 1. **the Duke of Cumberland** was the second son of George II. and Queen Caroline. He was wounded at Dettingen (1743): he was Commander-in-Chief of the allies in Flanders, and distinguished himself at Fontenoy. He was then recalled to oppose the Young Pretender, and after some slight reverses defeated Charles Edward utterly at Culloden (1746). In 1757 he was sent to command the army in Hanover: he suffered a signal defeat in 1757. He then resigned his commission, and lived the rest of his life in seclusion, his chief friend being Henry Fox. He died suddenly in 1765. Mr. Lecky says, "Of all the members of the royal family, with the exception of Queen Caroline, he was the only one who possessed any remarkable ability."

l. 5. **Reynolds,** Sir Joshua, the greatest English portrait painter and first President of the Royal Academy (b. 1723, d. 1792). His works are very numerous, about 700 have been engraved. The National Gallery possesses 23 of his works, of which we may mention the portraits of Admiral Keppel, Lord Heathfield, Lord Ligonier, Dr. Johnson, and himself; and also the "Age of Innocence," the "Holy Family," and the "Infant Samuel."

l. 6. **Nollekens,** Joseph, an eminent sculptor, was born in London in 1737. He studied in Italy, and on his return to London in 1770 he became a Royal Academician. He was a great favourite of George III. The National Portrait Gallery possesses his busts of Pitt, Fox, and Warren Hastings. He died in 1823.

l. 32. **humbug,** perhaps compounded of *hum*, to impose upon, to deceive, and *bug*, a hideous object, bugbear, bogie: (1) a piece of trickery, deceit, hoax, (2) one that practises such trickery or hoaxes.

Page 28, l. 4. **junto** (Sp. *junta*), a select Council or Assembly which deliberated in secret on any affairs of Government; a meeting of men for secret deliberation and intrigue for party purposes; a faction or cabal; as a junto of Ministers.

l. 31. **Sir John Cutler.** See Pope's *Moral Essays*, iii. 315, etc., to which Carruthers adds a note that Sir John Cutler was a wealthy citizen of the Restoration period, accused of rapacity on account of a large claim made by his executors against the College of Physicians, which he had aided by a loan.

Page 29, l. 11. **Craggs.** See p. 7, l. 8 *supra*, and note.

l. 16. **Doddington.** See p. 4, l. 2 *supra*, and note.

l. 33. **secret-service-money,** etc. Cf. p. 41, l. 2, etc., and p. 56, l. 15, etc.

Page 30, l. 20. the ministerial boroughs, sometimes called the Treasury Boroughs. The nomination to these was, of course, one means of corruption which the Duke meant to retain in his own hands. All such boroughs were subsequently swept away by the Reform Bill of 1832.

l. 26. Sir Thomas Robinson had been Minister at Vienna for 20 years, and was acceptable to George II. on account of his sympathy with the King's German policy. His rise to be Secretary of State and Leader of the House of Commons is described by Macaulay. Pitt and Fox united to ridicule Robinson until Fox was won over by a seat in the Cabinet. In 1755 Robinson retired to his former office of Master of the Wardrobe, and received a pension of £2000 on the Irish establishment. (See p. 33, l. 3 *infra*.)

Page 31, l. 3. the peace of Aix-la-Chapelle was signed in 1748, and closed the war of the Austrian succession. According to the terms of this peace, all conquests made during the war were to be restored. Spain retained their right of search. The Assiento treaty was confirmed for four years. The only concession made by France was the expulsion of the Pretender from her soil.

l. 10. Paymaster of the Forces, Pitt. **Secretary-at-War,** Fox.

l. 35. An English force was cut off in America. In order to protect the Ohio Company against the French in their trade with India, the Assembly of Virginia voted £10,000 on 16th January, 1754, to erect necessary fortifications at the confluence of the Alleghany and Monongahela rivers. The command of this expedition was entrusted to Colonel Joshua Fry and George Washington. Meanwhile, in advance of the action of the Burgesses, a company of men under Ensign Ward had been sent forward in haste to secure the position. Washington, in command of the main body, had reached the camp at Will's Creek, near Cumberland, when he learned that the French (under Contrecœur) had appeared in force before the works which Ward and his men had begun, and had demanded an immediate surrender. On 17th April, 1754, Ward surrendered, and that date has been taken as the beginning of actual hostilities in this final struggle of the French and English for the supremacy in America. (Bryant and Gay, iii. 260.)

Page 32, l. 8. Frederic the Second...uncle. Frederick the Great was the nephew of George II., being the son of his sister, Princess Sophia Dorothea.

l. 16. Legge (b. 1708, d. 1764) was son of the Earl of Dartmouth. He became Lord of the Admiralty in 1746, and Lord of the Treasury in 1747. In 1754 he became Chancellor of the Exchequer. He rebelled against Newcastle, as is described here; but he continued to adhere to Pitt in politics until his death.

Page 33, l. 12. Gerard Hamilton...nickname derived. The nickname was Single-speech Hamilton. He was elected M.P. for Petersfield in 1754, and in the following year delivered this remarkable speech. William Gerard Hamilton was introduced to Edmund Burke in 1759. He was by no means devoid of sense and acuteness, but in character he was one of the most despicable men then alive. He was described by one of Burke's friends as "a sullen, vain, proud, selfish, canker-hearted, envious reptile."

l. 15. **Pitt, who declaimed against the subsidies.** See p. 2, l. 27, and note.

l. 33. **the subsidiary treaties** are the treaties (mentioned on p. 32, l. 3, etc.) made for the seourity of Hanover.

Page 34, l. 7. Minorca was ceded to England by the Treaty of Utrecht. In 1756 it was recaptured by the French under the command of that old voluptuary the Duke of Richelieu. Admiral Byng was executed for failing to relieve it.

l. 11. **Port-Mahon** is the capital of Minorca, situated at the east side of the island, at the head of a capacious bay which forms one of the best harbours in Europe.

l. 31. **cant** (probably akin to Lat. *cantus*, singing, song, chant; Fr. *chant*, Lat. *cantare*, etc.) has many meanings.

(1) Singing, musical sound.

(2) Accent, intonation, tone.

(3) A whining manner of speaking, especially of beggars; a whine.

(4) The peculiar language or jargon of a class. (*a*) The secret language or jargon used by gipsies, thieves, professional beggars, etc., hence any jargon used for the purpose of secrecy. (*b*) The special phraseology of a particular class of persons belonging to a particular subject; professional or technical jargon (always depreciative or contemptuous). (*c*) The peculiar phraseology of a religious sect or class. (*d*) Provincial dialect; vulgar slang. (*e*) Attributively, with the previous meaning; cf. p. 23 of this Essay, "called by the *cant* name of the 'broad bottom.'"

(5) A form of words, a phrase. (*a*) A set form of words repeated perfunctorily or mechanically. (*b*) A pet phrase, a trick of words; especially a stock phrase that is much affected at the time, or is repeated as a matter of habit or form. This is the sense in which Macaulay uses it here.

(6) As a kind of phraseology. (*a*) Phraseology taken up and used for fashion's sake without being a genuine expression of sentiment; canting language. (*b*) Especially, affected or unreal use of religious or pietistic phraseology; language (or action) implying the pretended assumption of goodness or piety. (Extracts from Murray.)

l. 32. **Browne's Estimate** *of the Manners and Principles of the Times* (which appeared in 1757-8) is now hardly remembered, except by brief and disparaging notices in one of the later writings of Burke, and in this Essay of Macaulay; but it had once a wide popularity and a considerable influence on public opinion. Its author was a clergyman well known in the history of ethics by his answer to Shaftesbury, which contains one of the ablest defences in English literature of the utilitarian theory of morals. His object was to warn the country of the utter ruin that must ensue from a decadence of the national spirit, which he attributed mainly to an excessive development of the commercial spirit. He fully admits that constitutional liberty had been considerably enlarged, that a spirit of growing humanity was exhibited both in manners and in laws; that the administration of justice was generally pure, and that the age was not characterised by gross or profligate vice. Its leading quality was "a vain, luxurious, and selfish effeminacy," which was rapidly corroding all the elements of the national strength. "Love of our country," he complained, "is no longer felt, and, except in a few minds of uncommon greatness, the principle of public spirit exists not." He appealed to the disuse of manly occupations among the higher classes, to their general indifference to religious doctrines and neglect of religious practices to the ever-widening circle of corruption which had now passed from the Parliament to the constituencies, and tainted all the approaches of public life; to the prevailing system of filling the most important offices in the most critical times by family interest, and without any regard to merit or to knowledge. The extent of this evil, he maintained, was but too plainly shown in the contrast between the splendid victories of Marlborough and the almost uniform failure of the British arms in the late war, in the want of fire, energy, and heroism manifested in all public affairs, and, above all, in the conduct of the nation during the rebellion "when those of every rank above a constable, instead of arming themselves and encouraging the people, generally fled before the rebels; while a mob of ragged Highlanders marched unmolested to the heart of a populous kingdom." He argued with much acuteness that the essential qualities of national greatness are moral, and that no increase of material resources could compensate for the deterioration which had in this respect passed over the English people. (Lecky, vol. ii., ch. iv. 89, etc.)

l. 33. **Cowper's Table Talk.** The passage referred to begins about l. 400, and is as follows:

"*A*. The inestimable estimate of Brown,
Rose like a paper-kite, and charm'd the town;
But measures, plann'd and executed well,
Shifted the wind that raised it and it fell.
He trod the very self-same ground you tread,

And victory refuted all he said.
B. And yet his judgment was not framed amiss,
Its error, if it err'd, was merely this,—
He thought the dying hour already come,
And a complete recovery struck him dumb."

l. 34. **in Burke's Letters on a Regicide Peace.** The passage (vol. v., p. 157) is as follows: "I remember in the beginning of what has lately been called the seven years' war, that an eloquent writer and ingenious speculator, Dr. Brown, upon some reverses which happened in the beginning of that war, published an elaborate philosophical discourse, to prove that the distinguishing features of the people of England had been totally changed, and that a frivolous effeminacy was becoming the national character. Nothing could be more popular than that work. It was thought a great consolation to us, the light people of this country (who were and are light, but who were not and are not effeminate), that we had found the causes of our misfortunes in our vices. Pythagoras could not be more pleased with his leading discovery. But whilst in that splenetic mood we assured ourselves in a sour, critical speculation, of which we were ourselves the objects, and in which every man lost his particular sense of the public disgrace in the epidemic nature of the distemper; whilst, as in the Alps, Goitre kept Goitre in countenance; whilst we were thus abandoning ourselves to a direct confession of our inferiority to France, and whilst many, very many, were ready to act upon a sense of that inferiority, a few months effected a total change in our variable minds. We emerged from the gulf of that speculative despondency; and were buoyed up to the highest point of practical vigour. Never did the masculine spirit of England display itself with more energy, nor ever did its genius soar with a prouder pre-eminence over France, than at the time when frivolity and effeminacy had been at least tacitly acknowledged as their national character, by the good people of this kingdom."

Page 35, l. 24. the Duchy of Lancaster. The revenues of the Duchy of Lancaster were reckoned by Burke (in 1780) at an average of £4000 a year.

l. 25. **a tellership of the Exchequer.** A *teller* of the Exchequer is one of the four officers whose business it is to receive and pay all moneys due or belonging to the crown, and to give to the clerk of the pell a bill to charge him therewith; to pay persons to whom money is due by the king; and also to make books of receipts and payments. (Craig.)

Page 36, l. 16. The Great Seal was put into commission. An office is said to be in commission when it is placed by warrant in the charge of a body of persons, instead of the regular constitutional administrator. Some offices, as those of Treasurer and Lord High Admiral, are now permanently administered in this way by Lords Commissioners. Cf. Clarendon, *Hist. Reb.*, iii. (1843), 84/2, "The treasury was for the present put into commission." Ht. Martineau, *Hist. Peace* (1877), iii., v. i., 200, "The great seal was for some time in commission, from the difficulty of finding a Chancellor."

l. 18. **Pitt had lately married** Lady Hester Grenville, the sister of Lord Temple (1754).

l. 26. **Pitt, who sat for one of the boroughs which were in the Pelham interest.** At the general election which took place in 1754 Pitt accepted a nomination to the Duke of Newcastle's pocket borough Aldborough. In 1756 he sat for Oakhampton.

l. 31. **the Reform Bill** of 1832 disfranchised pocket boroughs.

Page 37, l. 5. **cabal.** See p. 81, l. 4 *infra*, and note.

l. 11. **crassa ignorantia**, dense, inexcusable, criminal ignorance; for, in the eyes of the law, ignorance of what any man of discretion not only may but is bound and presumed to know cannot be urged as an excuse. "Ignorantia eorum quae quis scire tenetur non excusat," and again, "Ignorantia facti excusat, ignorantia juris non excusat."

l. 35. **Marie Louise**, or Maria Louisa, the daughter of Francis I., Emperor of Austria, was married to Napoleon Buonaparte in 1810; and in 1811 she gave birth to a prince, afterwards called the King of Rome.

Page 38, l. 2. **Faubourg St. Antoine** is one of the poorer districts of Paris.

l. 22. **The King disliked Pitt, but absolutely hated Temple.** In a conversation with Lord Waldegrave the King stated with amusing frankness his opinion of their merits. He complained that Pitt made him long speeches which might be very fine but were greatly beyond his comprehension, and that Pitt's letters were affected, formal, and pedantic: that as to Temple, he was so disagreeable a fellow that there was no bearing him: that when he attempted to argue, he was pert and sometimes insolent: that when he meant to be civil, he was exceeding troublesome: and that in the business of his office he was totally ignorant.

l. 24. **Vatel**, or Vattel, wrote *Droit des Gens, ou Principes de la Loi Naturelle Appliqués à la Conduite et aux Affaires des Nations et des Souverains.* It was first published in 1758 and became the text-book of universities; it was republished again and again, and translated into most of the European languages.

l. 29. **at Oudenarde** in Belgium (11th July, 1708) the Duke of Marlborough and Prince Eugene defeated the French, under the Dukes of Burgundy and Vendôme. Before Marlborough had even got all his army into position he ordered his cavalry to charge, so that if the enemy had any thought of retiring without a battle this might prevent them. In this first charge the

Electoral Prince of Hanover, afterwards George II., distinguished himself.

l. 36. **Common Council**, the administrative body of a corporate town or city : a town or city council. In England (since the Act of 1835) retained as title only in the case of London. Cf. *Eng. Elect. Sheriffs*, "38 Sheriffs of London have been always chosen by the Mayor, Aldermen, Common Council and Liverymen." Wellington in *Gurw. Desp.*, v. 403, "You see the dash which the Common Council of the City of London have made at me." (Murray.)

Page 40, l. 19. **the great French writers of his time**, viz. : Rousseau and the Encyclopædists, Montesquieu, Voltaire, Diderot, d'Alembert, Helvetius, Condillac, the Abbé Raynal, and others.

l. 21. **The City of the Violet Crown.** Cf.

ὦ ται λιπαραὶ καὶ ἰοστέφανοι
καὶ ἀοίδιμοι "'Ελλάδος ἔρεισμα"
κλεινὰι 'Αθῆναι.   Pindar, fr. 46.

parodied by Aristophanes :

ὑμᾶς . . . .
πρῶτον μὲν ἰοστεφάνους ἐκάλουν.   *Acharn.*, 637.
λιπαραὶ καὶ ἰοστέφανοι 'Αθῆναι.   *Knights*, 1329.

the City of the Seven Hills, Rome. The seven hills were Palatine, Quirinal, Capitoline, Aventine, Caelian, Viminal, Esquiline. Hence the name *Urbs Septicollis*.

Page 41, l. 2. **secret-service-money.** See p. 29, l. 33, etc.

Page 42, l. 15. **Newcastle felt all that jealousy of Fox... two of a trade.** The proverb is "two of a trade seldom agree"; illustrations of which will be found in Ray's *Proverbs*, Gay's *Old Hen and the Cock*, and Murphy's *Apprentice*, act iii.

l. 31. **Lord Waldégrave.** James Earl Waldégrave, one of the Lords of the Bedchamber, was made Warden of the Stannaries in 1571, and in the next year was appointed Governor to the Prince of Wales.

Horace Walpole (*Memoirs of King George II.*, vol. i., p. 291) says that "The Earl was a man of pleasure, understood the Court, was first in the King's favour, easy in his circumstances and at once undesirous of rising, and afraid to fall. He said to a friend, 'If I dared I would make this excuse to the King ; Sir, I am too young to govern and too old to be governed.' But he was forced to submit. A man of stricter or of more reasonable sense could not have been selected for the employment: yet as the Whig zeal had caught flame, even this choice was severely criticised. Lord Waldégrave's grandmother was daughter of King James : his family were all Papists and his father had been but the first convert."

In 1754 he was entrusted with negotiations for a projected change of ministry. In 1757 he was appointed First Lord of the Treasury. Walpole describes the appointment thus: "In this distress the King (probably by the suggestion of Mr. Fox) sent for Lord Waldegrave, and commanded him to accept that high and dangerous post. The public was not more astonished at that designation than the Earl himself. Though no man knew the secrets of Government better, no man knew the manœuvre of business less. He was no speaker in Parliament, had no interest there, and, though universally beloved and respected where known, was by no means familiarised to the eyes of the nation. He declined as long as modesty became him : engaged with spirit, the moment he felt the abandoned state in which his master and benefactor stood" (*Memoirs*, iii. 26). But in the course of four or five days Fox and Waldegrave were compelled (with the reluctant acquiescence of the King) to abandon this projected ministry.

Page 43, l. 5. **Leicester House** stood in the N.E. corner of Leicester Square and was so-called after Robert Sydney, Earl of Leicester, father of Algernon Sydney, of Henry Sydney (the handsome Sydney of De Grammont's *Memoirs*), and of Lady Dorothy (the Saccharissa of the poet Waller). In 1718, when the Prince of Wales (afterwards George II.) had quarrelled with his father and received the royal command to quit St. James's, he bought Leicester House and made it his London residence. Pennant calls it very happily "the pouting place" of princes, for here in Leicester House, when the breach between George II. and his son Frederick, Prince of Wales, was too sore and too wide to heal, the Prince took up his residence as his father had done before him.

l. 9. **Pelham** held office without any strong opposition from 1743 to 1754. Cf. p. 49, l. 3 *infra*, "The Parliament was as quiet as it had been under Pelham."

l. 10. **Godolphin** was minister from 1702-1710 (see p. 8, l. 29 *supra*, and note) while Marlborough won his great victories abroad.

l. 32. **Aix**, a small island between the mainland of France and Ile d'Oleron, nearly opposite Rochefort.

Rochefort, an important seaport and third naval arsenal of France, at the mouth of the Charente, about twenty miles south of La Rochelle : in 1758 a large fleet and army were sent against Rochefort, but the expedition failed through the timidity of the commander, Sir John Mordaunt ; it succeeded only in destroying the fortifications of the little island of Aix.

l. 33. **St. Maloes**, or St. Malo, a seaport town of France on the English Channel, on the right bank of the estuary of the Rance. A powerful expedition of ships and sailors was sent against St.

Malo in 1758; but it resulted only in the destruction of some French shipping.

l. 35. **Cherbourg**, a seaport and naval arsenal of France, in the department of La Manche: in 1758 it was attacked and occupied, its docks were destroyed, its shipping was burnt; but this success was speedily counterbalanced by the disaster which befell some British troops which had landed at St. Cas.

Page 44, l. 4. Louisburg, the capital of the island of Cape Breton, was taken by General Amherst in 1758; the French fleet in the harbour was utterly destroyed, and the island of Cape Breton became a part of our empire.

l. 5. **the Court of Versailles.** Cf. "The fops and intriguers of Versailles," on p. 48, l. 22.

l. 8. **Kensington Palace** was originally the seat of Heneage Finch, Earl of Nottingham and Lord Chancellor of England; whose son, the second Earl, sold it to King William III. very soon after his accession to the throne. William III., and Queen Mary, Queen Anne, her husband Prince George of Denmark, and King George II. all died in this palace. Her present Majesty was born in it (1819), and here she held her first council.

l. 15. **war of the Grand Alliance**, *i.e.* the war of the Spanish succession. The Grand Alliance was between England, Holland, and the Empire against France and Spain; the war was to settle the succession to the Spanish throne.

l. 16. **Goree**, a station near Cape Verd, west coast of Africa, was taken from the French by the English in 1759.

l. 17. **Guadaloupe**, a West India isle, taken from the French by the English in 1759.

Ticonderoga was upon a point of land washed on the north, east, and south by the waters of Wood's Creek, the entrance to Lake Champlain and to Lake George. The French fortress here was besieged unsuccessfully by Abercromby in July, 1758, but was taken by Amherst on 26th July, 1759.

Niagara is at the head of Lake Erie; Colonel Prideaux appeared before it on the 6th July. The work was pushed forward with great vigour, but Prideaux was killed by the carelessness of one of his soldiers very early in the siege, and the command devolved on Sir William Johnson. The French garrison under Pouchot surrendered on 24th July, 1759.

l. 19. **Cape Lagos** on the coast of Portugal. Here Admiral Boscawen defeated the French Admiral de la Clue, who was in command of the Toulon squadron on its way to join the French fleet at Brest.

l. 20. **Wolfe on the heights of Abraham.** See p. 17, l. 17, and note.

l. 30. **The Brest fleet ... Hawke.** At Brest a strong French fleet under Conflans was blockaded by our ships under Hawke. The English were driven off by the equinoctial gales, and the French Admiral came out with twenty-one ships of the line and four frigates. He was intending to attack a British squadron near Quiberon Bay, but the appearance of Hawke to the rescue drove Conflans to the mouth of the Vilaine (the rest of the story is told best in Macaulay's own words).

Page 45, l. 14. **Cortes,** or Cortez, was born in 1485, at Medellin in Estremadura, and, after studying the law, quitted it for the military profession. In 1511 he went with Velasquez to Cuba; and when the conquest of Mexico was determined upon he obtained the command of the expedition. He set sail in 1518 and began the enterprise which resulted in the foundation of the town of Vera Cruz (1519) and the complete subjugation of Mexico and the Mexican territories.

Pizarro visited Peru in 1531 and succeeded in conquering it; in January, 1535, he laid the foundation of Lima, and named it the " City of the Kings."

l. 17. **Chandernagore** was a settlement of the French East India Company on the Hooghley, about twenty miles from Calcutta.

l. 18. **Clive.** See Macaulay's *Essays*, p. 502, etc.

Pondicherry to Coote. In 1762 Sir Eyre Coote gradually deprived Lally of all his conquests, and in 1761 captured Pondicherry, the chief French Settlement in the Carnatic.

l. 19. **Bengal, Bahar, Orissa.** Bengal is the chief Presidency of India; Behar (or Bahar) lies to the north, and Orissa to the south-west of Bengal: the kingdom of Orissa extends from the mouth of the Ganges to that of the Godávarí. These provinces form a princely dominion, and became subject to the English East India Company in 1765, by the treaty of Allahabad for a quit-rent of about £300,000.

the Carnatic is a district of Southern Hindustan extending along the whole coast of Coromandel.

l. 20. **Acbar,** or Akbar (b. 1542, d. 1605), the real founder of the Mughal dynasty. His great idea was the union of all India under one head. A good account of him is given by Colonel G. B. Malleson, C.S.I., in the series of books entitled *Rulers of India*.

l. 21. **Aurungzebe,** the Mogul emperor of Hindustan. He subdued Golconda, the Carnatic, Bijapur, and Bengal, and routed the pirates who had infested the mouth of the Ganges: he flourished from 1659 to 1707.

l. 23. **the King of Prussia,** Frederick the Great.

Page 46, l. 2. he would conquer America for them in Germany. By defeating the French in Germany he would make it easier to conquer them in America.

l. 18. **fiddle-faddle**, a reduplication of *faddle*, nonsense, trifling, a foolish fuss.

l. 32. **Prince Ferdinand of Brunswick.** Cf. Lecky, vol. ii., ch. vii., p. 412. "The Hanoverian army was armed anew. The command was given to Prince Ferdinand of Brunswick, one of the best generals of the Russian service. It was soon after reinforced by 12,000 English under the Duke of Marlborough, and it bore a chief part in defending the side of Germany conterminous to France. Pitt at the same time disregarding all his former denunciations of German subsidies, obtained an annual subsidy of nearly £700,000 for Frederick, which during the next few years was punctually paid."

l. 33. **Crevelt**, Creveldt, or Crefeld near Cleves (West Prussia). Here Prince Ferdinand of Brunswick defeated the French under the Count of Clermont (1758).

l. 34. **Minden**, in Westphalia. The English, Hessians, and Hanoverians under Prince Ferdinand of Brunswick defeated the French under Marshal de Contades. The French army mustered more than 50,000 men, while the British and German army was about 36,000 strong. The French lost about 7000 men and 30 cannon.

Page 48, l. 2. The success of our arms... The ardour of his soul had set the whole kingdom on fire, etc. With this passage we might compare Lecky, ii., ch. vii. 403, "Pitt had just confidence in himself. I am sure, he said on one occasion to the Duke of Devonshire, that I can save the country and that no one else can." If he did not possess to a high degree the skill of a great strategist in detecting the vulnerable parts of his opponents and in mapping out brilliant campaigns, he had at least an eagle eye for discovering talent and resolution among his subordinates, a rare power of restoring the vigour of every branch of administration, and, above all, a capacity unrivalled among statesmen of reviving the confidence and the patriotism of the nation, and of infusing an heroic daring into all who served him. "No man," said Colonel Barré, "ever entered his closet who did not come out of it a braver man."

l. 18. **Lord George Sackville**, who commanded the English cavalry at Minden, through a nervousness of which there are very few examples in English military history, disobeyed at a critical moment of the battle the order to charge, and thus saved the French from absolute destruction. He was pronounced by a court-martial guilty of disobedience, and unfit to serve the Crown in any military capacity whatever; and although great family influence and very considerable abilities raised him in the following reign to a high position, his reputation was irrevocably blasted. (Lecky, vol. ii., ch. vii., p. 432.)

l. 22. **The fops and intriguers of Versailles** is equivalent to "the Court of Versailles" on p. 44, l. 5. *Fop* (akin to Ger. *fopper*, to make a fool of one), a foolish fellow that seeks admiration of his showy dress; a coxcomb; a dandy.

Page 49, l. 28. **zenith**, that point of the heavens which is vertical to the observer; it is used figuratively for the highest point of prosperity or success.

THE EARL OF CHATHAM.

Page 50, l. 1. **More than ten years ago ... known to us.** In a letter to Mr. Napier (editor of the *Edinburgh Review*) dated August 14th, 1844, Macaulay says that he had undertaken an altogether unmanageable subject (viz., a review of Burke's *Life and Writings*). He then continues thus: "It is absolutely necessary that I should change my whole plan. I will try to write for you, not a history of England during the earlier part of George the Third's reign, but an account of the last years of Lord Chatham's life. I promised or half-promised this ten years ago, at the end of my review of Thackeray's book. Most of what I have written will come in very well. The fourth volume of the Chatham correspondence has not, I think, been reviewed. It will furnish a heading for the article."

A week later Macaulay writes, "The article on Chatham goes on swimmingly. A great part of the information which I have is still in manuscript.—Horace Walpole's *Memoirs of George the Third's Reign*, which was transcribed for Mackintosh; and the first Lord Holland's *Diary*, which Lady Holland permitted me to read."

Page 51, l. 1. **the great religious schism of the sixteenth century**, *i.e.* the Reformation, begun in England by Tyndale in the reign of Henry VIII., completed by Cranmer and others in the reign of Edward VI. (1547), annulled by Mary (1553), and restored by Elizabeth (1558).

l. 30. **Dante** (b. 1265, d. 1321), the great poet of Italy. His chief works, *The Vita Nuova, Convito*, and *Divina Comedia*, have been translated into English by various hands. The *Divina Comedia* is divided into three parts: *Inferno, Purgatorio*, and

Paradiso. The passage to which Macaulay refers here is in *Inferno,* Canto xxv. The narrative ends thus:
"That done the smoke was laid;
The soul, transformed into the brute, glides off
Hissing along the vale and after him
The other talking splutters." (Cary's translation.)

Malebolge means the horrible dark place; it was the eighth circle of Dante's *Inferno,* which contained in all ten bolgi or pits. In *Inferno,* Canto xviii., it is described thus:
"There is a place within the depths of Hell
Call'd Malebolge, all of rock dark-stain'd
With hue ferruginous, e'en as the steep
That round it circling winds."

Page 52, 1. 16. the Comptroller's staff, the office of controller. *Comptroller* is an erroneous spelling of *controller,* introduced about 1500, and formerly frequent in all senses; still retained in certain official designations, while in others it has been changed to the ordinary spelling, *e.g.* in Whitaker we find "Comptroller of the Household," "Comptroller of Accounts," "Comptroller and Treasurer," "Comptroller and Auditor-General," etc., etc.; but "Controller of the Navy," "Controller of H.M. Stationery Office," etc. The duty of a *Comptroller* or *Controller* is to examine and verify accounts.

the Great Wardrobe. Mastership of the Great Wardrobe was a high and lucrative office. Horace Walpole tells us that in 1754 Lord Hilsborough was Comptroller of the Household, and Lord Barrington Master of the Great Wardrobe in the room of Sir Thomas Barrington.

l. 18. **Locke,** John (b. 1632, d. 1704), wrote three *Letters concerning Toleration, Essay concerning Human Understanding, Two Treatises of Government, Thoughts concerning Education, The Reasonableness of Christianity.* He was, indeed, one of our most eminent philosophers and upholders of both Civil and Religious Liberty. He might be called the interpreter of the Revolution of 1688-9.

Milton, John (b. 1608, d. 1674), the great Puritan poet and champion of freedom. His chief poetical works are *Paradise Lost, Paradise Regained, L'Allegro, Il Penseroso, Lycidas, Comus, Samson Agonistes,* and *Sonnets.* His principal prose works are *Two Books on Reformation in England, Areopagitica, Eikonoclastes, Defence of the People of England,* etc., etc. (See Macaulay's *Essays,* pp. 1-28.)

l. 19. **Pym,** John (b. 1584, d. 1643), was one of the managers of Buckingham's impeachment, and took a prominent part in the debates on the Petition of Rights. He moved the impeachment of Strafford, and was the chief manager of his trial. He was a strong Presbyterian, though not at first disposed to go the whole length of the Root and Branch party. The Protestation and Grand Remonstrance were particularly his work. In his Essay on Sir William Temple (p. 421) Macaulay writes to this effect: "Nor could the new chiefs of parties lay claim to the great qualities of the statesmen who had stood at the head of the Long Parliament: Hampden, Pym, Vane, Cromwell are discriminated from the ablest politicians of the succeeding generations by all the strong lineaments which distinguish the men who produce revolutions from the men whom revolutions produce."

l. 19. **Hampden.** See p. 2, l. 36 *supra*, and note.

the thirtieth of January, the anniversary of the execution of Charles I. in 1649.

l. 20. **the man in the mask**, etc., the executioner and the assassin.

l. 24. **the iron tyranny of Strafford and Laud.** Thomas Wentworth, Earl of Strafford (b. 1593, d. 1641), was noted for his scheme of "Thorough" by which he attempted to make Charles I. an absolutely despotic and irresponsible ruler. This system failed in England, for it required a standing army; but in Ireland it was more successful. He was made Lord-Deputy of Ireland in 1633; his government there was despotic and cruel; and he raised a large army which was no doubt intended for the support of tyranny in England.

Macaulay has sketched his character thus: "He was the first Englishman to whom a peerage was a sacrament of infamy, a baptism into the communion of corruption. As he was the earliest of the hateful list so was he also by far the greatest; eloquent, sagacious, intrepid, ready of invention, immutable of purpose, in every talent which exalts or destroys nations pre-eminent, the lost Archangel, the Satan of apostasy."

William Laud, Archbishop of Canterbury (b. 1573, d. 1645), was the son of a clothier, and rose by his own abilities and force of character to be Primate of England. He hated Calvinistic Puritanism, and maintained the Divine right of the Episcopacy, the direct spiritual inheritance of the Church, and the sacredness of the anointed King. His study and sometimes misguided zeal for conformity to the Church, and his endeavours to introduce the liturgy into Scotland, raised up many enemies against him in days when Puritanism was rife in the land. He was impeached by the Long Parliament, but acquitted by the Lords; a bill of attainder declaring him guilty of treason was then passed by the Lower House, and he was beheaded. His character has been variously drawn by opposite parties: Macaulay despises him as "a ridiculous old bigot"; others express for him almost unlimited reverence. The Bishop of Peterborough regards him as not more superstitious than his epoch, and as a positive benefactor of his age.

l. 31. **Who would have believed ... Jaquelin?** Guizot, François Pierre Guillaume (b. 1787, d. 1874), was in 1830 member of the Chamber of Deputies and leader of a popular movement against the Polignac Administration, which led to the fall of Charles X. But in 1840 he became Minister of Foreign Affairs to Louis Philippe, and from that time till the fall of that monarch in 1848 he was his most obsequious minister.

l. 32. **Villemain,** Abel François (b. 1790, d. 1870), was, along with Guizot, obnoxious to the Government of Charles X., owing to his liberal opinions: but in 1830 he was a member of the Chamber of Deputies. He won high distinction as a political orator, and was created a peer of France during the reign of Louis Philippe.

l. 34. **Genoude,** Antoine Eugène (b. 1792, d. 1849), was at one time Aide-de-camp to the Prince of Polignac. In 1825 he became editor of the *Gazette de France,* in which he upheld the cause of monarchy and religion.

de la Roche Jaquelin, Henri, Marquis (b. 1805, d. 1867), a peer of France, was a member of the Chamber of Deputies in 1842, and a member of the National Assembly in 1848.

Macaulay points out that it would have been hard to believe fifteen years ago (*i.e.* in 1829) that Guizot and Villemain, the upholders of liberal opinions against Charles X., would now (in 1844) be ranged on the side of Louis Philippe and monarchy, against men like Genoude, Aide-de-camp of Polignac, and de la Roche Jaquelin, a peer of France, who, for their part, had now changed over to the side of the Republicans.

Page 53, l. 6. **Sidney,** Algernon, (b. 1620, d. 1683), joined the parliamentarians against the King: when the High Court of Justice was formed for the trial of the King he was nominated a member; and though he was neither present when sentence was pronounced nor signed the warrant for the execution, he vindicated that measure. Subsequently (in 1683) he was arrested along with Lord William Russell and others for being implicated in the Rye House Plot; and when brought before Chief Justice Jeffreys he was found guilty and condemned, although the evidence was defective and illegal.

l. 7. **Jeffreys,** George, generally known as Judge Jeffreys (b. 1648, d. 1689), was noted for his arbitrary and inhuman administration of the law; two of the more distinguished victims of his illegal cruelty were Algernon Sidney and Sir Thomas Armstrong: he presided also at the trials of Titus Oates and Richard Baxter: he was one of the advisers and promoters of all the oppressive and arbitrary measures of James II.; and by a series of judicial murders on the "Bloody Assize" he completed the destruction of the adherents of Monmouth, and was rewarded with the post of Lord High Chancellor in 1685.

l. 17. **the commission of the peace,** the authority given under the great seal empowering certain persons to act as Justices of the Peace in a specified district.

Page 54, l. 6. **the Mendip Hills,** in Somersetshire.
the Wrekin, in Shropshire.

l. 8. **Oxford,** etc. Robert Harley (b. 1661, d. 1724) was made Earl of Oxford and First Lord of the Treasury in 1710: the white staff is part of the insignia of office of the Treasurer. Oxford retained the office of Lord High Treasurer till 1714; but owing to the influence of Lady Masham, with whom he had quarrelled about a pension, he was dismissed from this post a few days before the death of Queen Anne.

l. 22. **Timoleon** belonged to one of the noblest families at Corinth. He was so ardent a lover of liberty that, when his brother Timophanes tried to make himself tyrant of their native city, Timoleon murdered him rather than allow him to destroy the liberty of the State. Subsequently Timoleon expelled almost all the tyrants from the Greek cities in Sicily and established democracies instead. He died B.C. 337.

Brutus, M. Junius, served under Julius Caesar in Gaul and in the civil war; but nevertheless in the cause of liberty and in order to free the State from a tyrant (as he thought) he joined the conspiracy which ended in the murder of Caesar in B.C. 44.

l. 27. **cant of patriotism.** See p. 34, l. 31 *supra,* and note.

l. 30. **the Rump,** a derisive epithet applied to the remnant of the Long Parliament which reassembled in 1659 after its dissolution by Richard Cromwell.

l. 35. **The banished heir of the House of Stuart headed a rebellion,** Charles Edward, the young Pretender, defeated by Duke of Cumberland (1646). See p. 27, l. 1 *supra,* and note.

l. 36. **the discontented heir of the House of Brunswick,** Frederick, Prince of Wales, son of George II., died 1751. See p. 12, l. 16 *supra,* and note.

Page 55, l. 12. **Minorca,** etc. See p. 34, l. 7 *supra,* and note.

Page 56, l. 2. **the memorable schedules A and B.** In the Reform Act of 1832 the towns and counties of England were classified under Schedules A, B, C, D, E, E 2, F, F 2, and G, for the purpose of electing Members of Parliament. Thus Schedule A comprised boroughs to cease to send members to Parliament. Schedule B comprised boroughs to return one member. Schedule C comprised new boroughs to return two members. Schedule D comprised new boroughs to return one member. Schedule E comprised places in Wales to have a share in elections for the shire towns or principal boroughs. Schedule E 2 comprised places sharing in the election of members, with the places therein, from which the seven miles are to be calculated. Schedule F comprised counties to be divided, and to return two knights for each division. Schedule F 2 comprised counties to return three members each. Schedule G comprised towns which are counties in themselves to be included in adjoining counties for county elections.

l. 3. **The great Whig families.** For a list of these see p. 58, l. 21, etc. *infra.*

l. 15. **secret service money.** See p. 29, l. 33, and p. 41, l. 2 *supra*, and note.

l. 22. **the great house at the corner of Lincoln's Inn Fields.** In his account of London (1793) Pennant writes of Lincoln's Inn Fields thus: "In the same square, at the corner of Queen Street, stands a house formerly inhabited by the well-known minister, the late Duke of Newcastle. It was built about the year 1686 by the Marquis of Powis, and called Powis House, and afterwards sold to the late noble owner. The architect was Captain William Winde."

l. 24. **lawn sleeves,** part of the official dress of a bishop. *Lawn* is contracted from Fr. *linon*, lawn, from *lin*, Lat. *linum*, flax.

"A saint in crape is twice a saint in lawn." (Pope.)

l. 30. **a prebend** (Fr. *prébende*, Pr. and Sp. *prebenda*, It. *prebenda*, *prevenda*, L. Lat. *praebenda* from Lat. *praebere*, to hold forth, afford, allow). The stipend or maintenance granted to a prebendary out of the estate of a cathedral or collegiate church with which he is connected.

l. 33. **potwalloper,** a voter in certain boroughs in England, where all who boil (wallop) a pot are entitled to vote. (Webster.)

Page 57, l. 5. **twenty years in Parliament, ten in office.** Pitt entered Parliament in 1735, he was admitted to office first as Vice-Treasurer of Ireland, afterwards as Paymaster-General in 1746. Macaulay is writing in round numbers.

l. 13. **or about the means of securing a Cornish corporation.** This is perhaps an allusion to the dispute about the election of Mitchell (*i.e.* St. Michael) in Cornwall (1755). Walpole describes the dispute thus: "Lord Sandwich, who would never be unemployed, but to whose busy nature any trifle was food, and who was as indefatigable in the election of an Alderman as in a Revolution of State, had been traversed at Mitchell in Cornwall, a borough belonging to his nephew (Courtney) by the families of Edgcombe and Boscawen. His candidates were returned by his intrigues, but a petition was lodged against them. He had scarce effected their return, but he applied to all parties for support against the cause should be heard in Parliament. . . . Fox eagerly supported him as a creature of the Duke." And at the second hearing of the petition Fox and Sandwich carried a division by 26.

l. 15. **arrogant humility**, an oxymoron. Cf. "Insaniens sapientia," γάμος ἄγαμος,
"His honour rooted in dishonour stood,
And faith unfaithful proved him falsely true."

l. 23. **tidewaiter**, an officer who watches the landing of goods to secure the payment of duties.

Page 58, l. 35. **who had married their sister.** Pitt married Lady Hester Grenville in 1754.

Page 59, l. 1. **the Bloomsbury gang**, a nickname of the Bedford faction, so-called from the Duke's House in Bloomsbury Square. In his *History of London* (1773) John Noorthouck describes Bloomsbury Square as follows: "This Square is embellished with many good houses, and the grass plots in the middle are surrounded with neat iron rails. The north side is entirely taken up with Bedford House, which is elegant, though low, having but one story, and was the design of Inigo Jones."

l. 10. **Sandwich**, Lord, was Bedford's oldest follower, and became Secretary of State in 1763. The King disliked him, some say because of his notorious profligacy. He had been plenipotentiary at the conference of Breda in 1747, and concluded the peace at Aix-la-Chapelle in 1749, and in 1751 "he had been hoisted to the head of the Admiralty by the weight of the Duke of Bedford, into whose affection he had worked himself by intrigues, cricket matches, and acting plays, and whom he had almost persuaded to resign the Seals in his favour." (*Memoirs*, i. 2.) Walpole says of his character: "Lord Sandwich was rapacious, but extravagant when it was to his own designs. His industry to carry any point he had in view was so remarkable that for a long time the world mistook it for abilities; but as his manner was most awkward and unpolished, so his talents were but slight when it was necessary to exert them in any higher light than in art and intrigue."

Rigby is mentioned by Horace Walpole as "The Duke of Bedford's Chief Counsellor." He acted in 1755 as an agent between Fox and the Duke of Bedford. In 1757, when Bedford was Lord Lieutenant of Ireland, Rigby was Secretary; his ascendency over both the Duke and Duchess of Bedford was absolute. Horace Walpole describes him thus: "Rigby had an advantageous and manly person, recommended by a spirited jollity that was very pleasing, though sometimes roughened into brutality: of most insinuating good breeding when he wished to be agreeable. His passions were turbulent and overbearing; his courage bold and fond of exerting itself. His parts strong and quick, but totally uncultivated; and so much had he trusted to unaffected common sense, that he could never afterwards acquire the necessary temperament of art in his public speaking. He had been a pupil of Winnington, and owed the chief errors of his life to that man's maxims, perniciously witty. . . . Rigby, whose heart was naturally good, grew to think it sensible to laugh at the shackles of morality; and having early encumbered his fortune by gaming, he found his patron's maxims but too well adapted to retrieve his desperate fortunes. . . . In short, he was a man who was seldom loved or hated with moderation; yet he himself, though a violent opponent, was never a bitter enemy. His amiable qualities were all natural; his faults acquired or fatally linked to him by the chain of some other failings."

l. 14. **Weymouth**, Lord, the head of the Thynnes of Longleat, was made Secretary of State in 1767. In 1769 he wrote a letter to the Surrey Magistrates at Lambeth advising them to be on their guard against riots and tumults and to make early application for a military force. Wilkes published this letter with a comment of his own, but without his name. This comment was decided by the House of Commons to be "an insolent libel." Weymouth retired from office in 1771. "He had, indeed, good natural abilities and an easy flow of eloquence, which, combined with a graceful person, pleased the House of Lords, but he wanted steady application, and had impaired both his fortune and his health by his taste for gaming and drinking." (Lord Mahon.)

l. 25. **William Murray.** See p. 26, l. 14 *supra*, and note.

l. 26. **Henry Fox.** See p. 11, l. 3 *supra*, and note.

Page 60, l. 8. **Hardwicke.** See p. 20, l. 34 *supra*, and note.

l. 9. **Legge.** See p. 32, l. 16 *supra*, and note,

l. 10. **Oswald**, James, a Scotchman, one of the Lords of the Treasury, and reviled by Wilkes in his *North Briton*. He was "master of a quickness and strength of argument not inferior to Fox or any speaker in the House. The rapidity of his eloquence was astonishing, not adorned, but confined to business." (Walpole, i. 59.)

l. 11. **Nugent**, Robert, was noted for his Bill of General Naturalisation of Foreigners (1751): he was bred a Roman Catholic, had turned Protestant, and not long after married Mrs. Knight, sister and daughter to the two Craggses. The King nominated him as a member for Bristol in 1753; but the Bristol men "begged to be excused." In 1754 he became one of the Lords of the Treasury. In 1755 he made an absurd speech in defence of Newcastle's Administration against the attacks of Pitt. He had all the boisterous good humour and love of banter characteristic of most Irishmen.

l. 11. **Charles Townshend.** See p. 8, l. 25 *supra*, and note.

l. 12. **Elliot**, Sir Gilbert, another Scot on the Treasury Board. Horace Walpole gave Elliot's Scotch birth as a conclusive reason why he should lead the House of Commons.

Barrington, Lord. William Barrington Shute, Viscount Barrington, was one of the Lords of the Admiralty in 1751, and in 1755 he was appointed Secretary at War. In the debate on Byng's sentence (1757) he spoke in justification of the 12th article of war being enforced in this case.

North, Lord, had lately been entrusted with the care of Prince George with the promise of an earldom; an amiable, worthy man, of no great genius unless compared with his successor. ... Lord North was removed to make way for Lord Harcourt (1751). (Horace Walpole.)

Pratt was subsequently (in 1757) made Attorney-General at the express desire of Pitt, and the next year Pratt prepared a bill for explaining and extending the Habeas Corpus, and ascertaining its full operation.

l. 18. **Lord George Sackville.** See p. 48, l. 18 *supra*, and note.

l. 19. **Bubb Doddington.** See p. 4, l. 2 *supra*, and note.

l. 27. **the Cocoa Tree.** The Tory Chocolate House of Queen Anne's reign is mentioned by Addison in the first number of *The Spectator*, Thursday, March 1st, 1718. A club called "The Cocoa-tree Club," from the place of meeting, was formed here about 1747.

l. 34. **The Journals of the House of Commons.** The official record of the proceedings of this department of the legislative body commenced November 8th, 1547. They were not kept with any degree of regularity until 1607. (Townsend, *Manual of Dates*.)

Page 61, l. 8. **The vigour and success with which the war had been waged in Germany.** "Frederick the Great's seven years' war might well have been another thirty years' war, if Pitt had not furnished him with an annual subsidy of £700,000, and in addition relieved him of the task of defending Western Germany against France." (*Encyclopædia Britannica*.)

l. 16. **his grandfather,** George II.; his father was Frederick, Prince of Wales.

l. 28. **the Emperor Francis.** Francis II., Emperor of the Romans, and first Emperor of Austria, King of Lombardy, etc., was born in 1768. In 1804, when France had been declared an empire, he assumed the title of hereditary Emperor of Austria. He declared war against France in 1792, and from this time till the defeat of Napoleon at Waterloo (1815) he was almost constantly in arms against France. In 1794 he defeated the French at Cateau, Landrecies, and Tournay; but in 1805 his army and that of Russia were destroyed by Napoleon; again in 1809 Napoleon gained a decisive victory against the Austrians at Wagram. Francis died in 1835, leaving a more extensive empire to his successor than any of his ancestors had ever possessed.

l. 29. his son-in-law, the Emperor Napoleon. Napoleon married the Archduchess Maria Louisa, daughter of Francis II. of Austria.

a ruler with no better title than Napoleon. Napoleon had no title whatever to the throne of France. He gained it by overthrowing the Government of the Directory (1799), whereupon he was raised to the supreme power by the title of First Consul.

l. 31. Richard Cromwell succeeded his father, Oliver Cromwell, in September, 1658; but he was incompetent to fill his father's place, and, having been compelled by his officers to dissolve the Parliament, he abdicated in April, 1659.

Page 62, l. 4. the Guelphs. The name of the ruling family of Hanover continues still in the two lines of Brunswick, the royal house of England, and the ducal house of Germany.

l. 33. bewray (M.E. *bewreien* from *be wreien*). Probably more or less of a conscious archaism since the seventeenth century; the ordinary modern equivalent is *expose*. (Murray.)

Page 63, l. 1. exchange St. James's for Hernhausen, *i.e.* exchange his palace in London for that in Hanover.

l. 18. the Revolution of 1688-9.

l. 19. the Act of Settlement. See p. 10, l. 10 *supra*, and note.

the risings of 1715 and 1745, in support of the old and young Pretender respectively.

l. 21. Derwentwater. James Radcliffe, the last Earl of Derwentwater, was a staunch adherent of the Stuarts. In 1715 he joined the army of the Pretender and marched to Preston, where he was defeated and taken prisoner. He was impeached for high treason, he pleaded guilty, refusing firmly to acknowledge the Hanoverian title and to conform to the Church of England, and was beheaded on Tower Hill in 1716.

Kilmarnock, one of the Scotch lords that joined Charles Edward, the young Pretender, marched with him to Derby, but was afterwards defeated at Culloden, taken prisoner, and executed for high treason.

Balmerino. Arthur Elphinston, Lord Balmerino, joined the Earl of Mar and served with him at Sheriffmuir. He then escaped to France, but returned to Scotland in 1733; when the young Pretender landed in Scotland, Elphinston was one of the first to join his standard. He was taken prisoner at Culloden by the Duke of Cumberland, and was brought to trial and executed along with Kilmarnock.

l. 21. **Cameron, Dr. Archibald,** suffered death at Tyburn. He had been forced into the rebellion by his brother Lochiel, had left his profession and family, and he attended his rash brother at Prestonpans and Falkirk, escaped with him, and was appointed physician to Lochiel's regiment in the French service. In 1753 he returned to Scotland, and as he was excepted by the Act of Indemnity was seized and executed as a rebel.

l. 22. **Born fifty years after the old line had been expelled.** George III. was born in 1738; James II. abdicated in 1688.

Page 64, l. 1. **Apis,** a god of the Egyptians whom they worshipped in the form of a calf.

l. 6. **Doge** (an Italian word akin to Lat. *dux*, a leader, and English, *duke*), the chief magistrate in the republics of Venice and Genoa.

Stadtholder (D. *stadhouder*, from *stad*, a city, town, and *houder*, a holder), the chief magistrate of the United Provinces of Holland.

l. 9. **Dido,** the Queen of Carthage, and widow of Sychaeus, becomes enamoured of Æneas, but is deserted by him.

l. 11. **recognised the vestiges of the old flame.** Cf. Virgil, *Aeneid,* iv. 23:

"Adgnoseco veteris vestigia flammae."

l. 12. **Harley,** the Chancellor of the Exchequer and Prime Minister of Queen Anne. (See also p. 54, l. 8, **Oxford,** *supra*, and note.)

l. 14. **The latitudinarian Prelates,** those with broader and more liberal views than were generally held by the supporters of Episcopacy.

l. 15. **Doddridge,** Philip (b. 1702, d. 1751), a distinguished dissenting divine; he was successively minister at Kibworth, Market Harborough, and Northampton. He established (1729) and presided over an academy for training young men designed for the ministry. He died of a pulmonary complaint when he had hardly reached his prime. He wrote *The Family Expositor, The Rise and Progress of Religion in the Soul, The Life of Colonel Gardiner,* and *Hymns.*

l. 16. **Whiston,** William (b. 1667, d. 1752), a divine and mathematician, was born at Norton in Leicestershire. He studied at Clare College, Cambridge, was chosen fellow of his college, and entered holy orders. In 1703 he succeeded Sir Isaac Newton as professor of mathematics, but having conceived doubts concerning the doctrine of the Trinity, and at length adopted Arian opinions, he was expelled from the University in 1710, and deprived of his office. He then removed to the metropolis, and gave lectures on astronomy ; but he was prosecuted as a heretic, and the proceedings were ultimately terminated by an act of grace in 1715. Being refused admission to the sacrament in his parish church, he opened his own house for worship, using a liturgy of his own composition. He subsequently distinguished himself by an abortive attempt to discover the longitude, and by his opinions on the millennium and the restoration of the Jews. His translation of the works of Josephus passed through many editions.

l. 17. **South**, Robert (b. 1633, d. 1716), was born at Hackney, educated at Westminster School and Christ Church, Oxford. In 1660 he was chosen public orator of the University, and successively became Chaplain of the Earl of Clarendon, Prebendary of Westminster, Canon of Christ Church, and Rector of Islip, in Oxfordshire. He preached before Charles II., but refused all offers of Church preferment. He would not take part in promoting the Revolution, and was never tired of preaching against the Dissenters.

Atterbury, Francis (b. 1662, d. 1731), was born at Milton Keynes, near Newport Pagnell, and was educated at Westminster School and Christ Church, Oxford. In 1691 he took holy orders, and adopted High Church principles; he was Chaplain in Ordinary to Queen Anne, Dean of Carlisle, preacher at the Rolls Chapel, a Canon of Exeter, Dean of Christ Church, Bishop of Rochester, and Dean of Westminster. His High Church principles were well known; and it is asserted that he boasted that, if a sufficient guard could be obtained, he would proclaim the Pretender; at any rate through his sympathy with the Pretender he involved himself in a "Bill of Pains and Penalties," and died an exile in Paris. (See Macaulay's *Miscellaneous Writings*, pp. 343, etc.)

Page 65, l. 8. **Duke of York.** Had Frederick the title of Duke of York as well as that of Prince of Wales?

Duke of Cumberland. Horace Walpole concludes his estimate of the Duke's character thus: "He despised money, fame, and politics; loved gaming, women, and his own favourites, and yet had not one sociable virtue."

the Queen of Denmark was the youngest daughter of George II., a princess of great spirit and sense, who died in the flower of her age in 1751.

l. 12. **Groom of the Stole**, the first lord of the bed-chamber in the household of the King of England.

l. 13. **John Stuart, Earl of Bute.** See p. 4, l. 19 *supra*, and note.

l. 18. **Scotch Representative Peers.** The Act of Union with Scotland in 1706 added to the House of Lords sixteen representative Peers from Scotland, elected at the beginning of every Parliament by the Scottish Peers.

l. 28. **Lothario**, one of the characters in Rowe's tragedy, *The Fair Penitent*. He is represented as a libertine and seducer, and is usually alluded to as "the Gay Lothario":
"Is this that haughty gallant, gay Lothario?" (Rowe.)

Page 66, l. 3. **Sir Charles Grandison**, one of Richardson's novels. In this character the author portrays his ideal of a perfect hero—a union of the good Christian with the perfect English gentleman.

l. 4. **Leicester House.** See p. 43, l. 5 *supra*, and note.

l. 11. **virtuoso**, a person skilled in the fine arts, antiquities, curiosities, and the like. "*Virtuoso* the Italians call a man who loves the noble arts and is a critic in them." (Dryden.)

Page 67, l. 1. **Filmer**, Sir Robert, was a Royalist of the time of Charles I., who said that there never was a time when men were equal. When there were only two in the world one was the master. When children were born Adam was master over them. Authority was founded by God Himself in Fatherhood. Out of Fatherhood came Royalty, the Patriarch was King. Filmer wrote several pieces that were published in the reign of Charles I. One of them boldly asserted that Parliament was an evil; they all maintained extreme views of the irresponsibility of Kings. (Morley.)

His chief works are *The Anarchy of a Limited or Mixed Monarchy* and *Patriarcha*.

l. 2. **Sacheverell**, Henry (b. 1672, d. 1724), an English divine, distinguished chiefly for his two famous sermons—one at Derby, the other at St. Paul's—in maintenance of the doctrine of non-resistance, the object of which was to create alarm for the Church, and to excite hostility against the Dissenters. He was impeached by the Whigs in the House of Commons, and was suspended from preaching for three years. The light sentence passed upon him was regarded as an acquittal, and the result of the trial was interpreted as a Tory triumph.

Perceval, the Right Hon. Spencer (b. 1762, d. 1812). He was a firm supporter of the measures of ministers during the life of Pitt, and of the Opposition during the administration of Fox. He became First Lord of the Treasury and Leader of the Tory Ministry in 1809. He was assassinated in 1812 on entering the lobby of the House of Commons, by a man named Bellingham.

Eldon, John Scott, Earl of (b. 1751, d. 1838), was educated at Newcastle Grammar School and University College, Oxford. He was called to the Bar in 1776. He entered Parliament in 1783 for the borough of Weobly and joined the party of Pitt. He became in turn Solicitor-General, Attorney-General, and Lord Chief Justice of the Common Pleas, and Lord Chancellor of England. In politics he was a staunch Tory.

l. 3. **Bolingbroke**, Henry St. John, Viscount (b. 1672, d. 1751), entered Parliament in 1700, became Secretary at War in 1704: resigned his office in 1708 : again formed part of the Ministry in 1710, and concluded the Peace of Utrecht. In 1712 he was created Viscount Bolingbroke ; but, dissatisfied that he was not raised to an earldom, he quarrelled with his colleagues, effected the dismissal of Harley, and himself became Prime Minister. After the death of Queen Anne the Whigs gained the ascendency. He, as a Tory, fled to France and became Secretary of State to James Edward, the Pretender. He was impeached and attainted, and it was not till 1723 that he was allowed to return to England. In 1725 his estates were restored to him, but he exerted all his talents against the Ministry until the fall of Sir Robert Walpole. He withdrew to France in 1735, but subsequently returned to England and died at Battersea in 1751. Lecky describes his character thus : " The genius and daring of Bolingbroke were indeed incontestable, but his defects as a party leader were scarcely less. No statesman was ever truer to the interests of his party, but by a strange contradiction no leader was ever less fitted to represent it. His eminently Italian character delighting in elaborate intrigue, the contrast between his private life and his stoical professions, his notorious indifference to the religious tenets which were the very basis of the politics of his party, shook the confidence of the country gentry and country clergy, who formed the bulk of his followers ; and he exhibited, on some occasions, an astonishing combination of recklessness and insincerity."

He was a political writer as well as a statesman. His chief works are *A Dissertation upon Parties, Letters on the Spirit of Patriotism, or the Idea of a Patriot King, and on the State of Parties at the Accession of George I.*

doctor, used in its literal sense of teacher, expounder.

l. 17. **the instrument which had called William and Mary to the throne**. The Declaration of Rights, "declaring the rights and liberties of the subject, and settling the succession of the crown," was made by the Lords and Commons of England to the Prince and Princess of Orange, 13th February, 1689. This declaration was embodied in the Bill of Rights passed by Parliament in the same year.

Page 69, l. 8. **the patriot Prince**, alluding to Bolingbroke's *Idea of a Patriot King*.

l. 13. **Sudbury**, in Suffolk, one of the old rotten boroughs: it was disfranchised for bribery in 1844.

Old Sarum. See p. 4, l. 36 *supra*, and note.

l. 14. **the privy seal** is affixed to all letters-patent for the grant of charters, pardons, etc., before they come to the Great Seal. *Privy Seals* are, therefore, equivalent to warrants from the King.

l. 15. **ship-money**, in old English law a tax imposed by the King upon sea-ports to provide ships in time of war. It fell into disuse and was included in the Petition of Right (1628) as a wrong to be discontinued. Charles I. revived this tax, demanding it in time of peace from inland towns, and not for the provision of warships. John Hampden refused to pay the tax, and this was one of the proximate causes of the Great Rebellion. It was abolished by Statute 16, Charles I., c. 14 (1640).

l. 21. **Dodingtons.** See p. 4, l. 2 *supra*, and note. George Bubb Doddington is one of the subjects of Browning's *Parleyings with Certain People of Importance in their Day*.

Winnington was first made Lord of the Admiralty, then of the Treasury, then Cofferer, and lastly Paymaster of the Forces, when Mr. Pelham was raised to the head of the Treasury. "Winnington had been bred a Tory, but had left them in the height of Sir Walpole's power; when that minister sunk, he had injudiciously, and to please my Lady Townshend, who had then the greatest influence over him, declined visiting him in a manner to offend the steady old Whigs; and his jolly way of laughing at his own want of principles had revolted all the graver sort, who thought deficiency of honesty too sacred and profitable a commodity to be profaned and turned into ridicule. He had infinitely more wit than any man I ever knew, and it was as ready and quick as it was constant and unmeditated. His style was a little brutal: his courage not at all so; his good humour inexhaustible; it was impossible to hate or to trust him. He died soon after by the ignorance of a quack, when he stood in the fairest point of rising, to the great satisfaction of Mr. Pelham, whom he rivalled and despised" (Walpole's *Memoirs*, i. 174). Again : "Winnington had unluckily lived when all virtue had been set to notorious sale, and in ridicule of false pretences had affected an honesty in avowing whatever was dishonourable" (iii. 66). (See also p. 11, l. 7 *supra*, and note.)

Page 70, l. 19. **Legge.** See p. 32, l. 16 *supra*, and note.

l. 29. **Montague**, Charles, Earl of Halifax (b. 1661, d. 1715), was born at Horton, in Northamptonshire; was educated at Westminster School, and at Trinity College, Cambridge; was appointed a lord of the Treasury in 1691, Chancellor of the Exchequer in 1694, and First Lord of the Treasury in 1697. On the accession of the Tory party he was impeached on a charge of peculation, etc., but these charges were dismissed. In 1714 he was again made Prime Minister. He reformed the currency, which had been reduced by clipping to far less than its normal value.

l. 30. **Godolphin**, Sidney, Earl of Godolphin (b. 1640, d. 1712), was educated at Oxford, and after the Restoration was made, by Charles II., a lord of the Treasury. In 1684 he became First

Lord of the Treasury. He was called to this office for the second time in 1690, and for a third time in 1700, and soon after the accession of Queen Anne he was appointed Lord High Treasurer. He was the intimate friend of the Duke of Marlborough, but passed gradually from the ranks of the Tory party into those of the Whigs; and after a long struggle with Harley was dismissed from office by the Queen in 1710.

l. 36. **House of Hapsburg**, a German princely family, to which belonged Maria Theresa.

House of Brandenburg. Brandenburg was a former margravate and electorate of the German Empire, the forerunner of the kingdom of Prussia.

Page 71, l. 1. **Silesia** was formerly a province of Poland; it was taken by the King of Hungary, 1478, and added to the Austrian dominion, 1526. It was conquered and lost several times during the Seven Years' War by Frederick II. of Prussia, but was retained by him at the peace in 1763.

l. 2. **the Main**, the most important of the right-hand tributaries of the Rhine.

l. 12. **commissary** (as a military term) is an officer or official that has charge of the supply of food, stores, and transport for a body of soldiers.

Prince Ferdinand. See p. 46, l. 32 *supra*, and note.

l. 15. **we borrowed, in four years of war**, etc. During the Seven Years' War (1756-1763) the National Debt was increased £53,141,024.

l. 28. **George Grenville.** See also p. 92, etc., *infra*.

Page 72, l. 5. **Vattel.** See p. 38, l. 24 *supra*, and note.

l. 20. **Onslow**, Arthur, was chosen Speaker of the House of Commons in 1728. During three-and-thirty years he filled that chair with higher merit, probably, than anyone either before or after him—with unequalled impartiality, dignity, and courtesy. He retired in 1761, and a vote was then passed acknowledging his services in the fullest terms, and another entreating the Crown to grant him some signal mark of its favour.

Page 73, l. 3. **the evil spirit whom Ovid described**, etc. The evil spirit is Envy, described in the *Metamorphoses* (Bk. ii., l. 760, etc.) as being sent by Minerva to taint with her poison Aglauros, the daughter of Cecrops. Ovid describes Envy's journey to Athens, and ends it thus (ll. 794-6):

" Et tandem Tritonida conspicit arcem,
Ingeniis opibusque, et festa pace virentem ;
Vixque tenet lacrimas ; qui nil lacrimabile cernit."

l. 30. **King of the Two Sicilies**, viz., the continental division of Naples and the Island of Sicily.

l. 31. **Maria Theresa**, the Archduchess of Austria, Queen of Hungary and Bohemia, and Empress of Germany. Other members of the coalition against her were Frederick the Great, the King of France, and the Elector of Bavaria; but England helped her to retain her rights.

Page 74, l. 22. **Havanna**, a seaport, and the citadel of Cuba, situated on a fine bay on the northern coast. It was taken by the English in 1762, but restored to Spain in 1763.

l. 23. **the Philippines**, or Philippine Islands, an archipelago lying between the China Sea on the west and the Pacific Ocean on the east; capital, Manilla.

Page 75, l. 15. **Gazette** (Fr. *gazette*, It. *gazzetta*, a Venetian coin, worth about ¾d., the price of the first newspaper at Venice), a newspaper: especially an official newspaper or journal published in London, Edinburgh, and Dublin, containing legal and state notices for the information of the public.

Page 76, l. 8. **No Newcastle salmon**. The Tyne was noted for its salmon.

l. 24. **Martinique**, an island of the lesser Antilles, West Indies; capital, Fort de France; chief port, St. Pierre. It now belongs to France, but at the end of the Seven Years' War and at two periods in the Napoleonic wars it was held by the English.

l. 28. **Manilla**. See p. 74, l. 23, **Philippines**, and note.

Page 77, l. 29. **Grub Street**, a London street still existing, but long known as Milton Street; it is in the parish of St. Giles, Cripplegate, and runs from Fore Street to Chiswell Street. Johnson explains it as "the name of a street in London much inhabited by writers of small histories, dictionaries, and temporary poems."

l. 33. **the starving poetasters of the Fleet**. *Poetaster* is a petty poet, a pitiful rhymester and writer of verses. *The Fleet* is the Fleet Prison, which, from 1641 till its destruction in 1846, was reserved entirely for debtors. These poetasters could not earn a livelihood by their miserable verses, and were consequently starving in the debtors' prison.

Page 79, l. 2. **Claremont**, an estate at Esher in Surrey, about 15 miles from London. In the reign of Anne, Vanbrugh purchased a piece of land here, and built himself a brick house of moderate dimensions, but in his usual fanciful style, and laid out the grounds with more than ordinary skill, if we may trust Garth's verses in *Claremont*:

"When Nature borrows dress from Vanbrugh's art."

This estate was afterwards bought by Thomas Pelham Holles, Earl of Clare (created Duke of Newcastle in 1715), who enlarged the grounds into a park, which Kent laid out, added a new wing to the house, and called the place after his then title, *Claremont*. The Duke died in 1768, and the following year Claremont was sold to Lord Clive, who pulled down the old mansion, and commissioned "Capability" Brown to erect a new and more magnificent one on the hill instead of the low site on which Vanbrugh's house stood. (*Handbook to the Environs of London*, by James Thorne.)

l. 14. **Lord Mansfield.** See p. 26, l. 14, **Murray**, and note.

l. 32. **The prime minister,** Lord Bute.

Lord Egremont was Secretary of State in Bute's ministry (1761), and again with Halifax in the ministry of George Grenville (1763). Chesterfield describes Lord Egremont as "proud, self-sufficient, but incapable." His speeches in Parliament, however, have been praised for their force and clearness. He had, moreover, besides his high rank and princely possessions, the advantage of a considerable following in the Tory party as the son of their late champion, Sir William Wyndham.

l. 34. **Sir Francis Dashwood,** created Baron le Despenser (d. 1781), the son of Sir Francis Dashwood by Lady Mary Fane, obtained his chief claim to celebrity in early life by his reckless immorality and profaneness. From such scenes as his "Franciscan Abbey" at Medmenham, Sir Francis was summoned to become Treasurer of the Chamber in 1761, in which office Bute found him so convenient a creature that on becoming Prime Minister he appointed him Chancellor of the Exchequer. Wilkes well understood the absurdity of the appointment when he said that "from puzzling all his life at tavern bills he was called by Lord Bute to administer the finances of a kingdom above one hundred millions in debt."

Page 80, l. 4. **the King over the water.** James II. and each of the Pretenders was toasted with this title by the Jacobites.

l. 21. **Hardwicke.** See p. 20, l. 34 *supra*, and note.

Page 81, l. 4. **cabal** (A.F. *cabala*, ad. med. L. *cab(b)ala*, It. Sp. Pg. *cabala*). (1) = Cabbala 1 : The Jewish tradition as to the interpretation of the Old Testament. (2) = Cabbala 2 : (*a*) Any tradition or special private interpretation. (*b*) A secret. (3) A secret or private intrigue of a sinister character formed by a small body of persons ; "something less than conspiracy " (J.). (4) A secret or private meeting, especially of intriguers or of a faction. *Arch.* or *obs*. (5) A small body of persons engaged in secret or private machination or intrigue ; a junto, clique, côterie, party, faction. (Murray.)

l. 33. **since the dagger of Felton had reached the heart of the Duke of Buckingham.** Felton entered the army at an early age, and served as a lieutenant under Sir Edward Cecil at Cadiz in 1625. Made reckless by poverty, and inflamed by the reading of the *Remonstrance of Parliament*, he assassinated (Aug. 23, 1628) the Duke of Buckingham, who had refused him the command of a company. (Cf. Dumas, *Les Trois Mousquetaires*.)

George Villiers, the first Duke of Buckingham, was the favourite both of James I. and Charles I.

Page 82, l. 2. **Strafford.** See p. 52, l. 24 *supra*, and note.

Falkland, Lucius Cary, Viscount (b. 1610, d. 1643), entered Parliament in 1640. On the trial of Strafford he interposed in behalf of moderation and delay. His purity and sensitiveness of character made him incapable of being a partisan, and also unfitted him for action in such stormy times. In 1641 the King succeeded, through the agency of Clarendon, in attaching Falkland to the Royalist cause, and made him Secretary of State. But Falkland distrusted the King and despised the Court, and the King feared him. Though he henceforth attended the King, his sympathies were on the side of freedom, and the distractions and calamities of his country broke his heart. He was among the first to fall at the first battle of Newbury (1643).

Clarendon, Edward Hyde, Earl of (b. 1608, d. 1674), was a zealous supporter of the King during the Civil War; he entered Parliament in 1640, and became Chancellor of the Exchequer, Privy Councillor, and chief adviser of the King. After the failure of the Royalist arms he joined Prince Charles in Holland; he contributed to the Restoration, accompanied Charles to London, and became Lord Chancellor. He was a staunch supporter of royalty, but at the same time the defender of his country's freedom from the abuses of kingly power. His *History of the Rebellion* is inaccurate, and not impartial.

Clifford, Thomas, Lord (b. 1630, d. 1673), was a member of the Cabal ministry in 1667, and took a prominent part in the Treaty of Dover, and in advocating the War with Holland. In 1672 he became Lord High Treasurer, but was compelled by the Test Act (1673) to resign this office (for he was one of the most zealous Catholics at Court), and shortly afterwards he died.

Shaftesbury, Anthony Ashley Cooper, Earl of (b. 1621, d. 1683), at the beginning of the Civil War sided with the King, but afterwards joined the Parliament. He sat in the Barebones and Protectorate Parliaments; was one of Cromwell's privy councillors, but subsequently quarrelled with Cromwell. He was sent to the Hague with Monk to invite Charles II. to return. For his services in bringing about the Restoration he was made a lord of the Treasury and Chancellor of the Exchequer. He was a prominent member of the Cabal ministry (1667). After the passing of the Test Act he joined the Opposition, and began intrigues with Monmouth. Owing to his violent opposition to the Crown he was sent to the Tower in 1677, and remained there for more than a year. When he again came into power he passed the Habeas Corpus Act, and supported the Exclusion Bill. He was again sent to the Tower on a charge of high treason in 1681; he was, however, acquitted and released. In the following year he was plotting with Sydney, Russell, and others, probably to place Monmouth on the throne. The conspiracy was discovered, and he fled to Holland, where he died. Dryden has satirised him thus:

"Of these, Achitophel was first,
A name to all succeeding ages curst;
For close designs and crooked counsels fit,
Sagacious, bold, and turbulent of wit,
Restless, unfixed in principles and place.
In power unpleased, impatient of disgrace;
A fiery soul, which working out its way,
Fretted the pigmy body to decay,
And o'er informed the tenement of clay.
A daring pilot in extremity,
Pleased with the danger, when the waves went high
He sought the storms: but for a calm unfit,
Would steer too nigh the sands to boast his wit."—Etc.

l. 3. **Lauderdale**, John Maitland, Duke of (b. 1616, d. 1682), took part with the Covenanters against the King, became one of the Scotch representatives in the Westminster Assembly, and commanded a Scotch infantry regiment at Marston Moor. In 1647 he was one of the Scotch Commissioners who signed the secret treaty with the King at Carisbrooke; he was with Charles II. at the battle of Worcester, and was taken prisoner and committed to the Tower. At the Restoration he obtained his liberty, and was appointed Secretary of State and High Commissioner of Scotland. For his attitude towards the Presbyterians of Fife and the South-west, see Scott's *Old Mortality*, Burton's *History of Scotland*, and Rankine's *History of England*. In 1670 he was a member of the Cabal ministry.

Danby, Thomas Osborne, Earl of (b. 1631, d. 1712), was appointed Lord Treasurer in 1673. It was by his advice that Charles II. persecuted the Nonconformists. In 1678 he was impeached by the Commons, and, though pardoned by the King, was committed to the Tower and not released till 1684. He joined in the invitation to the Prince of Orange in 1688, was named president of the Council in the following year, and in 1693 was created Duke of Leeds.

Temple, Sir William (b. 1628, d. 1699). See Macaulay's *Essays*, pp. 418-468.

Halifax. Macaulay refers to Sir George Savile, subsequently the first Marquis of Halifax (b. 1630, d. 1695), statesman, author, and orator, who was made Privy Councillor in 1672 for his services towards the restoration of Charles II. He was a papist, and on the accession of James II. was appointed President of the Council, but was dismissed for refusing his consent to the repeal of the Test Acts. He rejected the Exclusion Bill. In the Convention Parliament he was chosen speaker of the House of Lords, and at the accession of William and Mary was made Lord Privy Seal. He held this office from 1682-1685, and again in 1689. He wrote various political tracts, among which is one entitled, *Character of a Trimmer*. (See Macaulay's *History of England*, chap. ii.)

l. 3. **Rochester**, Lawrence Hyde, Earl of, was the second son of the great Earl of Clarendon ; he entered Parliament as member for the University of Oxford. He enjoyed the favour of Charles II., and was sent on various diplomatic missions to Paris, to John Sobieski, King of Poland, to the Imperial Court, and to the States of Holland. In 1679 he became First Lord of the Treasury. As a staunch Tory he opposed the Exclusion Bill. In 1684 he was removed from the Treasury through the influence of his rival Halifax. But on the accession of James II. Rochester was created Lord Treasurer, and practically Prime Minister. Rochester, however, was disinclined to support James II. in his efforts to restore Roman Catholicism ; he was in consequence dismissed, and his office was bestowed upon Sunderland.

In 1688 Rochester took the oath of allegiance to William III., and in 1700, through the influence of Harley, became Lord Lieutenant of Ireland. In Queen Anne's reign he acted as leader of the High Church Party, in 1710 was named Lord President of Harley's ministry, and died in 1711.

Sunderland. See p. 6, l. 17 *supra*, and note.

l. 11. **Carr**, Robert, Earl of Somerset, the favourite of James I., and murderer of Sir Thomas Overbury.

Villiers, George, Duke of Buckingham, the unworthy favourite of James I., by whom he was raised rapidly to the highest offices of the state. He conducted himself with so much pride and insolence as to excite popular hatred and disgust. In 1363, he accompanied Prince Charles on his visit to Spain to woo the Infanta. Through Buckingham's influence war broke out with Spain, and for the failure of the expedition to Cadiz he was impeached. He subsequently became the favourite minister of Charles I., and the ready instrument of his tyranny. For his death, see p. 81, l. 33 *supra*.

l. 20. **the Princess Mother**, Augusta of Saxe-Coburg, the wife of Frederick, Prince of Wales, and mother of George III.

l. 28. **The events of 1715 and of 1745.** See p. 63, l. 19 *supra*, and note.

l. 31. **barelegged mountaineers from the Grampians**, the 5000 Highlanders that marched with Charles Edward, the young

Pretender, as far south as Derby in 1745. The news of the arrival of this army at Derby reached London on Friday, the 6th of December, and that day was, therefore, known as Black Friday.

Page 83, l. 2. Temple Bar, a famous gateway before the Temple in London, which formerly divided Fleet Street from the Strand. It was removed in 1878 and re-erected at Waltham Cross, Herts.

l. 6. **Drummonds and Erskines, Macdonalds and Macgillivrays ... breeches.** These are names of families of Highlanders who spoke Gaelic and not English, who wore kilts and not trousers.

l. 14. **the princess in the Arabian tale ... Golden Fountain.** This is an allusion to the tale of "The Talking Bird" in the *Arabian Nights*.

l. 21. **Mæcenas,** the chief minister of Augustus, a great patron of literature, and friend of Horace and Virgil. Horace dedicates his first Ode to him, thus:

"Mæcenas atavis edite regibus
O et præsidium et dulce decus meum."

Cf. Hor. *Od.* II. xii. 9:
"tuque pedestribus
Dices historiis prœlia Cæsaris
Mæcenas."

And *Ep.* I. i. 1:
"Prima dicte mihi, summa dicende Camena."

l. 24. **Johnson,** Samuel, LL.D. (b. 1709, d. 1784), wrote *The Vanity of Human Wishes, Irene, Dictionary of the English Language, Rasselas, The Idler,* etc., etc. In 1762 he received from the King a pension of £300 a year, perhaps at the suggestion of Lord Bute. (See Macaulay's *Boswell's Life of Johnson,* in this series.)

l. 28. **Shebbeare,** John (b. 1709, d. 1788), a physician and political writer, was born at Bideford. He settled in London and began his career as a party writer. For his violence in this character he was pilloried once and imprisoned twice. Afterwards, under the administration of Lord Bute, he apostatised from the popular cause and obtained a pension. His chief works were *Letters to the People of England, The Marriage Act* (a satirical romance), *Lydia or Filial Piety, Letters on the English Nation,* and the *History of the Sumatrans* (a political satire).

l. 33. **Adam,** Robert, F.R.S. and F.S.A. (b. 1728, d. 1792), a celebrated architect, much employed upon the public buildings and noblemen's mansions of London. He and his brother built Adelphi Street, etc. At one time he represented the county of Kinross in Parliament.

l. 34. **Ramsay,** Allan (b. 1709, d. 1784), a Scottish portrait-painter, through the influence of Lord Bute was named first painter to George III. in 1767. His portraits of George III. and his Queen, Charlotte, have been acquired for the National Portrait Gallery.

l. 36. **Reynolds,** See p. 27, l. 5 *supra*, and note.

Mallet, David, a successful but unprincipled literary adventurer, was born about 1703. He came to London in 1723 as tutor to the family of the Duke of Montrose, and next year he published his ballad of "William and Margaret." He was the friend of Young, Pope, Thomson, and other eminent persons. He was patronised by Frederick, Prince of Wales. At the command of the Prince, he wrote, in conjunction with Thomson, the mask *Alfred*. In this mask was produced the song "Rule Britannia," but it is uncertain to which poet this song is to be attributed. He wrote also *Amyntor and Theodora, Truth in Rhyme, Gloria*. He died in 1765.

Page 84, l. 2. **John Home** (b. 1724, d. 1808), the author of *Douglas*, was born near Ancrum in Roxburghshire. Other works by him are *The Fatal Discovery, Alonzo*, and *Alfred*, as well as a *History of the Rebellion of 1745*.

l. 4. **the author of the Bard, and of the Elegy in a Country Churchyard** was Thomas Gray (b. 1716, d. 1771). In 1768 the Duke of Grafton presented him with the professorship of Modern History at Cambridge. In 1763 he had applied unsuccessfully for the professorship of Modern Languages.

l. 18. **chair,** a sedan.

l. 26. **A jack boot, generally accompanied by a petticoat.** The boot was a bad pun on Bute's name. The petticoat was the emblem of the Princess Mother.

l. 30. **Wilkes.** See p. 96 *infra*.

l. 31. **the mother of George the Third.** See p. 82, l. 20, **Princess Mother,** and note.

l. 32. **the mother of Edward the Third,** Isabella, Queen of Edward II., who, with her paramour, Roger Mortimer, deposed and imprisoned the King.

l. 33. **Churchill,** Rev. Charles (b. 1731, d. 1764), was at one time a clergyman, afterwards a town rake and associate of Wilkes. He wrote the *Prophecy of Famine*, which fanned into flame the old rancour between England and Scotland.

l. 35. **the Picts,** a people of disputed origin, who formerly inhabited the Highlands of Scotland and made frequent inroads into England. Their language was Celtic.

l. 36. **the Danes,** or the Northmen, were barbarians from Norway and Denmark, whose name was one of terror for many years to the peaceful dwellers in this country. We hear of the ravages of these sea-robbers in Northumbria before the end of the eighth century; but the first attack of the Danes in the south occurred in 832, in the reign of King Egbert, when a body of rovers sailed up the estuary of the Thames, plundered the Isle of Sheppey, and went off again in their ships with their booty.

Page 85, l. 2. in this year, etc., 1763.

l. 32. **Utopian.** In a work called *Utopia*, Sir Thomas More described an imaginary island as enjoying the greatest perfection in politics, laws, and the like. Utopia was an ideal state; hence *Utopian* means founded upon or involving imaginary perfection.

Page 86, l. 12. Henry Fox. See p. 26, l. 34, etc., *supra*.

l. 30. **Lady Sarah Lennox**, sister of the Duke of Richmond, and sister-in-law of Fox, was one of the most lovely women of the time. The King conceived a romantic passion for her. It was observed in the spring of 1761 that the King used almost every morning to ride along the Kensington Road while Lady Sarah, fancifully attired as a shepherdess, used to stand close by, on the lawn of Holland House, making hay. Finally, however, his Majesty, feeling the manifest objections that might attend his marriage with one of his own subjects, generously sacrificed his inclinations to the remonstrances of his mother and to the good of his people. Lady Sarah, on her part, with a high spirit suppressed whatever chagrin she may have felt. On the King's nuptials with the Princess of Mecklenburg she appeared as one of the bridesmaids. In the ensuing year Lady Sarah became the wife of Sir Charles Bunbury. (See Lord Mahon's *History*, chap. xli., and Lord Orford's *Memoirs of George III.*, vol. i., p. 64.)

Page 87, l. 4. the Princess of Mecklenburg, Charlotte, second sister of the Duke of Mecklenburg-Strelitz. "The character of this princess in after life, as Queen Consort of England for fifty-seven years, confirmed the soundness of the judgment which had raised her to that rank. An ever-present, yet unostentatious piety—to the King an affectionate reverence—to her children an unremitting care—prudence, economy, good sense and good temper were amongst her excellent qualities." (Lord Mahon, chap. xxxvii.)

Page 88, l. 2. Virgil's foot-race. Cf. *Aeneid*, v. 325, etc. Nisus, who is winning, trips up Salius, who is second, in order that his friend Euryalus may win the prize.

l. 28. **the ablest Prince of the blood.** Cf. p. 27, l. 1, **the Duke of Cumberland**, and note, *ad finem*.

Page 89, l. 22. his gold key, the badge of a Lord Chamberlain.

Page 90, l. 1. **tidewaiter**, p. 57, l. 23 *supra*, and note.

l. 2. **gauger**, an officer whose business it is to ascertain the contents of casks.

l. 4. **the Duke of Grafton**, the Duke of Newcastle, and the Marquis of Rockingham were dismissed from the Lord-Lieutenancies of their several counties in 1768.

l. 18. **patents.** All grants of offices, honours, pensions, and particulars of individual and corporate privileges received from the Sovereign are contained in charters, or letters-patent, that is open letters, *litterae patentes*. They were so-called because they are not sealed, but exposed to open view with the great seal pendent from the bottom, and were supposed to be of a public nature, and addressed to all the King's subjects.

l. 21. **Tellers of the Exchequer.** See p. 35, l. 25 *supra*, and note.

Justices in Eyre, *i.e. in itinere*, on journey. Henry II. divided England into circuits, and justices went on these circuits once in seven years. The courts in which they sat were called *assizes* (akin to Lat. *assideo*); Magna Charta provided for annual visits. In 1284 justices in eyre were superseded by judges of assize.

Page 91, l. 23. **the favourite**, Lord Bute.

l. 27. **a tax on cider** was proposed by Sir Francis Dashwood in the Budget of 1763. The amount was ten shillings on the hogshead, to be paid by the first buyer.

l. 32. **The Tory Johnson ... Excise.** The definition was "a hateful tax levied on commodities and adjudged not by the common judges of property, but by wretches hired by those to whom excise is paid."

Page 92, l. 1. **John Phillips** (b. 1676, d. 1708), wrote *The Splendid Shilling*, a burlesque of Milton's *Paradise Lost*, *Blenheim*, also in imitation of Milton, and *Cyder* in imitation of Virgil's *Georgics*.

l. 2. **the Cider-land had ever been faithful to the throne.** Its loyalty was chanted by Philips thus:

"Oh Charles! oh best of kings!

. . . .

Yet was the Cyder-land unstained with guilt;
The Cyder-land, obsequious still to thrones,
Abhorred such base, disloyal deeds, and all
Her pruning-hooks extended into swords!"

l. 11. **Dashwood.** See **tax on cider**, p. 91, l. 27 *supra*; also p. 79, l. 34, and note.

l. 31. "**Gentle Shepherd, tell me where.**" *The Gentle Shepherd* is the title of a Scotch pastoral comedy or dramatic poem by Allan Ramsay, published in 1725.

Page 93, l. 28. Lord Mansfield. See p. 26, l. 14 *supra*, and note.

Page 94, l. 31. his father-in-law. Bute married Mary, the daughter of Mr. Wortley Montagu, a gentleman of immense property, and the husband of the celebrated Lady Mary Wortley Montagu.

l. 33. He had obtained ... a British peerage for his son. His son was Lord Mount-Stuart.

Page 95, l. 3. Fox ... took refuge in the House of Lords as the first Lord Holland.

Page 96, l. 5. Mayor of the Palace. These officers existed from an early date among the Franks. The *major domus* was originally, as the name implies, the King's principal domestic, the master or comptroller of the household. He superintended the interior concerns of the palace, and exercised a certain authority over the leudes or antrustions, the confidential companions and vassals of the King. It was his duty to maintain order within the precincts of the court, to decide disputes among the nobles, and to direct the general economy of the royal establishment. The appointment was, of course, vested in the King, and held during his pleasure. Gradually, however, and in consequence of the jealousy which arose between the crown and the aristocracy, the Mayor of the Palace became the leader of the aristocratical faction and usurped political power; and by successive encroachments the office was at length wrested from the King and became elective in the hands of the nobles. A rival power was thus constituted in the State, the inevitable tendency of which was to supplant and overturn the Merovingian dynasty. Pepin of Landen, Pepin of Heristal, Ebroin, and Charles Martel were Mayors of the Palace. (See *The Student's France*, p. 56, etc.)

l. 6. A mere Childeric or Chilperic. Childeric was King of the Franks (about 458 to 481), but was deposed by his subjects to make way for Ægidius, the Roman general. After eight years' retirement to Thuringia he was recalled to his kingdom. Chilperic was King of Neustria (561 to 584); he, too, was condemned to lose his crown at the command of his subjects in consequence of the murder of his Queen, Galeswintha, and the advancement of his mistress, Fredegonda. He was afterwards replaced on the throne. "A mere Childeric or Chilperic" therefore denotes a monarch that is entirely at the mercy of his subjects, and holds his crown only so long as they permit.

l. 22. Aylesbury, one of the chief towns of Buckinghamshire.

Page 97, l. 11. The Times, our leading newspaper, founded in 1785 by John Walter, under the title of *The London Daily Universal Register*. The present name was adopted in 1788.

l. 11. Morning Chronicle was started in 1769 by William Woodfall, who combined all the functions of editor, reporter, and printer. In 1789 he was succeeded by James Perry. During the latter's régime such men as Coleridge, Lord Campbell, Campbell the poet, Sir James Mackintosh, Porson, and Hazlitt were contributors to *The Chronicle*. Perry died in 1821, and was succeeded in the editorship by John Black. Charles Dickens made his debût in newspaper work by contributing *Sketches by Boz* in 1835 to the *Evening Chronicle*. The paper, however, gradually decreased in circulation until it expired altogether (about 1860), after at one time having a very fair opportunity of rivalling *The Times*.

l. 21. **Court of Common Pleas** in ancient times followed the King's person and is distinct from that of the King's Bench. But on the confirmation of Magna Charta by King John in 1215, it was fixed at Westminster, and it continued to sit there until the new Law Courts were built in the Strand.

Chief Justice Pratt. See p. 60, l. 11 *supra*, and note.

l. 24. **the cider counties**, Worcestershire and Herefordshire.

Page 98, l. 10. **Buckingham House** or Palace, the royal residence at the western end of St. James's Park. It was settled by Act of Parliament in 1775 upon Queen Charlotte, and was hence known as the "Queen's House." It was remodelled under George IV., and considerable additions have been made by Queen Victoria, who began to occupy it in 1837.

l. 25. **Lord Hardwicke.** See p. 20, l. 34 *supra*, and note.

Page 99, l. 14. **Cornet Joyce**, leader of the 500 troops that in June, 1647, seized the person of Charles I., while in the custody of the Parliament at Holmby House.

President Bradshaw was President of the Court of 150 Commissioners appointed to try Charles I., and also the first President of the Council of State formed in 1648 after the execution of the King.

l. 19. **Pope's Essay on Man** is in four epistles, the first and second of which—"Of the Nature and State of Man, with respect to the Universe," and "Of the Nature and State of Man, with respect to Himself as an Individual"—appeared in 1732; the third epistle—"Of the Nature and State of Man, with respect to Society"—appeared in 1733; and the fourth—"Of the Nature and State of Man, with respect to Happiness"—appeared in 1734.

l. 20. **the Essay on Woman**, by John Wilkes and Thomas Potter (second son of the Archbishop of Canterbury), appeared in 1763. This work has little wit or talent to make amends for the blasphemy and lewdness with which it abounds. The *Essay on Man* was inscribed to Bolingbroke, and began, "Awake, my

St. John"; the parody was inscribed to Lord Sandwich, and began, "Awake, my Sandwich."

l. 21. Warburton's famous Commentary. William Warburton, Bishop of Gloucester (b. 1698, d. 1779), wrote *A Vindication of Pope's Essay on Man* (1740), and a Commentary on the same work (1742).

Page 100, l. 2. Lord March, afterwards Duke of Queensberry, is mentioned by Thackeray as one of the correspondents of George Selwyn, and as one "whose life lasted into this century; and who, certainly as Earl or Duke, young man or grey beard, was not an ornament to any possible society."

l. 12. He picked a quarrel with one of Lord Bute's dependents, etc. This was Mr. Samuel Martin, who had been Secretary of the Treasury under both the Duke of Newcastle and Lord Bute. (See Mahon, ch. xlii.)

l. 25. **catch,** a humorous canon or round, so contrived that the singers catch up each other's sentences.

l. 27. **the Beggar's Opera,** by John Gay (1688-1732), first acted at Lincoln's Inn Fields in 1727, was the first and perhaps the best specimen of English ballad opera. It was, indeed, so successful and popular that "It made Rich the manager gay, and Gay the poet rich."

l. 28. **Macheath** is the highwayman hero of *The Beggar's Opera*, "a fine, gay, bold-faced ruffian," as Scott calls him, "who is game to the last."

l. 29. "**That Jemmy Twitcher should peach me I own surprised me**" is in Act iii. *ad finem*, and is spoken by Macheath to Ben Budge and Mat of the Mint. *Peach* means to accuse of crime, to inform against (akin to *impeach*).

Page 101, l. 10. general warrants. In the early part of the eighteenth century, when an offence had been committed against the Government, general warrants were issued for the apprehension, not of individuals specified by name, but of any persons whom the public officers might, on investigating the matter, suspect of having been concerned in it. Such a warrant was issued for the apprehension of all persons concerned in the authorship, printing, and publication of No. 45 of the *North Briton*, under which forty-nine persons, including Wilkes himself, were arrested on suspicion and committed. Wilkes, being a member of the House of Commons, was released by a writ of *Habeas Corpus*, and actions were immediately brought by him against the Under-Secretary of State, and, also under his directions, by the committed printers against the messengers that had arrested them. In the course of these latter actions Lord Mansfield and the other judges of the King's Bench pronounced the warrant illegal, declaring that no degree of antiquity could give sanction to a usage bad in itself. This decision gave a death-blow to general warrants.

l. 28. **Henry Conway** was leader of the English centre of Prince Ferdinand's army at Kirch-Denkern in 1761, when the French, under Duke de Broglie, were repulsed with great loss. In April, 1764, because he had given a conscientious vote against the Government on the question of general warrants, he was deprived both of his post in the royal bedchamber, and also of his regiment. But in 1765 he was not only recalled, but was made Secretary of State along with the Duke of Grafton in Rockingham's ministry.

Page 103, l. 5. **the treaty negotiated by St. John**, the peace of Utrecht, 1713.

l. 6. **the treaty negotiated by Bedford**, the peace of Paris, 1762.

l. 23. **Hayes** is in Kent, twelve miles S.E. from London. Close by the church is Hayes Place, at one time the residence of Pitt. When purchased by Pitt in 1757, Hayes Place was an old mansion, formerly the seat of the Scotts, afterwards of the Harrisons, with a very few acres of ground attached. Chatham pulled down the house and built a new one, and added about one hundred acres to the grounds, which he laid out in a way to extort the warm praise of Horace Walpole. Here the younger William Pitt was born, May 28th, 1759. On coming into possession of Burton Pynsent in 1766, Pitt sold Hayes Place to the Hon. Thomas Walpole, but he soon repented; and when the following year he was prostrated by illness he became possessed with the belief that only the air and scenery of Hayes would save him. At length, somewhat reluctantly, Mr. Walpole consented to reconvey the property to him. And here Pitt spent most of the rest of his life, and died, May 11th, 1779. (*Handbook of the Environs of London*, by James Thorne.)

Page 104, l. 22. **Statute Book** contains all Acts of Parliament printed at full length.

Term Reports contain accounts of all the cases tried in various courts, with the decision of the judge in each case. They, therefore, supply interpretations of doubtful points contained in the Statute Book.

l. 32. **from the shore of the Great Lakes to the Mexican Sea.** The great lakes are Lake Superior, Lake Michigan, Lake Huron, and Lake Erie.

Page 106, l. 3. **junta.** See p. 28, l. 4, **junto**, and note.

l. 13. **Coligni** was taken prisoner by the Spaniards at the siege of St. Quentin. He and the Prince of Condé were defeated by the Duke of Guise at the Battle of Dreux. He suffered defeat also at Jarnac and Moncontour, and was murdered in the massacre of St. Bartholomew (24th August, 1570).

William the Third was defeated by the Prince of Condé at Senef. He suffered defeat also at Steenkirk and Neerwinden. He was, however, victorious against James II. at the battle of the Boyne, while the resistance of the Scotch was crushed at Killiecrankie. But Macaulay's statement is more or less true of his campaigns on the continent.

l. 14. **Marshal Soult** was wounded and taken prisoner by the Germans at Genoa in 1799. He was repulsed with loss from the walls of Corunna in 1808. He suffered defeat by Wellington at the Douro, by Beresford at Albuera; and between 1813 and 1815 he suffered many reverses at Bayonne, in the Pyrenees, on the Nive, at Orthez, Toulouse, and Waterloo.

l. 30. **Potsdam**, the capital of the Government district of Potsdam, province of Brandenburg, Prussia, situated at the junction of the Nuthe with the Havel, sixteen miles south-west of Berlin.

Page 107, l. 2. **gaugers.** See p. 90, l. 2, *supra*, and note.

Page 108, l. 15. **Extinxti te meque,** etc. See *Aeneid*, iv. 683-4. This is part of the lament of Anna, the sister of Dido, for the death of the latter.

l. 27. **Spitalfields weavers,** etc. In 1765, on the very day that the Regency Bill was passed, there came up for discussion in the Lords a measure which had been carried through the Commons with little notice. It was for imposing as high duties on Italian silks as were paid on the French. The purpose of this Bill was, of course, to obtain as far as possible a total prohibition of foreign silks. The Duke of Bedford spoke against the measure, and it was thrown out. In spite of this the Spitalfields weavers appeared at Whitehall in unruly numbers, carrying red and black flags, and shouting invectives against the Peers. They stopped many of their Lordships' carriages, amongst others those of the Chancellor. They then proceeded to lay siege to Bedford House, on the north side of Bloomsbury Square. The military were then called out, the Riot Act was read, and the mob dispersed by a party of cavalry.

Page 109, l. 3. **Mr. Mackenzie.** James Stuart Mackenzie, Lord Bute's brother, held the office of Privy Seal of Scotland. Grenville and his brother Ministers insisted, in 1765, upon the dismissal of Mr. Mackenzie. The King yielded most reluctantly to this demand; but he surrendered at last, for he felt that he ought not, for the sake of one private gentleman, to run the risk of plunging the whole realm into confusion.

l. 11. **Isle of Wight.** In November, 1647, Charles I. took refuge in the Isle of Wight, where he remained till November, 1648, to all intents and purposes a prisoner in Carisbrook Castle; he was then carried off by a troop of soldiers to Hurst Castle.

l. 18. **The Duke of Devonshire,** etc. See p. 2, l. 26, **Duke of Newcastle,** *supra*, and note.

Page 111, l. 4. **Hampden at Chalgrove.** See p. 2, l. 36, *supra*, and note.

l. 5. **Russell on the scaffold in Lincoln's Inn Fields.** William Russell (b. 1639, d. 1683) was the third son of the fifth Earl (later the first Duke) of Bedford. His elder brothers died before him, and he was often known by the courtesy title of Lord Russell. He became an active member of "The Country Party" in 1673; a leading opponent of Danby and the Duke of York; a privy councillor (1678-80) and supporter of the Exclusion Bill. The Court Party brought an action against him for high treason. He was tried and condemned for pretended complicity in the Rye House Plot. He was beheaded in Lincoln's Inn Fields, July 23, 1683.

l. 10. **Lord John Cavendish**, the youngest of the Duke of Devonshire's brothers, was well-read, held in just esteem for his truth and honour, and resolute in his views, though shy and bashful in his manner. "Under the appearance of virgin modesty," says Horace Walpole, "he had a confidence in himself that nothing could equal." Burke, however, had no great opinion of Lord John's abilities or application. He wishes that his friend could be induced to "show a degree of regular attendance on business," and he adds, "Lord John ought to be allowed a certain decent and reasonable portion of fox hunting; but anything more is intolerable."

l. 11. **Sir George Savile** was one of the members for Yorkshire, 1768, and brought forward a measure commonly called the Nullum Tempus Bill, for securing the property of a subject at any time after sixty years' possession from any dormant pretension of the Crown. Ten years later he proposed, and Dunning seconded, the Roman Catholic Relief Bill. In 1779 he vigorously but unsuccessfully opposed Wedderburn's measure to suspend for six months all exemptions from impressment into the Royal Navy. In 1780 he supported Rockingham in his plans for Economical Reform. He attended the Great Meeting at York, and afterwards presented to the House of Commons the great Yorkshire petition praying for reduction of all exorbitant emoluments, and for the abolition of all sinecure places; he moved that the names at least of all holders of pensions for life, or patent places, should be laid before the House. During the Gordon Riots his house (Savile House, in Leicester Square) was attacked, looted, and burned. Savile was through the whole of his political career distinguished for upright and unsuspected independence.

l. 15. **Marquess of Rockingham's** inability to express his opinions in debate was so great that he could seldom be persuaded or provoked to rise. One night, after Lord Sandwich had been plying him in vain with much raillery and eloquence,

Lord Gower whispered—"Sandwich, how could you worry the poor dumb creature so?" In estimating his worth as a statesman, we must remember that he had the advantage of following one of the most unpopular of Ministers, and of employing, as his private secretary, Edmund Burke, whose genius has cast a flood of light upon his administration, and imparted a somewhat deceptive splendour to his memory. (See Mahon and Lecky.)

Page 112, l. 14. Dowdeswell, Mr. William, "was acknowledged to be well-informed and upright, but there was some foundation for the epithet—'dull Dowdeswell'—which Lord Chatham once applied to him." (Mahon.)

l. 15. **General Conway.** See p. 101, l. 28 *supra*, and note.

l. 20. **Augustus Duke of Grafton** (b. 1735, d. 1811) was appointed Secretary of State in 1765, but the following year he resigned, and soon after became Lord of the Treasury, which post he held till 1770. During his administration he was frequently attacked in the letters of Junius. (See also p. 90, l. 4, *supra*.)

l. 26. **Charles Townshend.** See p. 8, l. 25 *supra*.

l. 28. **mere lutestring; pretty summer wear.** Lutestring, a lustrous silk; "the price of lutestring" (*Spectator*, No. 21). A curious corruption of lustring or lustrine; "lustring or lutestring, a sort of silk" (Kersey). F. *lustrin*, lustring (Hamilton). Ital. *lustrino*, lutestring (a shining silk), tinsel (Meadows), so-called from its glossiness. Ital. *lustrare*, to shine. Lat. *lustrare*, to shine. (Skeat.)

Page 113, l. 1. a little treatise. Edmund Burke's *Philosophical Inquiry into the Origin of our Ideas of the Sublime and Beautiful*, published in 1756.

l. 7. **Turk's Head**, the name of several coffee-houses formerly in London, one of which on the Strand was frequented by Dr. Johnson and other celebrities of the eighteenth century.

l. 8. **Dr. Johnson.** See p. 83, l. 24 *supra*, and note.

l. 18. **Edmund Burke** (b. 1729, d. 1797) was educated at Trinity College, Dublin, entered the Middle Temple, and coming to London in 1750 began literary work. He wrote *A Vindication of Natural Society* (1756); *A Philosophical Inquiry into the Origin of our Ideas of the Sublime and Beautiful* (1757). In 1758 he projected the *Annual Register*, and for some years wrote the whole of it. In 1765 he became Lord Rockingham's private secretary, and entered Parliament as member for Wendover. He took a leading part in debate, and distinguished himself by his speeches on the American question, on Catholic emancipation, on economical reform, and on the prosecution of Warren Hastings. He subsequently became Paymaster of the Forces and Privy Councillor. He retired from Parliament in 1794. Other writings of his are *Reflections on the French Revolution* (1790), *Letters on a Regicide Peace* (1796-7), *Letters to a Noble Lord* (1796).

l. 35. **Gazette.** See p. 75, l. 15 *supra*, and note.

Page 114, l. 29. **Charles's writ of shipmoney.** See p. 69, l. 15 *supra*, and note.

l. 30. **James's proclamation dispensing with the penal laws.** James II. had appointed certain officers in the army who were Roman Catholics. This was in direct violation of the Test Act. The Parliament, in November, 1686, respectfully informed the King that he had committed an illegal act. James then laid claim to a dispensing power, which was in fact an assertion of the sovereign's rights to abrogate express laws by the exercise of his prerogative, and to render the Monarchy absolute.

The powers of the Crown as to interference with legislation were finally determined by the Bill of Rights (I. Will. and Mar., sc. ii., ch. ii.), which laid down as follows: "That the pretended power of dispensing with laws, or the execution of laws by regall authority, as it hath been assumed and exercised of late is illegall."

Page 115, l. 5. **Lombard Street,** a street in the City, London, where the Lombard merchants of the Middle Ages established themselves before the reign of Edward II. It has always been an important commercial centre, and is now a great banking centre.

l. 9. **the Toleration Act** was passed in 1689 and granted liberty of worship to dissenting ministers, provided (1) they took the oath of allegiance to the sovereign ; (2) an oath in repudiation of the doctrine that princes excommunicated by the Pope might be deposed or murdered ; (3) they signed a declaration that no foreign prince, prelate, or potentate had or ought to have any ecclesiastical or spiritual jurisdiction within the realm ; (4) they subscribed a declaration against transubstantiation and the invocation of saints.

the Habeas Corpus Act, passed in 1679 (st. 31, Car. 2, c. 2) through the efforts of Shaftesbury, enacted that prisoners must be produced in court for trial within a limited period, varying from three to twenty days, according to the distance to be traversed ; that no one must be imprisoned beyond the seas ; and that once tried and acquitted no one shall be committed to prison again on the same charge.

ll. 17-20. **doctrines ... inculcated by Burke, in orations, etc.** See Burke's *Speech on American Taxation* and *Speech on Conciliation with America* in this series.

l. 23. **the waters of Bath.** Bath, a town in Somersetshire, situated on the Avon, was the Roman Aquæ Solis (baths of the sun). It is one of the leading watering places in England, noted for its saline and chalybeate hot spring. It was a very fashionable resort in the eighteenth century, owing in a great measure to the influence of Beau Nash.

l. 26. **Massachusetts and Virginia.** Massachusetts is the most northern of the New England States; capital, Boston. Virginia is one of the southern States; capital, Richmond.

l. 31. **Strafford ... resistance to the liturgy of Edinburgh.** The forcing of the Liturgy on Scotland produced the enthusiastic resistance of the Covenanters in 1638. (See also p. 52, l. 24, **Strafford, and note.**)

Page 116, l. 16. **the King's friends. The character of this faction has been drawn by Burke.** See *Thoughts on the Cause of the Present Discontents.*

Page 117, l. 29. **Dodington.** See p. 4, l. 2 *supra*, and note.

l. 30. **Sheridan,** Richard Brinsley (b. 1751, d. 1816), a distinguished statesman, wit, and dramatist, was educated at Harrow and at the Middle Temple, but was not called to the Bar. His first dramatic work was *The Rivals* (1775), followed by *The Duenna* (1775), *School for Scandal* (1777), and *The Critic* (1779). In 1780 he entered Parliament as member for Stafford. He attained great celebrity as an orator, especially during the impeachment of Warren Hastings. In 1806 he became Treasurer of the Navy and a Privy Councillor. He had been the boon companion of the Prince Regent, and on the passing of the Regency Bill he was admitted to extraordinary intimacy and confidence by the Regent. At the General Election of 1806 he was chosen member for Westminster. The latter part of his life was embittered by misfortunes, the fruit of his own improvidence, and much of it was spent in miserable attempts to avoid his creditors. But his name will live as one of the most brilliant of perhaps the most brilliant group of orators the world has ever seen.

Page 118, l. 25. **sycophant** (Gr. συκοφάντης from σῦκον, a fig, and φαίνειν, to show), (1) originally an informer in Athens, who sought favour by denouncing those that stole figs, or exported them contrary to law, etc. (2) A tale-bearer or informer generally (*obs.*). (3) A base parasite; a flatterer of princes and great men: hence also a deceiver, an impostor.

Page 120, l. 29. **The House of Commons ... condemning the use of general warrants ... condemning the seizure of papers in case of libel.** In 1765 Lord Camden, as Chief Justice of the Common Pleas, decided in the case of Entick v. Carrington that a Secretary of State had no power to issue *a general search warrant* for the discovery and seizure of a person's books and papers. (See also p. 101, l. 10, **general warrants,** and note.)

O

Page 121, l. 13. **prorogation** (Lat. *prorogatio*), the continuance of parliament from one session to another ; adjournment.

Page 122, l. 16. **a peerage on ... Chief Justice Pratt.** Charles Pratt was raised to the peerage as Earl Camden in 1765.

l. 28. **Rigby.** See p. 59, l. 10 *supra*, and note.

Wedderburn, Alexander, afterwards Lord Loughborough, and later still Earl of Rosslyn (b. 1733, d. 1805), at the beginning of his political career attached himself to his countryman, Lord Bute, whose star was then in the ascendant. By Lord Bute's influence was he brought into parliament, and with Lord Bute's bodyguard was he numbered. As such he was lashed by Churchill in one of his satires :

"A pert prim prater of the Northern race,
Guilt in his heart, and famine in his face,
Mute at the Bar and in the Senate loud," etc.

After Bute's retirement from office Wedderburn joined the Opposition. But when at last Lord North proposed to him to become Solicitor-General, the pleasing offer was readily accepted. "This must be confessed," says Lord Campbell, "to be one of the most flagrant cases of *ratting* recorded in our party annals."

Page 123, l. 4. **Locke.** See p. 52, l. 18 *supra*, and note.

Sidney. See p. 53, l. 6 *supra*, and note.

l. 9. **Ormond,** James Butler, second Duke of, was grandson of the Duke of Ormond that strenuously tried to uphold the authority of Charles I. in Ireland. He was brought up a Tory, but joined the Prince of Orange on his arrival in England; became his intimate friend, and served under him in Ireland and in Flanders. He was in favour with Queen Anne, and after the disgrace of Marlborough became her Commander-in-Chief. He was a strong Tory, but of no military ability.

l. 30. **Wallenstein,** the hero of a drama, called after his name, published by Schiller in 1799. It has been translated into English by Coleridge.

l. 36. **a villa at Hampstead,** called at that time *North End House* (now known as *Wildwood House*). Chatham was here in 1766 and again during the period when he remained "inaccessible and invisible," and "afflicted by a strange and mysterious malady ... able at intervals to take the air upon the heath, but still at all times inaccessible to all his friends." This time he came to North End shattered in health, March, 1767 ; but, deriving no benefit, returned to Burton Pynsent in September. Whilst here, though Prime Minister, he "would see no one on business, except once the Duke of Grafton, at the King's urgent entreaty." (Mahon and Horace Walpole.)

Page 124, l. 3. **Bengal.** See p. 45, l. 19 *supra*, and note.

l. 4. **Tanjore** is a district of British India in the Madras presidency. It is known as the garden of South India, being well watered by an elaborate system of dams, cuts and canals in connection with the rivers Cauvery and Coleroon. It belonged to the Mahrattas from 1678 to 1799, when it was ceded to the East India Company.

Burton Pynsent, the estate in Somersetshire, left to Pitt by Sir William Pynsent.

Page 125, l. 13. **Lewis the Fourteenth**, King of France, called the "Grand Monarque," a haughty despot, whose characteristic saying was, "L'Etat, c'est moi."

l. 26. **that family league which was now the favourite plan at Stowe**, a reconciliation between Chatham and the Grenvilles. Stowe is a village in Buckinghamshire, three miles north-west of Buckingham. Stowe House was the seat of Lord Temple. This estate belongs to the same family still, the Duke of Buckingham being its present owner. It was, during his exile from France, the home of the Comte de Paris, who died there a few months ago. The grounds of Stowe House are laid out in a most elaborate fashion, and are ornamented with several temples which Macaulay here calls "pavilions and summer houses."

Page 126, l. 10. **In spite of all these difficulties, a ministry was made ... which ... contained no four persons who had ever in their lives been in the habit of acting together.** Burke has described this "chequered and speckled" administration with great humour, speaking of it as "indeed a very curious show, but utterly unsafe to touch and unsure to stand on."

l. 22. **Pratt, now Lord Camden.** See p. 60, l. 12 *supra*, and note.

l. 23. **Lord Shelburne.** See p. 17, l. 25 *supra*, and note.

l. 24. **Duke of Grafton.** See p. 90, l. 4 *supra*, and note.

l. 26. **Conway.** See p. 101, l. 28 *supra*, and note.

Page 127, l. 9. **On the very day on which the new prime minister kissed hands**, *i.e.* of his sovereign.

Page 128, l. 2. **the Monument**, a column in London, north of the Thames, near London Bridge. It was erected to commemorate the great fire of 1666, and stands close to the spot where the conflagration started. It was built by Wren, and is 202 feet high.

l. 9. **William Pulteney.** See p. 7, l. 33, *supra*, and note.

l. 21. **Versailles**, the capital of the department of Seine-et-Oise, about eleven miles south-west of Paris, is noted for its famous palace, for many years the home of the royal family of France.

l. 21. **St. Ildefonso**, a village, containing La Granja, a royal palace of the King of Spain, in old Castile, built in a mountainous country, by Philip V., in imitation of Versailles.

Page 129, l. 3. **Saunders**, Admiral Sir Charles, was present with the fleet in America when Wolfe took Quebec, and was paid some well-earned compliments by Pitt. Immediately on his return from America, without waiting for orders, he sailed from Plymouth to join Hawke at Quiberon and take part in that action, but arrived too late.

Keppel, Augustus (b. 1725, d. 1786), accompanied Commodore Anson round the world, and afterwards rose through all the ranks of the service to be Admiral. In 1778 he commanded the Channel fleet, which engaged the French fleet off Ushant: Keppel expected to renew the action on the next day, but the enemy had retired. This affair gave great dissatisfaction to the nation, which was aggravated by Sir Hugh Palliser, the second in command, preferring charges against Keppel for misconduct and incapacity in the recent action. The Court Martial, however, decided that, far from having sullied the honour of the service, Keppel had acted in all respects as became a judicious, brave, and experienced officer.

l. 6. **The Duke of Portland** was afterwards the head of the Coalition Ministry of 1783.

l. 7. **Lord Besborough, Postmaster**, resigned this office very soon, in consequence of Chatham's overbearing behaviour and language to him, which provoked Conway to exclaim that "such language had never been held westward of Constantinople."

l. 32. **In a few months they were able to dictate their own terms.** See p. 131 and p. 134, etc., *infra*.

l. 36. **The harvest had been bad.** This was in 1766. Chesterfield writes on the 1st of August of that year: "There never was so wet a summer as this has been in the memory of man; we have not had one single day since March without some rain, and most days a great deal."

Page 130, l. 2. **embargo** (from the Spanish and Portuguese *embarga* to hinder or detain, the root of which is the same as that of *bar*, barricade) is in its special sense a detention of vessels in a port; it also means an order from Government forbidding the departure of goods from a port.

l. 5. **At last an act was passed to indemnify**, etc. "The Opposition, urged especially by Earl Temple in one House and by Mr. Grenville in the other, called for an Act of Indemnity to the ministers. This the ministers at first disdained and refused, but finally accepted and passed." (Lord Mahon.)

l. 12. **He bade defiance,** etc. In one of the stages of the Bill (of Indemnity) Lord Chatham spoke for the second time, and took occasion in his most lofty tone to say that he would set his face against even the proudest connection in the land. These words of the great Dictator (as his enemies now began to call him) gave much offence and drew him into a short but angry altercation with the Duke of Richmond. "I hope," cried Richmond, "the nobility will not be brow-beaten by an insolent minister." (See Lord Mahon's *History,* and Lord Orford's *Memoirs of George III.*)

l. 18. **browbeat,** to bear down with haughty looks or with arrogant speech.

Page 131, l. 2. **Alderman Beckford** was a man of neglected education, noted in the House of Commons for his loud tones and faulty Latin, but upright and fearless and ever prompt and ready; and of much commercial weight and especial popularity in the City of London, which he represented in Parliament.

l. 5. **Burke thundered against the ministers.** He painted Lord Chatham as a great "Invisible Power that had left no minister in the House of Commons." "But perhaps," he cried, "this House is not the place where our reasons can be of any avail. This great person who is to determine on this question may be a being far above our view; one so immeasurably high that the greatest abilities" (here he indicated Townshend), "or the most amiable disposition" (here he pointed to Conway), "may not gain access to him; a being before whom thrones, dominations, princedoms, virtues, powers" (here he waved his hands over the whole Treasury Bench behind which he sat), "all veil their faces with their wings." (Lord Orford's *Memoirs of George III.*)

l. 12. **when he reached the Castle Inn at Marlborough ... Footmen and grooms ... livery.** Lord Mahon denies the truth of this story.

Page 133, l. 1. **malingering** (Fr. *malingre* from *mal,* and O. Fr. *haingre,* akin to Lat. *æger*), feigning to be ill in order to avoid duty.

Page 134, l. 34. **Lord North,** Frederick North, Earl of Guildford, generally known as Lord North (b. 1732, d. 1792), was educated at Eton and at Trinity College, Oxford. He was in 1767 appointed Chancellor of the Exchequer, and in 1770 First Lord of the Treasury.

l. 36. **Corsica,** under Pascal Paoli, had risen in insurrection against the rule of the Genoese. So long and so successful was this resistance that in May 1768 the Genoese concluded a treaty with the Duke de Choiseul agreeing to cede their rights on Corsica for a sum of money to France. Large reinforcements were then sent from France, and Paoli, notwithstanding a resolute resistance, was overpowered, and Corsica was thus conquered by the French without any interference on the part of England.

Page 135, l. 23. **Junius** was the assumed name of a writer of a series of letters in the *Public Advertiser*. These letters contained attacks on most men in high places, *e.g.* the Duke of Grafton, Lord Granby, the Duke of Bedford, Lord Mansfield, etc., etc. The mystery of the authorship of these letters has never been solved beyond question; but they are generally attributed to Sir Philip Francis.

Sir William Draper was a General in the Army and Knight of the Bath, who took up the cudgels against Junius in defence of Lord Granby.

l. 24. **Blackstone,** Sir William, often called Doctor Blackstone because he practised in Doctors Commons, was in 1769 Solicitor-General and Member for Westbury. He was the author of *Commentaries on the Laws of England*. In the House of Commons he maintained the legal incapacity of Wilkes. He was answered by Mr. Grenville from a passage of those Commentaries, where all the rightful grounds of disqualification were enumerated, and where no such case as Wilkes's was assigned. Junius assailed him thus: "For the defence of truth, of law and reason, the Doctor's book may be safely consulted; but whoever wishes to cheat a neighbour of his estate, or to rob a country of its rights, need make no scruple of consulting the Doctor himself." (Letter xiv., June 22, 1799.)

l. 25. **had so mangled the reputation of the Duke of Grafton.** Junius addressed no less than ten of his letters to the Duke of Grafton, abusing him for his want of application to business, his fondness for Newmarket, and Nancy Parsons, etc., etc.

l. 27. **Euston** Park is about 10 miles north-west of Bury St. Edmunds in Suffolk. The house was built by Lord Arlington in the reign of Charles II., and stands in a well-timbered and well-watered park. It descended to the Grafton family through the marriage of Isabella, daughter of Lord Arlington, with the first Duke of Grafton, Henry Fitzroy, son of Charles II. Walpole wrote in 1753, "Euston is one of the most admired seats in England, in my opinion, because Kent has a most absolute disposition of it. Kent is now so fashionable that, like Addison's *Liberty*, he can 'make bleak rocks and barren mountains smile.' I believe the duke wishes he could make them green too. The house is large and bad. It was built by Lord Arlington, and stands, as all old houses do, for convenience of water and shelter in a hole; so it neither sees nor is seen. He has no money to build another. The park is fine, the old woods excessively so; they are much grander than Mr. Kent's passion,—clumps; that is sticking a dozen trees here and there till a lawn looks like the ten of spades."

Page 136, l. 11. a State of the Nation. In 1768 Mr. Knox, lately the Secretary of Mr. Grenville, and writing under his eye, published a pamphlet, entitled, *The Present State of the Nation*. In 1769 Burke published his celebrated answer, *Observations on a Late Publication, entitled " The Present State of the Nation."* In one passage Burke refers to Grenville thus: "Some ravens have always indeed croaked out this kind of song. They have a malignant delight in presaging mischief, when they are not employed in doing it; they are miserable and disappointed at every instance of the public prosperity: they overlook us like the malevolent being of the poet—"Tritonida conspicit arcem," etc. (for the rest of the quotation see p. 73, l. 3, **the Evil Spirit,** etc., and note).

l. 30. **Stowe.** See p. 125, l. 26, and note.

Page 137, l. 22. **Lord Camden.** See p. 60, l. 12, and p. 126, l. 22, and note.

Lord Shelburne. See p. 17, l. 25, and p. 126, l. 23, and note.

Colonel Barré, a soldier of fortune, born in Dublin of humble parents, was "found out, pushed and brought into Parliament by Lord Shelburne (in 1761); he had not sat two days in the House before he attacked Mr. Pitt." He became a very ready debater; he subsequently joined the side of Pitt and voted against the Stamp Act (1765), and, the following year, was appointed to one of the lower offices in the Government. It was Colonel Barré that moved in the House of Commons that the remains of Pitt should be interred at the public charge. In 1780 he declaimed against the Pension List. In 1782 he was appointed Treasurer of the Navy, and in the same year a pension of no less than £3,200 a year was granted to him by Lord Rockingham.

l. 23. **Dunning,** John (b. 1731, d. 1783), after serving his clerkship in his father's office, studied for the Bar. He was counsel for Wilkes; and in 1768 was appointed Solicitor-General: in the same year, through the influence of Lord Shelburne, he was returned to Parliament as Member for Calne. In 1778 he seconded Sir George Savile's Roman Catholic Relief Bill. He became Chancellor of the Duchy of Lancaster in 1782, and was raised to the peerage as Lord Ashburton.

l. 31. **Garrick.** See p. 16, l. 34, and note.

Talma, Francis Joseph (b. 1763, d. 1826). This French tragic actor was born at Paris, spent his childhood in England; he formed one of an amateur French company which performed at Hanover Square Rooms, and was at one time on the point of appearing at Drury Lane Theatre. He returned to Paris, however, and made his début at the Théatre Français in the character of Séide in Voltaire's *Mahomet*.

Page 138, l. 3. Murray ... Lord Mansfield. See p. 26, l. 14 *supra*, and note.

l. 24. **a colonial senate**, the Congress of Philadelphia (1774), consisting of delegates selected by the Provincial Assemblies. Except Georgia, all the colonies which existed before the Peace of 1763 were represented.

l. 25. **the colonial militia crossed bayonets with the British regiments** at Lexington, April 19th, 1775, and at Bunker's Hill the same year.

l. 29. **separated themselves by a solemn act from the Empire**, *i.e.* by the Declaration of Independence, on July 2nd, 1776, whereby it was declared that "these United Colonies are, and of right ought to be, free and independent States ; that they are absolved from all allegiance to the British Crown, and that all political connection between them and the State of Great Britain is and ought to be totally dissolved."

Page 139, l. 3. Quebec. See p. 17, l. 17, **General Wolfe**, and note.

l. 4. **Minden.** See p. 46, l. 34, and note.

the Moro. In 1762 an expedition, commanded by General the Earl of Albemarle and Admiral Sir George Pocock, was sent against Havannah, the richest and most important town of Cuba. Its harbour was one of the best in the world. It was the centre of the whole trade of the Spanish West Indies. The entrance to the harbour was defended by two strong forts, deemed well-nigh impregnable, the forts of Puntal and of Moro. It was against the Moro that the English first directed their attack. They landed near Havannah, and after much labour, during which several men dropped down dead with heat, thirst, and fatigue, batteries were constructed on land. The siege began on the 12th June, but the besieged made many vigorous sallies, and held out till the end of July. On the 30th of that month a practicable breach was effected in the fort, and the English troops marched up to the assault. The enemy did not on this occasion display the same intrepidity as in their former sallies ; many threw down their arms, and cried for quarter ; many others rushed headlong towards the river, where they perished. Yet their officers set them a most gallant example, and it was not until both the first and the second in command (Don Luis de Velasco and the Marquis de Gonzales) had fallen mortally wounded that the besiegers stood victorious on the summit of the castle wall.

Thus the Moro was conquered, and Havannah fell a few days afterwards. Nine noble ships were taken, five others were destroyed during the siege, or in the docks, and the treasure taken is said to have amounted to not less than three millions sterling. (See Mahon and Lecky.)

l. 16. **Pennsylvania and Virginia**, two of the United States.

l. 17. **the House of Bourbon** (from which came the royal houses of France, Spain, and Naples) derives its origin from the Archambauds of Bourbon in Berry. Negotiations had been carried on for some time between the Americans, the French, and the Spanish, and in 1778 two treaties of Commerce and Alliance were signed at Paris by the three Commissioners, Franklin, Deane, and Lee, on the part of America, and by M. Gérard, Secretary of the King's Council, on the part of France. Consequently, in England there now began to prevail a great and growing desire that Lord Chatham might be restored to the head of affairs—to avert a war with the House of Bourbon, or to make that war triumphant as the last, and to preserve, if it yet could be preserved, the unity of the empire.

Page 140, l. 18. the treaty by which, a few years later, the republic of the United States was recognised was signed at Paris on the 3rd of September, 1783.

l. 22. **The Duke of Richmond**, far unlike Lord Chatham, had become eager to close the American contest by a surrender of the British sovereignty. He gave notice of an address to his Majesty for 7th of April (1778), entreating the King instantly to withdraw his fleets and armies from the Thirteen Revolted Provinces, and to make peace with them on such terms as might secure their good will. (Lord Mahon, ch. lvii.)

l. 31. **His son William**, generally known as the younger Pitt, was the second son of the Earl of Chatham. Born in 1759, he became M.P. in 1782, Chancellor of the Exchequer in 1782, Prime Minister from 1783 to 1801, and again in 1804 until his death in 1806.

l. 32. **Lord Mahon.** Charles Earl Stanhope of Mahon (b. 1753, d. 1816) married Lady Hester Pitt, daughter of the Earl of Chatham. He distinguished himself at the time of the French Revolution by openly avowing republican sentiments, and by laying aside the external ornaments of the peerage. As a man of science he ranked high, and was the author of many inventions, particularly of a method of securing buildings from fire, an arithmetical machine, a new printing press, a monochord for tuning musical instruments, and a vessel to sail against wind and tide.

l. 33. **the Chancellor's room.** Was this at the end of Westminster Hall? (See Plan and Appendix.)

Page 141, l. 13. He lost the thread of his discourse, etc. "I will never consent," he cried, "to deprive the Royal offspring of the House of Brunswick, the heirs of"—(here he faltered for some moments while striving to recall the name)—"of the Princess Sophia, of their fairest inheritance," etc., etc. (See Lord Mahon, chap. lvii.)

Page 142, l. 28. her magnificent cathedral, St. Paul's.
l. 35. **Colonel Barré.** See p. 137, l. 22 *supra*, and note.
Duke of Richmond. See p. 140, l. 22 *supra*, and note.
Lord Rockingham. See p. 111, l. 15 *supra*, and note.
l. 36. **Burke.** See p. 113, l. 18 *supra*, and note.
Savile. See p. 111, l. 11 *supra*, and note.
Dunning. See p. 137, l. 23 *supra*, and note.
Page 143, l. 1. **Lord Camden.** See p. 60, l. 12, and p. 126, l. 22 *supra*, and note.
l. 2. **young William Pitt.** See p. 140, l. 31 *supra*, and note.
After the lapse of ... twenty-seven years. The younger Pitt died in 1806, and was laid in his father's grave.
l. 6. **Chatham sleeps near the northern door of the church,** in the north transept, called now " the statesmen's aisle."
l. 9. **Mansfield.** See p. 26, l. 14 *supra*, and note.
Fox. This is Charles James Fox (b. 1749, d. 1806), the third son of Henry Fox, and rival of the second Pitt. In the introduction to *Marmion*, Scott writes :
" Drop upon Fox's grave the tear
'Twill trickle to his rival's bier ;
O'er Pitt's the mournful requiem sound
And Fox's shall the notes rebound."
l. 10. **Grattan,** Henry (b. 1750, d. 1820), was born at Dublin, and entered the Parliament of Ireland in 1775, where he immediately made a name by his patriotic speeches, demanding freedom of trade and a free Parliament for Ireland. The latter years of his parliamentary life were chiefly devoted to a warm and energetic support of Catholic emancipation.
Canning, George (b. 1770, d. 1827), entered Parliament in 1793. He became Secretary for Foreign Affairs in 1807, and to him may be justly ascribed the line of British policy in Spain, which destroyed the hopes of Napoleon and led to his overthrow. In 1816 he was President of the Board of Control, and in 1822 was again chosen as Secretary for Foreign Affairs. In 1827 he became Prime Minister.
Wilberforce, William (b. 1759, d. 1833), was elected member for Hull in 1770. In 1787 he began to distinguish himself by his exertions for the abolition of the slave trade, which was finally decreed by the British legislature in 1807. He never relaxed his efforts to emancipate the negro from slavery, and he lived to see the second reading of the Emancipation Act carried by the House of Commons in 1833.
l. 12. **High over those venerable graves towers the stately monument of Chatham.** It is 33 feet high, and is said to have cost £6000.

l. 13. **his effigy, graven by a cunning hand.** The sculptor was John Bacon. The effigy represents Chatham, in his parliamentary robes, addressing the House.

l. 16. **The generation which reared that memorial of him has disappeared.** The monument was set up in 1779. It bears this inscription : " Erected by the King and Parliament as a testimony to the virtues and ability of William Pitt, Earl of Chatham, during whose administration, in the reign of George II. and III., Divine Providence exalted Great Britain to a height of prosperity and glory unknown to any former age. Born November 15, 1708. Died May 11, 1776." *Bacon, sculptor.*

CHRONOLOGICAL TABLE

1708. Birth of William Pitt.
1709. Battle of Malplaquet.
1710. Harley and Bolingbroke, Tory Ministers.
1709-1710. Sacheverell Riots and Trial.
1713. Treaty of Utrecht.
1714-1727. George I., King.
1714-1716. Lord Townshend, Chief Minister.
1715. Oxford, Ormond, and Bolingbroke impeached.
Riot Act passed.
Jacobite Rebellion (the first Pretender).
Battles of Sheriffmuir and Preston.
Death of Louis XIV.
1716. Septennial Act passed.
1717-1721. General (Earl) Stanhope, Chief Minister.
1717. Triple Alliance (Great Britain, France, Holland).
1718. Quadruple Alliance (Great Britain, France, Holland, German Empire).
Spanish Fleet destroyed off Cape Passaro.
1719. Jacobite Invasion of Scotland foiled.
1720. South Sea Bubble bursts.
Title of Prime Minister or Premier.
1721-1742. Robert Walpole, Prime Minister.
1723. Bishop Atterbury banished.
Wood's halfpence.
1723-1724. The Drapier's letters (Dean Swift's).
1724. The Craftsman.
1725. Treaty of Hanover (Great Britain, France, Prussia).
1726. Pitt enters Trinity College, Cambridge.
1726-1729. War with Spain.
1727. Death of George I.

CHRONOLOGICAL TABLE. 221

1727-1760. George II., King.
1730. Methodism begins.
Pitt obtains a Cornet's Commission in the Army.
1733. Walpole's Excise Bill fails.
Bourbon Family Compact (France and Spain).
1735. Pitt entered Parliament as member for Old Sarum.
1736. Porteous Riots at Edinburgh.
1737. Queen Caroline dies.
1738. Walpole procured Pitt's dismission from the Army.
Pitt became Groom of the Bedchamber to the Prince of Wales.
1739. Pitt spoke against Hanoverian subsidies and against the Spanish Convention.
War with Spain.
1740-1744. Anson's voyage round the world.
1740. War of Austrian Succession begins.
1742. Walpole resigns office.
Pitt spoke in favour of a motion for investigation of last ten years of Walpole's Administration.
1742-1743. Earl of Wilmington, Prime Minister.
But the chief power is in the hands of Pulteney and Carteret.
1743. Second Family Compact.
Battle of Dettingen.
1744-1754. Henry Pelham, Prime Minister.
1744. Duchess of Marlborough died and left Pitt £10,000.
1745. Battle of Fontenoy.
Jacobite Rebellion (the Young Pretender).
Battle of Prestonpans.
March to Derby.
1746. Battle of Falkirk.
Battle of Culloden.
Broad-bottomed Ministry formed.
Pitt became Vice-Treasurer for Ireland.
Soon afterwards Paymaster-General of the Forces.
1747. Pitt sat for Seaford.
1748. Peace of Aix-la-Chapelle.
Madras ceded to England.
1750. National Debt reduced.
1751. Frederick, Prince of Wales, dies.
1752. New style adopted.

222 WILLIAM PITT, EARL OF CHATHAM.

1753. Marriage Act passed.
1754-1762. Duke of Newcastle, Prime Minister.
1754. Pitt accepts membership for Aldborough (one of Newcastle's pocket boroughs).
1755. Braddock's defeat at Fort Duquesne by French and Indian Ambuscade.
1756-1763. Seven Years' War.
1756. Admiral Byng's failure off Minorca.
  Duke of Devonshire, Prime Minister.
  Pitt, Secretary of State.
1757. Battle of Plassey.
  Duke of Cumberland's surrender at Klosterseven.
1757-1762. Newcastle and Pitt (the "Coalition" Ministry).
1758. Louisburg (Cape Breton Island) captured.
1759. Battle of Minden.
  Wolfe's victory at Quebec.
  Admiral Hawke's victory at Quiberon Bay.
1760. Conquest of Canada.
  Battle of Wandewash.
  George II. dies.
1760-1820. George III., King.
1761. Third Family Compact.
  Pitt resigns office.
  He obtains a pension of £3,000 a year for three lives; his wife was created Baroness Chatham.
1762. War with Spain.
  Duke of Newcastle resigns office.
  Havannah and Manilla captured.
1762-1763. Earl of Bute, Prime Minister.
1763. Peace of Paris.
1763-1765. George Grenville, Prime Minister.
1763-1774. Wilkes's agitations.
1765. Stamp Act passed.
  Pitt received legacy of Burton Pynsent and nearly £3,000 a year.
1765-1766. Marquis of Rockingham, Prime Minister.
1766. Stamp Act repealed.
  Pitt formed a Ministry; was raised to the peerage as Viscount Pitt and Earl of Chatham.
1766-1768. Earl of Chatham in office.
1767. Charles Townshend taxes America.

CHRONOLOGICAL TABLE. 223

1768–1770. Duke of Grafton, Prime Minister.
1768. Massachusetts and Virginia resist taxation.
British troops quartered in Boston.
1769–1772. Letters of Junius published.
1770–1782. Lord North, Prime Minister.
1770. Pitt (after nearly three years' seclusion) resumed his seat in the House of Lords.
1771. Right of reporting Debates acquired.
1772-1785. Warren Hastings.
1772. Mansfield decides that English soil makes free.
1773. Tea Riots at Boston.
1774. Congress meets at Philadelphia.
1775–1783. American War.
1775. Battle of Lexington.
Battle of Bunker's Hill.
1776. British troops evacuate Boston.
(July 4) American Declaration of Independence.
1777. Burgoyne capitulates at Saratoga.
1778. France and Spain in alliance with United States.
Death of Chatham.

APPENDIX.

p. 16, l. 30, etc. "His voice ... was heard through lobbies and down staircases to the Court of Requests, and the precincts of Westminster Hall."

p. 119, l. 21, etc. "The gallery, the lobby, the Court of Requests, the staircases, were crowded with merchants from all the great ports of the island."

p. 140, l. 33, etc. "He rested himself in the Chancellor's room till the debate commenced, and then, leaning on his two young relations, limped to his seat."

To those that are familiar with only the present Houses of Parliament and their position with regard to Westminster Hall, these passages present considerable difficulty, in fact are quite unintelligible.

The annexed plan[1] is taken from a larger plan in Smith's *Antiquities of Westminster*, dated 1807. It shows how the House of Lords and House of Commons of that day stood in relation to Westminster Hall before they were destroyed by fire in October, 1834. Macaulay's first essay, *William Pitt, Earl of Chatham*, appeared in the *Edinburgh Review* in January, 1834, i.e. ten months before the fire; the Court of Requests was standing then, and the passage quoted above from p. 16, l. 30, etc., would be quite intelligible to his readers.

Macaulay's second essay, *Earl of Chatham*, was published in October, 1844, and although this was ten years after the destruction of the Court of Requests, he and his readers would be quite familiar with its site, and the passage quoted from p. 119, l. 21, etc., would not require any explanation for them.

In the *Antiquities of Westminster*, Smith writes the following passage: "On the same east side (of Palace Yard) stands the Court of Requests, of late, since the union of this Kingdom and Ireland, converted into a House for the Lords; but the principal entrance to it is from the passage at the south end of Westminster Hall, which passage at once serves to connect that Hall with the two Houses of Lords and Commons, and as a way to them all from old Palace Yard. Behind the Prince's Chamber

[1] See Frontispiece.

APPENDIX. 225

and the Court of Requests, or present House of Lords, whichever of the two it is called, are situated in different directions, the old House of Lords, the Painted Chamber adjoining it, and many other nameless rooms, which, together with the Prince's Chamber, the Court of Requests and a number of cellars under the whole mass of buildings, were unquestionably part of the old palace."

With regard to "The Chancellor's Room," mentioned in p. 140, l. 33, the plan again shows us that the Courts of Chancery and of King's Bench used to sit at the end of Westminster Hall, nearest to the old House of Commons. We may presume therefore that the Chancellor had a room there, in which it would be convenient for Chatham to wait on this occasion until the debate began, and from which it would not be impossible for him, "leaning upon his two young relations, to limp to his seat."

It will not perhaps be out of place here to point out that the annexed plan shows that there have been in Westminster at least three buildings known at different times as the House of Lords: (1) the House of Lords above Guy Fawkes' cellars; (2) part of the Court of Requests, previously known as White Hall, and after "the Union of this Kingdom and Ireland, converted into a House for the Lords," which was destroyed by fire in 1834; (3) the present House of Lords, built close on to the Thames, almost parallel with Westminster Hall.

INDEX TO THE NOTES.

A

Acbar, 174.
Act of Indemnity, 212.
Adam, 197.
Aislabie, 151.
Aix, 172.
Aix-la-Chapelle, Peace of, 164, 166.
Anatomie Vivante, 159.
Annual Register, 145.
Apis, 186.
Apophthegms, 160.
Argyle, Duke of, 154.
Arrogant humility, 182.
Atterbury, 187.
Aurungzebe, 174.
Aylesbury, 201.

B

Bahar, 174.
Balmerino, 185.
Bard, Author of the, 198.
Barelegged mountaineers, 196.
Barré, Colonel, 215, 218.
Barrington, Lord, 184.
Bath, 208.
Beckford, Alderman, 213.
Beggar's Opera, 203.
Belisarius, 148.
Bengal, 174, 210.
Besborough, Lord, 212.
Bewray, 185.

Blackstone, 214.
Blear-eyed, 145.
Bloomsbury gang, 182.
Blues, 150.
Bolingbroke, 157, 189.
Boroughs, Ministerial, 166.
Boswelliana, Lues, 145.
Bounties for perjury, etc., 146.
Bourbon, House of, 217.
Boys, The, 162.
Bradshaw, President, 202.
Brest fleet, 174.
Broad bottom, 164.
Brougham, Lord, 158.
Browbeat, 213.
Brown's "Estimate," 168.
Brutus, 159, 180.
Buccaneer, 162.
Buckingham House, 202.
Burke, 169, 207, 218.
Burke's character of Walpole, 160.
Burke's criticism of Brown's "Estimate," 168.
Burke thundered against the ministers, 213.
Burton Pynsent, 211.
Bute, 149, 187.

C

Cabal, 170, 193.
Cæsar, 150.

INDEX TO THE NOTES. 227

Camden, 209, 210, 211, 215, 218.
Cameron, 186.
Campbell, John, Duke of Argyle, 154.
Canning, 218.
Cant, 167, 180.
Carnatic, 174.
Carr, 196.
Carteret, 152.
Catch, 203.
Cavendish, Lord John, 206.
Chalgrove, 147, 206.
Chancellor's room, 217, and appendix.
Chandernagore, 174.
Cherbourg, 173.
Chesterfield, 153.
Childeric, 201.
Chilperic, 201.
Churchill, Rev. Charles, 198.
Cider counties, 202.
Cider-land, 200.
Cider tax, 200.
City of the Seven Hills, 171.
City of the Violet Crown, 171.
Claremont, 192.
Clarendon, 194.
Clifford, 194.
Clive, 174.
Cocoa Tree, 184.
Cocytus, 150.
Coligni, 204.
Colonial militia, 216.
Colonial senate, 216.
Columns, 145.
Commissary, 191.
Commission, The Great Seal in, 169.
Common Council, 171.
Comptroller's staff, 177.
Conway, Henry, 204, 207, 211.
Coote, 174.
Coriolanus, 159.
Cornet, 146.
Corsica, 213.
Cortes, 174.
Court of Common Pleas, 202.

Court of Requests, 159, and appendix.
Cowper's "Table Talk," 168.
Coxe, Archdeacon, 158.
Craggs, 152, 165.
Crassa ignorantia, 170.
Crevelt, Creveldt, Crefeld, 175.
Cromwell, Richard, 185.
Cumberland, Duke of, 165, 187.
Cutler, Sir John, 165.

D

Danby, 195.
Danes, 198.
Dante, 176.
Dashwood, Sir Francis, 193, 200.
Declaration of Independence, 216.
Declaration of Rights, 189.
De la Roche Jaquelin, 179.
Denmark, Queen of, 187.
Derwentwater, 185.
Devonshire, Duke of, 205.
Dido, 186.
Dispensing with penal laws, 208.
Doctor, 189.
Doddridge, 186.
Dodington, 148, 165, 184, 190, 209.
Doge, 186.
Dowdeswell, 207.
Draper, Sir William, 214.
Duchy of Lancaster, 169.
Dunning, 215, 218.

E

Egremont, Lord, 193.
Eldon, 188.
Elegy in a Country Churchyard, 198.
Elliott, Sir Gilbert, 184.
Embargo, 212.
Essay on Man, 202.
Essay on Woman, 202.

Euston Park, 214.
Evil Spirit, etc., 191.
Excise Bill, 154.
Extinxti te meque, etc., 205.

F

Falkland, 194.
Faubourg St. Antoine, 170.
Felton, 193.
Ferdinand of Brunswick, Prince, 175, 191.
Fiddle-faddle, 175.
Filmer, 188.
Fleet, The, 192.
Foot-race, Virgil's, 199.
Fop, 176.
Fox, Charles James, 160, 218.
Fox, Henry, 155, 164, 183, 199, 201.
Francis, The Emperor, 184.
Frederick, Prince of Wales, 157, 180.
Frederick the Great, 166, 184.

G

Garrick, David, 160, 215.
Gauger, 200, 205.
Gazette, 192, 208.
General warrants, 203.
Genoude, 178.
Gentle Shepherd, 200.
Gifford, John, 145.
Godolphin, 153, 172, 190.
Gold Key, 199.
Goree, 173.
Grafton, Duke of, 200, 207, 214.
Grand Alliance, 178.
Grandison, Sir Charles, 188.
Granville, Lord, 157, 191.
Grattan, 218.
Groom of the Stole, 187.
Grub Street, 192.
Guadaloupe, 173.
Guelphs, 185.
Guizot, 179.

H

Habeas Corpus Act, 208.
Halifax, 195.
Hamilton, Gerard, 167.
Hampden, John, 147, 156, 178, 206.
Hampstead, Villa at, 218.
Hardwicke, Lord, 162, 183, 193, 202.
Harley, 153, 157, 186.
Havanna, 192.
Hawke, 174.
Hayes, 204.
Henry IV. (of France), 158.
Hernhausen, 185.
Home, John, 198.
House of Brandenburg, 191.
House of Hapsburg, 191.
Humbug, 165.
Hume, David, 155.
Hunt, 159.

I

Ildefonso, St., 212.
Independence, Declaration of American, 216.
In esse, 146.
In posse, 146.
In spite of Gods, men and columns, 145.
Isle of Wight, 205.

J

Jack boot, 198.
January, The thirtieth of, 178.
Jeffreys, Judge, 179.
Jemmy Twitcher, 203.
Johnson, Samuel, 197, 200, 207.
Journals of the House of Commons, 184,
Joyce, Cornet, 202.
Junius, 214.
Junta, 204.
Junto, 165.
Justices in Eyre, 200.

INDEX TO THE NOTES.

K
Kensington Palace, 173.
Keppel, 212.
Kilmarnock, 185.
King of Prussia, 174.
King over the water, 193.
King's friends, The, 209.

L
Lagos, Cape, 173.
Lambert, Daniel, 159.
Lakes, The great, 204.
Latitudinarian Prelates, 185.
Laud, 178.
Lauderdale, 195.
Lawn sleeves, 181.
Lear, 148.
Legge, 166, 183, 190.
Leicester House, 172, 188.
Lennox, Lady Sarah, 199.
Lincoln's Inn Fields, 181.
Locke, John, 177, 210.
Lombart Street, 208.
Lothario, 188.
Louis XIV., 211.
Louisburg, 173.
Lues Boswelliana, 19.
Lutestring, 207.

M
Macheath, 203.
Mackenzie, 205.
Mæcenas, 197.
Mahon, 217.
Main, The, 191.
Malebolge, 177.
Malingering, 213.
Mallet, David, 198.
Manilla, 192.
Mansfield, William Murray, Earl of, 164, 193.
March, Lord, 203.
Maria Theresa, 192.
Marie Louise, 170.
Maritime right (of search), 161.

Marlborough, Duchess of, 163.
Mars, 150.
Marshal Soult, 205.
Martinique, 192.
Mask, The man in the, 178.
Massachusetts, 209.
Mayor of the Palace, 201.
Mecklenburg, Princess of, 199.
Mendip Hills, 180.
Milton, 177.
Minden, 175, 216.
Minorca, 167, 180.
Montague, 190.
Monument, The, 211.
Morning Chronicle, 202.
Moro, The, 216.
Mother of Edward III., 198.
Mother of George III., 198.
Murray, William, 164, 183, 215.
Muses, 150.

N
Napoleon, 185.
Neptune, 150.
Newcastle, Duke of, 147, 162.
Niagara, 173.
Nollekens, Joseph, 165.
North, Lord, 184, 213.
Nugent, Robert, 183.

O
Oakhampton, 150.
O'Brien, Giant, 159.
October Club, 156.
Old Sarum, 149, 189.
Onslow, Arthur, 191.
Orissa, 174.
Orleans, Regent, 149, 158.
Ormond, 210.
Oswald, James, 18
Oudenarde 170.
Oxford, 180.

P
Parliamentary History, 145.
Parricides in Rome, 151.

Patents, 200.
Patriot Prince, 189.
Patriots, The, 156.
Peace, Commission of the, 180.
Peach, 203.
Pelham, 149, 152, 155, 172.
Pennsylvania, 217.
Pepys, 161.
Perceval, 188.
Petticoat, 198.
Philippines, 192.
Philips, John, 200.
Picts, 198.
Pitt s ardour, 175.
Pitt's constituency, 170.
Pitt's desertion of Newcastle, 147.
Pitt's monument, 218.
Pitt's inconsistency, 146, etc.
Pitt's opposition to Hanoverian Subsidies, 147.
Pitt's tendency to gout, 150.
Pitt's wife, 170, 182.
Pitt, William, the younger, 217, 218.
Pizarro, 174.
Placeman, 162.
Poetasters, 192.
Polish Count, 159.
Pondicherry, 174.
Pope's "Essay on Man," 202.
Portland, Duke of, 212.
Port-Mahon, 167.
Potsdam, 205.
Potwalloper, 181.
Powis-house, 181.
Pratt, 184, 202, 210, 211.
Prebend, 181.
Pretender, 164.
Prince of Wales, Frederick, 157.
Princess in the Arabian Tale, 197.
Princess Mother, 196.
Prorogation, 210.
Pulteney, William, 152, 156, 211.
Pym, John, 177.

Q

Quebec, 216.
Queensberry, Duke of, 203.

R

Rainham Hall, 153.
Ramsay, 198.
Reformation, The, 70.
Reform Bill, 170.
Regent Orleans, 149, 158.
Register, Annual, 145.
Rembrandt, 148.
Requests, Court of, 159, and appendix.
Revolution (1688), 157, 185.
Reynolds, Sir Joshua, 165.
Richmond, Duke of, 217, 218.
Rigby, 182, 210.
Robinson, Sir Thomas, 166.
Rochefort, 172.
Rochester, 196.
Rockingham, Marquis of, 206, 218.
Rump, 180.
Russell, Lord William, 156, 206.

S

Sacheverell, 188.
Sackville, Lord George, 175, 184.
Saint Simon, 149.
Sandwich, Lord, 182.
Sandys, 149.
Sarum, Old, 149.
Saunders, 212.
Savile, Sir George, 206, 218.
Schedules A and B, 180.
Scotch Representative Peers, 187.
Seal, Privy, 189.
Secret-service-money, 165, 171, 181.
Settlement, Act of, 154, 185.
Shaftesbury, 194.

INDEX TO THE NOTES. 231

Shebbeare, 197.
Shelburne, Lord, 160, 211, 215.
Sheridan, 209.
Ship-money, 190, 208.
Sicilies, The Two, 191.
Sidney, Algernon, 179, 210.
Silesia, 191.
Somers, Lord John, 148, 157.
Soult, 205.
South, Robert, 187.
South Sea Act, 151.
Spain, Peace with, 146.
Spitalfields weavers, 205.
Stadtholder, 186.
Stanhope, 151.
Stanley, 160.
State Paper Office, 144.
Statute Book, 204.
St. John, 157.
St. Malo, 172.
Stowe, 211, 215.
Strafford, 178, 194.
Subsidiary treaties, 167.
Subsidies, Pitt declaimed against, 147, 163, 167.
Sudbury, 189.
Sunderland, 151, 196.
Sycophants, 209.

T

Talma, 215.
Tanjore, 211.
Tellership of Exchequer, 169, 200.
Temple, 195.
Temple Bar, 197.
Tergiversation, 148.
Term Reports, 204.
Thackeray, Rev. F., 144.
Themis, 150.
Ticonderoga, 173.
Tidewaiter, 182, 200.
Times, The, 201.
Timoleon, 180.
Tindal, 158.

Toleration Act, 208.
Tomline, Bishop, 145.
Ton, 154.
Townshend, Charles, 153, 184, 207.
Treaty negotiated by St. John, 204.
Treaty negotiated by Bedford, 204, 217.
Turk's Head, 207.
Twitcher, Jemmy, 203.

U

Urn, 150.
Utopian, 150, 199.

V

Vails, 164.
Vatel, 170, 191.
Versailles, 173, 211.
Villemain, 179.
Villiers, George, 196.
Virgil's foot-race, 199.
Virginia, 209, 217.
Virtuoso, 188.

W

Waldégrave, Lord, 171.
Wallenstein, 210.
Walpole, Horace, 154.
Walpole, Lord Horatio, 155.
Walpole, Sir Robert, 151.
Warburton, 203.
Wardrobe, The Great, 177.
War of the Grand Alliance, 173.
Warrants, General, 203, 209.
Wedderburn, 210.
Westminster Hall, 159, and appendix.
Western Squire, 156.
Weymouth, Lord, 183.
Whiston, 186.

Wilberforce, 218.
Wilkes, 198.
William III., 205.
Winnington, 155, 190.
Wolfe, General, 160, 173, 216.
Wordsworth, 148.
Wrekin, 180.
Wyndham, Sir William, 156.

Y

York, Duke of, 187.
Yonge, Sir William, 155.

Z

Zenith, 176.

www.ingramcontent.com/pod-product-compliance
Lightning Source LLC
Chambersburg PA
CBHW031751230426
43669CB00007B/578